THAI
STICK

THAI STICK

Surfers, Scammers,
and the Untold Story
of the Marijuana Trade

Peter Maguire and Mike Ritter

Foreword by David Farber

Columbia University Press
New York

COLUMBIA UNIVERSITY PRESS
Publishers Since 1893
New York   Chichester, West Sussex
cup.columbia.edu

Library of Congress Cataloging-in-Publication Data
Maguire, Peter (Peter H.)
Thai stick : surfers, scammers, and the untold story of the marijuana
trade /
Peter Maguire and Mike Ritter.
     pages   cm
Includes bibliographical references and index.
ISBN 978-0-231-16134-3 (cloth : alk. paper) —
ISBN 978-0-231-53556-4 (electronic)
1. Marijuana industry—Thailand. 2. Drug traffic—Thailand—
History. 3. Smugglers—Thailand—Biography. I. Ritter, Mike.
II. Title.

HD9019.M382T553   2014
363.4509593—dc23   2013008590

Cover design by Phil Pascuzzo
Cover image by iStockphoto

CONTENTS

FOREWORD

When Innocence
Must Become Experience

DAVID FARBER

In the broken-down realm of the American domestic empire of the 1960s and 1970s, a self-selected crew tried their hand at living free and unencumbered by the dictates of social convention and legal authority. From a polite distance, the label "counterculture" was attached to the most obviously disaffiliated of this particular mixed bag of heroic cultural rebels, drug-addled dropouts, predatory longhairs, idealistic communards, and clueless day trippers. The label was useful in promoting full-color magazine spreads of hippies and flower power marketing campaigns but said little about the lived experience of people who had decided to organize their lives outside of the day-in-and-day-out of institutional life in America. That new life, often enough, began as an innocent lark. It rarely ended that way.

The young people who went on this trip to a place with no name had their reasons, and those reasons were not all the same. Those with artistic visions and, in some cases, talent found pattern and inspiration in the long lineage of bohemian avatars that spoke across the generations, preaching of a rucksack revolution and Eastern mysteries. Others found their source in outlaw territory—1 percent motorcycle clubs and old-school gangsters. And in an age when black, brown, and yellow colonized people were overthrowing centuries-old yokes of oppression, a percentage of white youths saw a world in which every old hierarchy of control was up for grabs. The evil lie of Vietnam played its part too, as did every other vestige of state-sponsored Cold War horror, especially the grotesque threat of atomic Armageddon. But all were not driven by despair or high-minded pursuit of Truth. Even as troubles came down the road, the sixties was a triumphal time of consumer plenty and unprecedented prosperity, and some young folks simply wanted to extend their egos and their pleasures as far as their gifts and their courage would take them. There were pushes and there were pulls, and nobody said you had to pick just one path or lineage of rebellion—plenty of people mixed and matched, and that haphazard mélange made the era what it was.

For those who chose to live out their disregard for the status quo in the 1960s and early 1970s—whatever their formula for rebellion—the near-sacramental use of cannabis, LSD, and other hallucinogens gave a commonality of expression and practice to the collective mission. For many, it was the drugs that opened up their personal rabbit hole. Without those particular drugs, the cultural rebellion would have looked and felt and been different. Illegal drugs gave the counterculture its style, its attitude, and its dead certainty that living outside the law was a material necessity. Those drugs and the peculiarities of the times combined to create an anthropologically specific liminal realm, an illegal nation that crossed borders, in which the rules had to be made as the game was played.

Much has been made, then and now, of the most visible of the counterculture's pied pipers. Timothy Leary, who was simultaneously charlatan and shaman, appeared on TV and in gentlemen's magazines pitching LSD. Allen Ginsberg, in his robes and beard, was everywhere, spreading mystical good cheer. The Diggers organized the Haight-Ashbury; the Yippies made their political play; and famous rock bands from the Grateful Dead to the Jimi Hendrix Experience to the Beatles disseminated their druggy truths and half-baked claims to millions of young people who wanted something more than what their parents and teachers and bosses offered them. Whatever role these marketers of cultural rebellion played—and it was not inconsequential—they offered only a road map, not the trip itself. The high-octane fuel had to come from somewhere else.

The counterculture's means of production was, above all else, mind drugs, especially LSD and cannabis. Producing those drugs for the multiplying number of young people who wanted in on the experience was, for a relatively small bunch of intrepid risk takers, an opportunity to make a living out of a way of life. Like the counterculture itself, these drug operatives were shape shifters; they could not and did not stay stuck in time. They made the counterculture possible and they got made by it. But the life they chose, supplying the drugs that made tens of millions see the world in a different light, put them outside the law. And outside the law, hard men and hard choices abounded. Nobody stayed innocent, and many of the men who signed up as drug smugglers and dealers, especially at the tail end of the "love generation," never expected or wanted anything else but a life of hard kicks and out-of-the-box adventure. For most, hippie ethos aside, money played a not-insignificant role—either as source for life-expanding good times or as tool for an extended voyage into the best an outlaw life had to offer.

Nearly a half century after this business was begun, we are still patching together the history of an epic undertaking. Given the scale, scope, and creative genius of the illegal drug industry in the 1960s and mid-1970s, how little is known about it is astounding. It's like only vaguely knowing how the steam engine changed the world in the nineteenth century. The countercultural inventors and their international compatriots of this critical form of "deviant globalization" changed the trajectory of modern economic development, even as they opened up the mind's eye of a generation of young people in the United States, Western Europe, and other points around the world.

The story you are about to read should—and there are no other words for it—blow your mind. The men—and the relatively few women—you are going to meet took chances on land and sea to make a market in highly potent marijuana. They went from smuggling small loads of weed across the Mexican border to introducing massive shipments of Thai sticks to an international market looking to get stoned in ever more precise and potent ways. These smugglers—"scammers," as they called themselves—were a mixed bag: a wild bunch of surfer Robin Hoods, crooked watermen looking for their main chance, happy-go-lucky pirates, sweet-talking, back-stabbing narcissists, and deadly sociopaths.

Southern California is the point of departure for this tale but almost immediately the high-quality cannabis trade became an international, cross-cultural bonanza. Surfers looking to fund their next big wave safari jump-started the business, bringing high-grade marijuana across the Mexican border. Quickly, the action spread. The hippie trail to points east, especially to the hash regions of Afghanistan, offered up a top-quality product that sparked an international hunt for further supply even as smugglers burnished their tradecraft, rigging up false-paneled vehicles and tuned-up suitcases. Friendships, or at least convivial partnerships, across cultures spawned deal after deal. The Vietnam War put Southeast Asia into play as servicemen, vets and civilian contractors discovered premium cannabis at bargain prices in unorganized village markets, especially in Thailand. Local fixers and middlemen provided their services to the growing cast of scammers. A core group maintained a certain allegiance to the ethos that had, at least in part, built the demand for their wares. But as the loads got bigger and the profits more lucrative, the game and the cast changed. Gangsters in Hawaii and hard men all over insisted on a growing cut of the action as they provided the wherewithal to move the loads into the distribution supply lines. A few of the original scammers set up shop in exotic ports of call, still chasing waves and setting up multiton deals. Some people got rich, some got set up, and some died.

By the mid-1970s, the countercultural scene that had given impetus, style, and even purpose to the early scammers' adventures in drug smuggling was fast disappearing. The DEA and the "War on Drugs" made their world more dangerous. Higher stakes changed the business and the men who operated it. Then, too, the advent of cocaine as generational fuel, and as the smugglers' own drug of choice, played a vital role in darkening their way of life. So, too, did a new cast of heavies: tough men from different lands and cultures began their rule of the international, illegal drug trade.

Anybody who passed through this world, even as a casual participant, knows that sometimes it demanded a price people could not pay. People did stupid things on drugs. They got caught and went to jail. Most of us of a certain age have such sad, small-time stories to tell. I know people who never came back from one acid trip too many. A friend who got high every day stepped off a roof and died. Another went to Thailand with a wad of cash in his pocket and was found dead with a needle in his arm that he had not put there. The Kodachrome tales herein, of the heavy scammers of this long-ago time, tell of years in prison, risk and death on the high seas, and lives broken by the promise of just one more load. The dark side of this high adventure shadows everything that happened during these years. But it does not overshadow the brazen, creative, extraordinarily courageous spirit of the scammers who made it their mission to smuggle in massive loads of high-quality cannabis from the far points of the globe to meet a generation's need to get totally stoned.

ACKNOWLEDGMENTS

It is difficult to thank the many who have helped this project come to frui-
tion over the past sixteen years. Without a doubt, our greatest debt is to
the many narrators who shared their stories with us. Mike Ritter and I
were able to talk to a huge cross-section of historical actors. Smugglers,
Thai pot growers, law enforcement agents, Vietnam-era intelligence pro-
fessionals, smugglers turned confidential informants, prosecutors, defense
lawyers, and even some of Southeast Asia's regional power brokers spoke
very candidly with us both on and off the record. Without their trust and
cooperation, we never could have completed this book. A special thanks
goes to Mike Carter, whose epic tale of the *Ancient Mariner* is as good a
sea story as I have ever heard. The late Craig Williams was a true Hawaiian at heart who taught us about life and faced death with courage and
humor. His former partner Mike Ferguson was also a great supporter who
grew into a close friend. He provided critical information and made some
important introductions. David Ortiz never failed to offer leads when we
thought we had reached dead ends. Bob "Butch" Martin sailed loads of
contraband in both the Pacific and the Atlantic and never lost perspective.

James "Abdul" Monroe*'s easygoing nature and natural storytelling ability always entertained us. Ritter's original Thai connections, Lek and Jo, are indomitable spirits who were and remain an inspiration. Retired DEA agent Jim Conklin was also extremely generous with his time and provided an altogether different perspective on the marijuana trade. Other retired DEA agents and confidential informants greatly added to our story. A number of narrators agreed to speak with us on the condition that we changed or omitted their names. They added greatly to our story and helped to fill in a number of historical blanks. The names that have been changed are indicated in the text with an asterisk on first appearance.

Numerous academics also contributed to this book. Without the oral history training both Ritter and I received from Ron Grele at Columbia University, we could not have embarked on such an ambitious project. My former professor and friend Anders Stephanson and our late advisor, James Patrick Shenton, provided invaluable support. I was fortunate to have Peter Dimock as an editor at Columbia University Press; he helped make sense of what at times seemed like an unmanageable amount of research. Leslie Kriesel, my other editor at Columbia University Press, has suffered through four books with me now. Her keen eye and easygoing nature have made her pleasure to work with. Anne Routon at Columbia University Press did an admirable job convincing her skeptical board that a book about pot smuggling belonged in the Columbia catalogue. She also assigned Anders Stephanson to be one of my readers; his challenging and incisive readings of the manuscript were always a pleasure to receive. My other Columbia University Press reader, Anne McClintock, was also incredibly helpful. "Good enough" is not in her vocabulary, and it was a pleasure to be pushed by a brave intellectual like her. When she sensed I was hedging about my own personal involvement with the subject, she called me out and forced me to disclose more fully my own proximity to, and participation in, this underground economy.

Mike Ritter and I could have never imagined the seismic shifts in the American legal terrain that came in the wake of 9/11 and how they would affect us. When law enforcement took a renewed interest in Ritter, and in our project, we were very fortunate to have the calm, steady, and cynical counsel of Andy Patel, Nat Smith, and Kris Larsen. Over great meals in Manhattan, Andy advised me about our limited legal options and the outlook of a new generation of law enforcement agents.

The many researchers and journalists I worked with during my time in Cambodia and Southeast Asia were also incredibly generous. Without Chris Riley, who invited me to Cambodia in 1993, I never would have learned of the Americans captured by the Khmer Rouge. His associate Doug Niven provided invaluable assistance with my research over the years. My late fixer and friend, Sok Sin, also played a key role in my research for many years. Craig Etcheson was and remains a trusted colleague whose research abilities are second only to his gastronomic skills. Historian David Chandler was also very supportive and encouraging in the early days of this project. Documentation Center of Cambodia head Youk Chhang and his former researchers Sorya Sim and Meng Tre also greatly added to my knowledge of S-21 Prison. Thanks also to Michael Hayes, Chris Decherd, Lisa Miller, Anthony Alderson, and Sylvain Vogel. Not only did Sylvain provide a home away from home, he was also a demanding martial arts training partner.

In Hawaii, many were especially helpful and supportive of this project, but nobody more than Mary Kennedy and Frank "Bamboo" Opperman. My landlords became close friends, and their Mokuleia compound will always hold a special place in my heart. Mokuleia equestrian Michael Daly was also extremely helpful to both Mike Ritter and myself. Another special thanks goes to Duc Nguyen and Minh Nga Vu, the proprietors of Duc's Bistro. The restaurant provided a safe harbor at a very tumultuous time in the project. Their generosity, grace, and delicious food allowed us to forget about our legal woes for a few hours each week.

Others who provided help and support over the years: Leonard Brady, John Milius, Martin Splichal, Mike Perry, Stan Pleskunas, Robert Worth Bingham, Im Chan, Van Nath, Karl Deeds, Jason Frye, Patricia Dietrich, Steven Niles, Alaric Valentin, George Greenough, Gary Chapman, Joe Pietri, Ed Vulliamy, David Eisenbach, Mark Lytle, Peter Hutton, Tom Sherrit, K. K. Jackson, Jon Bush, Pat Falby, John Ryle, Dave Kattenbus, Jason Blum, Terry Dawson, Bill Boyum, Dion Wright, Preston Piccus, Redman, Nicholas Schou, Roland Neuveu, Al Rockoff, Roger Deutsch, Ron Steel, Martin Sugarman, Sara Powers, Dion Wright, Kevin Doyle, the *Bangkok Post*, *High Times*, and *The Surfers Journal*. Last, but not least, thanks to my wife, Annabelle Lee, whose grace under pressure is unequaled and has accompanied me on adventures that few others would.

INTRODUCTION

When I first moved to New York to start college in 1984, people would look at my photo album and tell me that I was crazy because there were so many pictures of empty waves. Today, when I see images of the dirty, slate-gray tubes of Santa Monica State Beach, the greenish brown walls of Rincon, the long rights at Rattlesnake Point, the backlit tubes of Broken Head, and the cobalt blue mountains at Mokuleia, I see old friends. Not only did these waves have more predictable personalities than most people I knew, they were there for me when my mother, father, friends, and girlfriends were not.

I am a professional historian, but I have been a surfer for much longer; my experiences and the sport's popular perception are impossible to reconcile. Behavior that today might earn a temporary restraining order or charges of hate crimes was then just part of California localism, strange regional prejudices every bit as inbred and paranoid as anything in Appalachia or the Ozarks. La Jolla, San Clemente, Newport, Huntington, Long Beach, Palos Verdes, Manhattan Beach, Venice, Santa Monica, Topanga, Malibu, Oxnard, Ventura, Santa Barbara, Big Sur, Santa Cruz—each had

The author surfing Oahu's North Shore. Photo: Kevin Robinson

its own distinctive surfing style and hierarchy, complete with an ethos, icons, and enforcers. It was once a closed society, a fact that Tom Wolfe discovered when he tried to write about La Jolla's Windansea Surf Club and never got past the Pumphouse.[1]

Growing up on the Southern California coast before it was completely overrun, my friends and I thumbed our collective noses at Frederick Jackson Turner's "Frontier Thesis" because the Pacific Ocean, our frontier, was alive and well. We felt like pioneers, with the Pacific Rim as the Ponderosa of our imaginations. As William Langewiesche has pointed out in his book *The Outlaw Sea*, "the ocean is a realm that remains radically free." It is also a place of risks, rewards, and consequences, in which action speaks louder than words. Before they allowed me to ride a board, my parents made sure I was an exceptionally strong ocean swimmer. While we all surfed, we aspired to be "watermen" who could also dive, ocean paddle, sail, and operate boats in the surf. Many of us became junior lifeguards and hoped one day to compete for a spot in the L.A. County Lifeguards.

Many mornings I left my house before sunrise and wound down Santa Monica Canyon on a bike or skateboard in time to see the coyotes scampering into the brush after gorging themselves on neighborhood cats. Once I got to the stairs at the top of the canyon, I could spy the waves through the eucalyptus trees. My board lived at a friend's house, and even with the ocean just a few hundred meters away, I could only surf with friends because it took two of us to carry one board. After we wrestled our surfboards down to the beach, we surfed until the "meatball" or black ball, no surfing flag was hoisted at 10 a.m. and then rode inflatable mats or bodysurfed for the rest of the day.

Although technology, in the form of lightweight fiberglass surfboards and wetsuits, had already transformed the surfing/waterman's subculture into something much more mainstream, nothing did more to soften surfing than the invention of the surfboard leash (the cord that connects a surfer to his or her board). Prior to the cord, if you fell, at the very minimum, you had to swim for your board. If you lost your board at a world-class wave like Maui's Honolua Bay or Australia's Lennox Head, more often than not, it was smashed to pieces on the rocks. In the precord days, you had to pay to play, and the most experienced and talented surfers got the best waves. Above all, "it was a culture based on respect," recalled San Diego surfer Stan Pleskunas. "Respect was earned, respect was based on what you did in the water, not how well you could bullshit on the beach."[2]

The waterman ethos was still strong in the early 1970s. Cords were frowned on when I began surfing at State Beach. Although the waves were decidedly mediocre, I got to see another side of life there. Not only was it home to the world's best volleyball players, there were also resident winos, an openly gay beach, and some of the most physically beautiful people in the world. Although the towering bronzed gods ruled the volleyball courts, they would all stop and take notice when a dark-haired, gap-toothed man carried his board to the water. Even my father, a former surfer and a man not easily impressed, pointed to him slyly and whispered through clenched teeth, "Dora." In stark contrast to the gym-cut Adonises on the volleyball courts, Mikolos Chapin Dora was of medium height and medium build. Yet when he surfed the very ordinary beach break, it was not a sport—it was a performance. I later learned that Dora, one of the world's most famous surfers, was wanted by Interpol and an international fugitive. His cons and scams allowed him to extend his adolescence into his fifties.[3]

Though we loved the ocean and riding the waves, there was a darker reason so many of us were drawn to surfing. Our parents were members of the "Me" generation, and while most of us came from solidly upper middle-class families, we were coming of age in the odd, rootless rubble of the 1960s. By the 1970s, the quest for utopia had given way to hedonism and narcissism. One neighbor had a primal scream room and another a bisexual butler who serviced both mom and dad. Our days at the beach were a welcome relief from big, lonely houses ruled by maids and nannies. Surfing was a refuge of sense: not only was there a distinct hierarchy with clear-cut rules, the sea provided a source of consistency and stability at an uncertain time in our young lives.[4]

There were no surf schools or soft surfboards in the early 1970s—only trial and error within a very rigid caste system where "kooks" like us sat at the very bottom. Kooks were relegated to the worst waves and were constantly harassed. If we got in the way or accidentally dropped in on someone else's waves, the consequences were immediate. It was not uncommon to get slapped or dunked underwater and kicked out of the water or "sent in." On my first trip to the Hawaiian Islands at age fourteen, I committed a minor breach of surfing etiquette and a massive grown man slapped me in the face, held me underwater, and when he finally brought me to the surface, said, "Fuckin' haole, outta da watta!"

If one graduated from kook to gremmie, there were still years of hazing to endure. Our elders held us to very high standards that one day we would be expected to maintain. It was not enough to be able to surf. There were aesthetic standards and unwritten rules that changed with every few miles of coastline. Just because you were accepted in Malibu did not mean you got a pass in La Jolla, Oxnard, or Santa Barbara. With the sole exception of esoteric Marxist factions, the surfing world best illustrates Sigmund Freud's law of "the narcissism of small differences." Where I started surfing, wetsuits were black, surfboards were white, and initially, cords were for kooks. By the late 1970s, these rules began to loosen in my region; however, this thaw was not universal. One afternoon, after I got what I thought was an especially good wave at Rattlesnake Point, an older surfer paddled up to me. I was expecting a compliment, but instead he said, "Oh, I see you got your cord and your booties there. Wouldn't want to lose your board or cut your feet." I looked at him in disbelief as he continued his diatribe: "No, no, don't get me wrong, I think that booties and cords are great—every kook ought to have them!" With that, he paddled away, and I saw that he wore no cord, booties, or even a wetsuit. He was surfing's equivalent of a dry fly catch-and-release specialist; to him I was a lowly bait caster with a Folger's coffee can full of worms.[5]

While surfing is a lifelong practice, like martial arts or yoga, it is also like sex because it is so sensual and fleeting. As a result, many surfers are selfish hedonists who will drop everything else under the right set of climatic circumstances. Time and freedom are by far the most valuable commodities when living a life dictated by the weather. Although physically attractive, serious surfers make very bad boyfriends and husbands because they are married, first and foremost, to the sea. After I broke a date with one of my favorite high school girlfriends, she tabled an ultimatum—the surfboards or her? I was offended by the question.

Our extreme confidence in the ocean often translated to a dangerous sense of freedom and arrogance on land. At fourteen, I was busted by Customs at the Tijuana border trying to smuggle fireworks. At sixteen, I was sneaking onto private and government property to surf waves guarded by barbed-wire fences, no trespassing signs, and men with guns. At nineteen, I moved to Australia and never looked back. There was very little we were not willing to do if it enabled us to surf perfect, uncrowded waves.

Whether it was bringing a few cases of Canadian whiskey through the surf during Prohibition, poaching some illegal Mexican lobsters for mobsters in Vegas, working on the gambling boats anchored in international waters off Santa Monica Pier, or offloading a load of Thai marijuana, California watermen had always been part of the black market. Fast money bought time and freedom. As journalist C. R. Stecyk III has written, those who knew "both the lay of the land and the nuances of the sea always found lucrative employment functioning as guides, facilitators, and transporters in this underground economy."[6]

Just as common as the "June Gloom" fog during my formative years of surfing in California was the distinctive smell of burning marijuana at the beach. In fourth grade, I saw my first bag of pot. My friends and I used to walk to our local surfboard shop to stare longingly at surfboards we would never own. Although Zeppelin or the Stones throbbed from large teak cabinet speakers, often there was not an employee in sight, and not even the resin and coconut surfboard wax could mask the odor of marijuana smoke. One afternoon a long-haired, well-traveled surfer came into the shop, and after exchanging warm greetings and elaborate handshakes with the shopkeeper, he threw a big plastic bag filled with greenish-brown plant matter onto the counter and said, "Thai sticks, bro." That same summer, my friend Alex Kecht* found his older neighbor's stash of Thai sticks and stole one. It looked like a small cigar because the buds were so neatly and uniformly tied to a small bamboo stick with a thread of the plant's fiber. We broke the stick in half, wrapped it in a piece of notebook paper, and began to puff away. The ensuing intoxication, though not unpleasant, was so intense that I did not smoke pot again for several years.

By fourteen I was surfing well enough to cadge rides up the coast with older surfers. As a gremmie, I sat in the truck's bed, and when the cab's split rear window opened, they passed me a big, oily, burritolike joint of Thai that we smoked down to the roach. By the time we reached Westward Beach, I was so stoned that I felt like crawling under the truck and hiding. However, the combination of cold water, powerful waves, and peer pressure quickly sobered me up. By sixteen, marijuana was my daily bread, without which no surfing session was complete. Although there was a Western Surfing Association, a National Scholastic Surfing Association, a Christian Surfing Association, and probably even a Republican surfing organization, my peers and I were members of the Marijuana Surfing Association. Not all surfers smoked pot—some were adamantly opposed to it—but for us, pot and surfing went hand in hand. Not only was smoking an anesthetic that dulled life's sharp edges, it was, above all, an effective time killer for our endless waiting. Whether it was for a swell to come, the tide to drop, or the wind to change, we seemed to be always waiting for something.

I am old enough and honest enough to remember the Thai sticks that flooded my beachside town each summer—a surfer's equivalent of the Beaujolais nouveau. What Yale's Skull and Bones society once was to American politics, our subset of the Californian, Hawaiian, and Australian surfing tribes was to Thai marijuana smuggling. By the 1980s, the arrival of the Thai marijuana fleet in California marked the start of summer. Because so many watermen were employed in different aspects of the trade, we had Thai sticks before anyone else.

Thai sticks. Photo: Michael S. Ferguson

Thai pot was as important a part of our long summer surfing expeditions to Baja's remote point breaks as wetsuits, surfboards, or sleeping bags. Because we knew we would be searched by the Mexican Army and federales at checkpoints up and down the peninsula, we rolled dozens of joints that we hid in the Speedos we wore under our swim trunks. We knew that while the macho Mexicans would frisk us, they would never touch our crotches. For as young and as stoned as we were, we held up well under questioning. One frustrated federale, after spending forty-five minutes tearing my truck apart, stared into my friend's bloodshot eyes and said, "You say you have no *mota*, but your eyes say yes."

At a remote and windblown point break far down the Baja peninsula, I saw a Cessna 172 land on a rough dirt strip and begin unloading surfboards. The pilot and his friend, skilled older surfers, rode waves for a few hours and then flew away. Every afternoon of the swell, the same Cessna flew in for the best waves of the day and returned to Cabo in time for happy hour. I asked my friend how they were able to winter on the North Shore and summer in Baja with no visible means of support. "Because," he replied in a hushed and slightly reverential tone, "they're scammers." To us pot-smoking teenagers, scammers were heroic Robin Hood characters. They trafficked only in pot and surfed more world-class waves than anyone else.

While the pedestrian scammers paddled bales of pressed Mexican across the border, the elite had moved on to Southeast Asia, where the risk-to-reward ratio was much greater. Because of our proximity to the sources, it was very easy for surfers to make large amounts of money fast by middle-manning deals between the marijuana haves and have-nots. Like so many surfers, I was saving my money for an international surfing safari; although I had a full-time summer job, my income was supplemented by brokering pot deals. As criminally powerful as Crips and other black gangs were, they had a very hard time getting their hands on good pot because it was largely controlled by upper-middle-class white boys who refused to deal with them. I had developed some deep ties through sports and work to powerful black families in the Venice and Crenshaw areas and foolishly believed that I somehow was immune to the rules of the game.

I would meet my surfer connection at a McDonald's in Malibu, eat a burger, and leave with a duffle bag full of pot. From there I would drive down to the "Ghost Town" section of Venice. Formally known as Oakwood, Ghost Town is a black neighborhood less than a mile from the beach that had been set aside by Venice founding father Abbot Kinney as a neighborhood where blacks could own property. I had grown up playing sports with the scion of one of the most prominent criminal families there.

Kevin "KK" Jackson and I first met in Pop Warner Football as ten-year-olds and were reunited in high school, where we became close friends. By the 1960s, Oakwood was a ghetto and Jackson's parents, aunts, and uncles had established their reputations as thugs and career criminals long before the Crips. "My mother was a gangster, man, I seen her cut muthafuckas up, shoot muthafuckas," said KK. "Get a trick—I didn't know it was a trick at the time—in the house, rip off his money, and then tell me and my cousins to chase him out because he's beating her. I didn't know what the game was until I got older, and I was like, 'Damn! My mother!'" The crime for which his family would become infamous occurred in 1965 when his mother, Uncle Bernard, and Aunt Shirley mugged and murdered a Santa Monica city councilman's son. They were all arrested, tried, and sentenced to lengthy prison terms.[7]

KK Jackson was raised by his grandparents, and most of his childhood weekends were spent driving from San Quentin, to Soledad, to Folsom, to Sybil Brand to visit family members. By the time his Uncle Bernard got out of prison, he was a muscle-swollen "OG" (Original Gangster). His second-floor apartment just off the strand in Venice was always full of tattooed musclemen doing curls in the living room and silicone-enhanced blondes they referred to as "freaks," who looked like they had just stepped from the pages of *Hustler Magazine*. In this buzzing hive of criminal activity, KK and his brothers and cousins learned the rules of the game. "He methodically got all the kids my age at that time into drugs, because everybody was at his house," Jackson recalled. "'This is a gram, this is an eighth. You take this to that muthafucka down the street and he gonna give you an envelope.'" I was the only student in our school who was a regular visitor to Uncle Bernard's; little did I know that I was on a first-name basis with the heaviest gangsters in Venice. "That whole crew hangin' out at his place were cutthroats and killers, we didn't know—we didn't know we was in the lion's mouth," said Jackson.

By his senior year of high school, KK was one of West L.A.'s most promising point guards. Not only did he lead Crossroads High School to their first California Interscholastic Federation (CIF) basketball championship, he was named All-CIF, *L.A. Times* All-Westside, All-CIF Southern Section, Delphic League Player of the Year, and team MVP. Although he received a basketball scholarship to San Jose State, he was also a fast-rising member of the Venice Shoreline Crips. KK and Uncle Bernard would buy whatever pot I was willing to sell them, break it into minuscule half-gram bags, and make a small fortune. Nobody ever laid a finger on me because nobody wanted to kill the golden goose.

KK was not my only inner-city connection. Other times I left the Malibu McDonald's, took the Coast Highway south to the Santa Monica Freeway, got off in Crenshaw, near the Watts border, and drove to one of the tidy row houses, where my friend Rod Smith* lived with his parents. I met Rod when working as a construction laborer on the graveyard shift on a downtown Los Angeles high rise. Aside from the elevator operator, I was the only white on the shift and got hired because of my father's eminent position on the project. The previous summer I had been a lifeguard in Malibu Colony and had planned to lifeguard again, but after crashing a car, I owed my dad money, and he had other ideas about my summer job.

One of my first nights, the foreman, Lee Smith*, paired me with base-ball legend Carl Jones. Darryl Strawberry's former teammate from Cren-shaw High School, Carl was said to have been nearly as good as Straw-berry, and everyone was surprised when he was not drafted by a major league baseball team. After high school, he went to work with his father, Thedo Jones, in high-rise construction and his other lucrative, construc-tion-related side businesses. By the time I met him, Carl was already a legend in the industry for his superhuman feats during massive concrete pours.[8] He was not very happy when he was told to teach me how to oper-ate a big forklift. Our job was to dump the smaller garbage bins into larger, rectangular, open-topped Dumpsters known as "rolloffs."

Before jumping into the giant rolloff to freebase cocaine, Carl pointed to the forklift's pedals and said, "That's the gas, that's the brake, that's the clutch." Almost as an afterthought, he pointed to a lever and said, "That's the muthafucka that make the muthafucka go up and down." With those instructions I was set loose, dumping drywall and concrete into the con-tainer where he was freebasing. Aside from the three or four holes the fork punched in the side of the bins, I did surprisingly well. My teacher was so happy with my performance that he invited me in for a hit of base. Cocaine had already claimed a few of my friends, and although I was very wary of it, I didn't want to be rude. Carl handed me a plastic pipe, placed a rock on top of a piece of Brillo pad in the bowl, and lit it with a Bacardi 151-soaked torch. I drew the acrid smoke deep into my lungs. The ensuing ten-minute high was such a high, and the subsequent low was such a low, that I vowed at that moment never again to smoke cocaine, and I never did.

One night our foreman's son Rod and I were shoveling broken con-crete when he pulled out what looked like a toothpick inside a paper cover. "Pete, let's smoke this little old joint," he said as he sparked it. Seeds popped as he hit the nasty Mexican. Although it smelled unsmokable, I took a token hit and resumed working. No sooner had Rod finished the joint than our foreman, his dad, walked onto the floor. I had never seen the calm, quiet man so angry. "Sheet, y'all couple a shumhead muthfuckas!" he exploded. "Ain't got a hundred hours between you and you smokin' on my flo'!" While we shoveled, Lee delivered an hour-long harangue and dressed us down for our stupidity. "Pete, yo' daddy a big wheel, what the fuck he gonna think when he find out you smoking weed on the job with the niggas?" Finally, lunch break came. "Smoke in your car, on your break, and not on my time!" he said, and never mentioned it again.

A week or so later, we were eating lunch by our cars and Rod pulled out another pinner joint. I had been waiting for this moment. I turned to my colleagues, let out an arrogant snort, and said, "Put it away, Rod. Man—that's not a joint." I took a big fat Thai joint from my truck's ashtray and handed it to him. "Now, *this* is a joint." Suffice it to say that none of the others had ever smoked pot of this quality, and the rest of the shift was especially unproductive. Although Carl was a heavy lifter when it came to cocaine, he got so stoned that he spent the remainder of the night supine, riding it out on a stack of drywall. Word got out that "Pete was connected," and my first request for a big bag of pot, at cost plus, came from my foreman, Lee.

After my summer job ended I was a regular visitor to the Smith house in Crenshaw. If my white Mustang was parked out front, it meant that they were open for business. My old foreman bought at least a quarter of whatever I brought at my cost—the tribute. His son broke up the rest into tiny nickel bags that he sold from the outdoor porch. Rod's parents had no problem with him selling pot, and there was nothing fleeting or furtive about it. Most nights we would drink beer and eat chicken or ribs as a steady stream of people came up on the porch. All of our customers were adults, most on their way home from work, and grateful for the opportunity to buy quality pot. The only time there was ever any tension was the evening two cars roared up to the house and came to skidding stops. I immediately thought there was going to be a drive-by shooting, and even Rod seemed alarmed. The car doors flew open, and young men with brass instruments and big drums began to spill out. It all made sense when I saw a cougar on one of the drums and immediately realized that they had just robbed Crenshaw High School. While Mrs. Smith had no problem with her son selling pot, hiding stolen property was not okay. She came out to the porch, whispered something in Rod's ear, and headed back inside. "Y'all ain't bringin' that shit in my house," Rod barked. They all stopped in their tracks. By now the cars had fled, and the felonious marching band left on foot.

Between my full-time construction job and my drives to the hood, I was able to save quite a bit of money and took an eight-month surfing trip to New Zealand, Australia, Nauru, Micronesia, Fiji, Rarotonga, and French

Polynesia. One week after I returned to Southern California in the late summer of 1984, I decided I could never live there again. I managed to wrangle an eleventh-hour admission to a small Northeastern liberal arts college and for the first time in my life became a serious student. What shocked me about New York was that it was easier to get heroin than decent pot. After my freshman year, I returned to California and spent the summer working construction and surfing in Baja. As I was getting ready to drive back to New York for the fall semester, I decided to bring a quarter pound of pot. Of course I had to make the pot pay for itself and called KK Jackson, who told me to meet him at Uncle Bernard's apartment, where he was now living. After a year in college, he had dropped out and returned to Venice to resume his life of crime.

It had been over a year since I had visited Bernard's apartment, and when the metal security door opened, something felt different. After I took an oversized Ziploc from my duffle bag, Bernard and his homies rushed me and started trying to grab handfuls of weed. I was appalled and immediately stuffed the pot back into the bag. "What the fuck is this? You wonder why you can never get any good pot when you pull this kind of nigg—" Mid-sentence, KK grabbed me by the arm and dragged me into one of the back bedrooms. He looked me dead in the eye and said, "Pete, you better break off some buds for those wolves or you ain't getting out of here with that bag." Although he appeared nervous, I knew how good a con man he was and figured it was a setup. Begrudgingly I handed over some buds and cursed him for his betrayal. A few minutes later he returned, still acting nervous. "Pete, they smoking now. Put your hand in that bag like you got a gun and go straight for the door. I made sure it's unlocked." Although I made it out of Bernard's spot unscathed, it would be twenty years before I spoke to KK again.

I broke my quarter pound into smaller, heat-sealed bags that I carefully wiped down with gasoline in case of dogs. Those bags went inside a large plastic bag that was secured to the underside of my driver's seat. I was taught always to assume that you would be searched, and if the police could find your stash, you deserved to get busted. I rolled two joints for the drive and covered over 900 miles the first day. Closing in on the New Mexico–Texas border, I lit my last joint and after I'd taken a few puffs, I accidentally dropped it. I turned on the interior light to look for the still burning joint and unbeknownst to me, passed a New Mexico state police-

Kevin Jackson, Richard J. Donovan Correctional Facility. Photo: Kevin Jackson

man going 85 m.p.h. Finally, I found the joint on the floor, took a couple more hits, and then noticed red lights so far behind me that I figured they were for someone else.

The lights gained at an alarming rate, and suddenly a spotlight filled my Mustang's interior with harsh white light. "Pull over and keep your hands on the steering wheel," the policeman said over his loudspeaker. Because the joint was still in my hand and the car reeked of pot, I did neither and instead slid the roach into my sock and rolled down both electrical windows. In a vain attempt to air out the car, I took a suspiciously long time to slow and stop. In my rearview mirror, I saw the tall, lean state policeman approaching with one hand on his flashlight and the other on his gun. The beam from his big Maglite® found my eyes and although I was nearly blinded, the sound of gravel crunching underfoot grew louder and stopped next to my window. The officer took one look at my bloodshot eyes, caught a whiff of the car's interior, and asked, "Son, are you transporting narcotics across state lines?" Terrifying thoughts jumped into my head and my brain did quantum-speed calculus: more than four ounces + crossing state lines = Dad/lawyers/never live it down. Once I recognized my proximity to deep trouble, I remembered the advice of my elders—"It's not over until the cuffs are on"—and settled into character. It was time to stonewall.

"No sir!" I barked like a nervous marine recruit at Parris Island.

"Son, I smell the fruity herbal aroma of marijuana, your eyes are bleeding, and you have a brown stain on your lip."

"No sir," I replied with even more conviction.

"Do I have your consent to search?"

Hoping to trip him up on a technicality, I did not reply and instead handed him the keys. He told me to get out of the car and open it or he would get a dog. I lifted the hatchback; the car was crammed with surfboards, duffle bags, and boxes of books and papers. When he unzipped the first duffle bag and found bundles of slides wrapped in paper and duct tape, certain that he had hit the drug motherlode, he ordered me up against the car and told me to spread my hands and feet. I followed his instructions and said, "Sir they are just slides." The policeman opened a few packages of Kodachromes and resumed his search. When he found a dozen blocks of white surfboard wax, he ordered me up against the car again. "Coconut surfboard wax," I said. "Smell it."

After twenty minutes, half of my belongings were sitting in the red New Mexico dirt, and he hadn't found so much as a seed. Because the search started in the back of the car, he was still a long way from the pot stashed under the driver's seat. I could sense the cop's frustration as he lay facedown in the back of the car, sniffing like a dog. By now, even the smell of the joint had faded, and for the first time I thought, *I might get out of this after all.* In that moment, under the dark desert sky, I told myself that if I got out of this jam, I would never put myself in this position again. The policeman finally got out of the back of my car, straightened his uniform, looked me sternly in the eye, and said, "Son, we are going to strike a little deal," and paused. Although I managed to maintain my composure, my mind started to race: where was he going with this? When he said, "You keep it under 55 while you are in New Mexico and we'll call it even," I nearly collapsed. Now came the hardest part: not jumping in his arms and promising never to do anything so stupid again. Instead, I kept a straight face and said, "Yes, sir," for the final time, and began putting my bags back in the car. Although I continued to smoke pot, I never trafficked in it again.

I began writing *Thai Stick* more than thirteen years ago, when I was a footloose bachelor who didn't mind taking risks and stepping on toes. Today, I live in the Bible Belt with my wife and two young sons. In addition to writing, I design and test boats for the U.S. military. Although my long hair, an ongoing source of father-son tension, is gone and my views are more conservative than they once were, there is a part of my past that I will not sweep under the rug and disavow. Growing up in Southern California during the 1970s and 1980s, drugs, mainly marijuana, were a big part of my life. In my case, marijuana was not a gateway to other drugs and didn't prevent me from finishing college and earning a Ph.D. with highest honors at twenty-eight.

After receiving my doctorate from Columbia University in 1993, I began working in Southeast Asia, documenting Khmer Rouge atrocities for a number of nonprofit organizations. During my first trip in 1994, I visited Tuol Sleng Prison in Phnom Penh, where approximately 15,000 to 20,000 men, women, and children entered and fewer than 20 survived. All were savagely tortured, and most were photographed in a series of eerie and sometimes gruesome portraits. Four Americans had been among those killed. When I found and read their confessions, I was stunned. Had I been a few years older, it could have been me. While some historians and journalists were speculating that they were CIA agents, I suspected they were pot smugglers.[9]

The following summer, I went camping at Rattlesnake Point, a remote surf spot on the Baja peninsula. Isolated and lawless, it had once been a favorite hideout for surfers on the lam. One long afternoon during a flat spell, Ned, a quietly impressive older surfer from Maui, stopped by our camp for a chat, and the conversation turned to my recent trip to Cambodia and the four Americans killed by the Khmer Rouge. Not only did he know two of them, he also confirmed they had been trying to smuggle pot. Although the details were hazy, Ned said that his friend Mike Ritter was living in Thailand at the time of their captures and knew more.

Ritter's personal history is not unique. His life is in many ways a template for the surfer scammer. The Santa Barbara native smuggled his first hash from Afghanistan in 1968 and became a partner in a hash oil ring in 1970. By the mid-1970s, the Californian had found his calling—Thai sticks. Year after year, scam after scam, he had only limited financial success. Finally, in 1986, he earned $5,000,000 from a successful Thai scam and retired. Now that he had the capital to enjoy "the surfing lifestyle," he did not recognize it. Unlike himself and his peers, who were content to subsist on fish, rice, water, and perfect waves, the modern surfers he ran into in Indonesia traveled in climate-controlled yachts with satellite phones, full bars, and little cultural interest beyond watching the video highlights of their last surf session. After a decade of international surfing surfaris and exotic travel, Ritter grew bored. When he divorced at fifty, he felt as though his life of scamming was catching up with him. Above all, he did not want to lead a double life anymore. In an effort to maintain his cover, Ritter shunned people and as a result, he said, "My life became solitary and lonely. I was not learning anything new. I wanted a fuller life; I wanted deeper relationships with people."

There had been a time when surfer smugglers were treated like heroes, but by the 1990s those days were over. Not only was law enforcement successfully hunting them down, their history was being disavowed by many of their former coconspirators and old customers, who had traded pot for Prozac. Even worse, some had become SUV-driving Republicans. Despite the seismic shifts in the social landscape, Mike Ritter remained proud of how he and his peers had crossed oceans and war zones and overcome tremendous obstacles to return with this precious commodity. The smuggler wanted to talk about his past—the frustrations, the failures, the triumphs. Like the moonshiners of the north Georgia mountains, Ritter did not consider smuggling morally wrong, just illegal because of an arbitrary law.[10]

Mike Ritter visited Cambodia as a tourist in 1997 and heard about my research on Tuol Sleng Prison at the bar of the Foreign Correspondents Club in Phnom Penh. My colleague Doug Niven and I had tracked down and interviewed the prison's staff and survivors. Included in the mountains of evidence were the "confessions" of the four American sailors captured on yachts in Cambodian waters. Ritter remembered when they vanished and had wondered about their horrible fate for more than two decades. The retired smuggler had good reason to fear the Khmer Rouge. He had piloted numerous boatloads of marijuana in the Gulf of Thailand and on more than one occasion, in Cambodian waters.

Mike Ritter and I both happened to be at Rattlesnake Point to surf a large swell generated by Hurricane Nora in September 1997. I had just returned from another trip to Cambodia with new information about the captured Americans provided by one of the prison's survivors. Ritter pulled up to a dusty cantina in a tricked-out sand rail (dune buggy) and introduced himself. Unlike some of the pot dealers I had met, the actual smugglers, those who moved the product, looked different. They were weatherbeaten, weary, and conspicuously inconspicuous. He was no exception. Although he was small and sinewy, he had the broad shoulders of a lifelong surfer and was remarkably fit for his age. With his wary eyes hidden behind sunglasses, Ritter was cool and noncommittal, but agreed to reach out to some old friends in Thailand and help me learn more. It would be many years before he told me that in 1978 he had been asked to supply one of the captured boats with marijuana. Within a month, Ritter confirmed that both boats had been on smuggling missions; he had found out who was running the operations and who probably supplied the marijuana.

That fall, Mike Ritter began interviewing retired smugglers to learn more about the Americans who had vanished off the Cambodian coast. I was amazed by the interviews and showed some of the transcripts to my former professor, Ron Grele, director of Columbia University's Center for Oral History. Considered by some the father of modern oral history, Grele was impressed enough by the first interviews to admit the smuggler to Columbia's prestigious summer oral history institute. During the summer of 1999, Ritter joined two dozen lawyers, journalists, graduate students, and historians to discuss works in progress and historical methodology. After his time at Columbia, Ritter wanted to better understand the historical currents that moved him and many of his generation to do what they did and asked for my help conducting a larger oral history of pot smuggling.

Grele warned both of us that we were operating in a legal no-man's land by interviewing former criminals about their criminal acts. Although Ritter could not talk about his own past without jeopardizing his freedom, a decade had passed since his last smuggling venture and almost everyone he knew was dead, busted, or broke. He thought the DEA was no longer interested in him and naïvely believed he had some form of immunity. As a result of Grele's warning, Ritter decided he would only tape interviews with convicted smugglers. Over the next four years, he conducted dozens of interviews with American and Thai smugglers and even some of the DEA agents who had busted them. Meanwhile, I was able to track down and interview some of the former Khmer Rouge sailors who had seen the Americans and their boats after they were captured at sea.

When Ritter asked me if I was interested in turning our research into a book, I was immediately interested. As a professional historian with a background in oral history, who had been a peripheral participant in the marijuana trade, I was in a unique position. Over the next decade, Ritter and I were able to engage these historical actors who lived outside the law and capture a forgotten dimension of an era that would otherwise go unrecorded and undocumented. Once the interviews were collected and transcribed, it became clear that the voices of the participants were critical for understanding the ethos of the times.

The subject of marijuana smuggling posed a narrative challenge. Who would best tell the story? Following the lead of British Marxist E. P. Thompson, we were most interested in capturing the voices of a voiceless group that was conspicuously absent from both oral history and the "new social history" (which studies the experiences of ordinary people in the past). Because marijuana smuggling is illegal, it is impossible to assemble historical evidence in a traditional way. There are no smuggling archives, and state records only document the victories of law enforcement. The only records of success are the fading memories of the surviving participants. Though the marijuana dealer's side of the story has been told many times, the smuggler's story has never been told satisfactorily. Despite the inevitable inaccuracies of decades-old memories, oral history is of unique value in understanding the past; as the great Italian historian Alessandro

Portelli points out, it "tells us less about the events as such than about their meaning."[11]

"True crime" is a strange, one-sided genre that consists mostly of law enforcement fairy tales and self-serving, Mr. Big soliloquies of greatness that omit all but the heroic narrator's myopic perspective. Although there is a substantial body of literature on marijuana, little has been written about the intricacies of smuggling by the men who were involved. In reviewing the literature on subject, we were stunned by the many significant factual errors in such books as *The Underground Empire*, *Reefermen*, *The Hunt for Marco Polo*, and many others. This should not have come as a surprise, I now realize. Members of this particular underground economy do not typically draw attention to themselves, much less write letters to the editor. Little did I know that we would conduct thousands of hours of interviews, and the smuggling history project would turn into a collaboration. More often than not, I would ask Mike Ritter a question and he would respond with an essay.

My relationship with Mike Ritter was tested and tempered by reversals of fortune that neither of us could have anticipated or imagined. As much as *Thai Stick* is a series of stories about smuggling and a brief utopian moment in twentieth-century American life, it is also a business history that would make an excellent case study for any MBA program, because the main elements are supply and demand, and overcoming logistics and marketing obstacles. But above all, the aim of this book is to show that many people, beyond those immediately involved, played a part in this narrative, whether they were aware of it or not. Many Americans want to forget that pot smugglers helped shape contemporary culture. They established the corrosive relationship between generations of American middle- and upper-middle-class youth and law enforcement that eroded our respect for the state.[12]

Pacific Coast, United States

Southeast Asia

1

SURFERS, SCAMMERS, AND THE COUNTERCULTURE

Today, the expression "waterman" has been reduced to a marketing cliché used to sell stand-up paddle boards and other detritus of the so-called "surfing lifestyle." There was a time when the word carried great weight, designating the maritime equivalent of a black belt in a great martial art. It was not enough simply to surf. A waterman had to have mastered all the aquatic arts: he was a skilled diver, canoe surfer, oarsman, meteorologist, sailor, ocean swimmer, body surfer, lifesaver, tandem surfer, fisherman, and board/boatbuilder who could ride any size surf on any craft put underneath him. Pioneer watermen like Duke Kahanamoku, Gene "Tarzan" Smith, Bill Bridgeman, and Dan Fowlie set a bar so high that their accomplishments only look more impressive over time.

Although the Duke was the greatest surfer and swimmer of the twentieth century—he won gold medals in the 1912 and 1920 Olympics—the Hawaiian most dramatically demonstrated his mastery in the sea when a fishing boat capsized in heavy surf off Corona Del Mar in 1925. Although seventeen fishermen drowned, the Duke singlehandedly saved eight in what the Newport Beach police chief called "the most superhuman surfboard rescue act the world has ever seen." Equipped with a compass, a hunting knife, and a pair of goggles, 6'6" hulk Gene "Tarzan" Smith paddled a surfboard 100 miles from Oahu to Kauai in 1940. Malibu surfer Bill Bridgeman was one of the point's original locals, but he became best known as the test pilot who flew higher and faster than Chuck Yeager. Not only did Bridgeman set the world speed record at mach 1.88 in 1951, that year he also set the world altitude record of 79,494 feet. These extraordinary men of action had one thing in common: they were not motivated by glory, fame, or money. If a fish needed catching, they caught it; if a wave needed riding, they rode it; and if a life needed saving, they saved it, because that is what watermen did.[1]

For the purposes of this story, waterman Dan Fowlie provides a useful example. Fowlie made so much money diving for abalone in La Jolla during the 1950s that he bought his first car at age thirteen, and by the end of high school he was making more money than his aircraft engineer father. Featured surfing on the cover of *Sports Illustrated* in 1954, he went on to make a fortune that he used to buy thirty kilometers of Costa Rican coastline, where he established one of surfing's Valhallas. Fowlie claimed that his money came from his Laguna Beach leather goods business, but a U.S. federal court disagreed, and sentenced him to thirty years in prison for conspiring to distribute marijuana and being part of a continuing criminal enterprise.

The surfers who became smugglers were mostly Dionysian men of action who rejected all things political in favor of a sensual, hedonistic life. When asked if he'd had strong political views during the 1960s and 1970s, Hawaiian smuggler Craig Williams replied bluntly, "No, I was too loaded [on] sex, drugs and rock and roll."[2] During the first four months of 1969, U.S. Customs busted six surfers trying to bring hash-filled surfboards into America. According to smuggler Jerry Kamstra, surfers and tourists "accounted for more marijuana reaching the U.S.A. during the 1960s than by any other method." For many young Californians, no trip to Baja was complete without a few waves at K-38, lobsters at Puerto Nuevo, beers at Hussong's Cantina, and a kilo stuffed in the panels of Mom's station wagon.[3]

Why did so many surfers smuggle pot? The simple and obvious reason is that surfers need time and money to chase waves. Inspired by the example of Bruce Brown's *Endless Summer*, generations of wave riders went on the road in search of the perfect wave. "Bruce Brown said it, being able to go to the beach and live," said one convicted surfer smuggler, "not just work and go home and watch TV. You get to live, you get to go surfing, you get to go to the beach, you're an independent."[4]

One organic result of surfer wanderlust during the 1960s and 1970s was an ever expanding, international network market for marijuana—South Africa, France, Bali, Australia, New Zealand, Hawaii, California—virtually anywhere there were waves. By the late 1960s, surfers had established an aquatic version of the Hippie Trail whose core group could be found in Europe during the fall; Hawaii or Africa during the winter; in Mexico or new, exotic destinations like Tahiti, Bali, or Mauritius during the summer. Unlike the Hippie Trail pilgrims, surfers had clear goals and destinations. Big-wave surfing legend Owl Chapman described the distinction: "They were like me, I wasn't like them," he said. "I was a hippie, but I was always a surfer first." The transition into the black market was not a stretch for thrill seekers who had traditionally come from the margins of American society. Not only did surfing provide excellent cover, but in a few nervous days or hours, one could earn enough money to pay for years of surfing dreams.[5]

Hawaii was one of the first and most important crossroads for marijuana smugglers. For generations of surfers, the islands were a proving ground where reputations were made and lost. By the late 1960s, many California surfers paid for their surf trips by smuggling Mexican marijuana and LSD to the most remote island chain on earth. Because the territory did not become a U.S. state until 1959; gambling and prostitution were legal well into the 1940s, and given the huge transient military population, vice was an important part of the economy. Although there was Mexican pot available, one early Hawaiian smuggler said everybody wanted Asian "ganja." A pool hall in Pearl City sold dime wrappers that contained five tiny joints, and it was by far the strongest pot anyone had ever smoked. Many of the first Thai loads were going to Hawaii because it was a hub for American soldiers coming from and going to Vietnam.

Initially, the Army Post Office (APO) and returning soldiers were the first to smuggle pot back from Southeast Asia. For those who had survived combat, what was one more risk?[6] Later, the pot trade would shift toward civilians sailing loads. Hawaiian-born surfer Terry Dawson* was among the first Americans to smuggle high-quality Southeast Asian

Presurf smoke, California. Photo: Jeff Divine

marijuana to Oahu. Dawson was forced to flee in 1967 after a Honolulu debutante's parents found their daughter naked by the pool, high on LSD, dancing with a statue, and babbling about "Terry's magic." They contacted the FBI, and before he could be apprehended, Dawson and 500 hits of LSD boarded an Alaska Barge Lines tug called the *Nez Perce* that was headed to Vietnam. Officially, the vessel had a shady government contract to deliver construction supplies that would take them all the way up the Mekong River to Phnom Penh, Cambodia. Unofficially, the tugboat with a red Indian on the stack was a black market PX that considered itself "a friend to all and foe to none." Typically, the wily old captain left cases of beer and cigarettes on remote river beaches and if the peace offering was accepted, the tug dropped anchor and sold cigarettes, beer, whiskey, food, and more exotic fare. The young American was amazed by the Eurasian prostitutes, American commandos, ROK Marines, ARVN paratroopers, CIA agents, and possible VC who came out of the remote jungles for a bit of R&R.[7]

Dawson flew to Vientiane, Laos, and in a stall in the central market saw the most beautiful, golden-yellow marijuana he had ever seen. "Mamasan had the full line, in piles just like beans and rice," he recalled. "The hill tribes grew the pot on the little islands in the Mekong River." The American introduced himself to the betel nut-chewing woman who ran the stall and paid her for only the top buds of her finest plants. Dawson carefully instructed her son to break them up by hand and grind them into dust with a sieve. "Why do sticks? Why do branches? Why do leaves? It was a special product," wrote Dawson. "His family ground gigantic bales into the powdered marijuana I called the 'Golden Voice.'" Like most pot smugglers, although opium and heroin were readily available, Dawson refused to deal in any opiates. He believed that marijuana, hashish, and LSD were tools of enlightenment, while heroin and even alchohol were not. When the first ten pounds of Terry Dawson's Laotian "Golden Voice" arrived in Honolulu via the APO in 1968, it caused an overnight sensation and sold out in days for the unheard-of price of $1,000 per pound. "Already 'the voice' is a legend among Oahu's growing secret society of potheads. No other weed is anything like it," wrote Michael McPherson in his novel *Rivers of the Sun*. "It's ganja, the golden voice from Laos, the most powerfully psychedelic marijuana I've ever smoked, noted for its delayed effect."[8]

Although many Hawaiian surfers enjoyed drugs the utopian trappings of the California counterculture were conspicuously absent. Most Hawaiians were as likely to take LSD and go pig hunting as they were to contemplate a sunset. After Terry Dawson's first APO load sold out, Ralph Baxter, his local crime syndicate connection, informed him that he would be returning to Laos sooner than he had expected. This was an order that could not be refused if Dawson ever planned to bring pot into Hawaii again. If it weren't for his personal excesses, Ralph Baxter might have risen high in Japanese-Hawaiian organized crime syndicate. The half-Japanese former architecture graduate student turned armed robber was a formidable predator who liked to take LSD before holding up high-stakes poker games with a stocking over his face and a .45 in his hand. A modern-day rōnin with angular features, long black hair, and piercing eyes, he "seemed unaffected by fear, emotion, or danger of any kind." His legend grew after an especially bold caper during the packed show of a well-known Hawaiian singer in a Waikiki hotel. When the lights and power suddenly went out, the band kept playing, and many thought it was part of the show. Seventy seconds later, when the power was restored, $20,000 cash was missing. "I was at the fore with Augustus Owsley Stanley III, the Laguna Brotherhood, Crane's Crew," wrote Terry Dawson, "and the likes of Ralph

Ralph Baxter. Photo: Michael McPherson

Baxter who overshadowed them all." Surfer scammers quickly learned to sell all of their pot when they arrived in Hawaii or get ripped off. For anyone trying to import drugs into the Hawaiian Islands, their greatest concern was not the police, it was fearsome predators like Baxter and a bevy of local thugs backed by corrupt elements of law enforcement and organized crime.[9]

Surfing's Mount Everest is a remote 55-kilometer stretch of beach on Oahu's North Shore. This rural, largely agricultural area could get mighty lonely with only one patrol car between Kahuku and Wahiawa. "They were rolling up all those guys on the North Shore and putting gasoline on them and telling them, 'Where's the stash or we're going to burn you alive and fuck your wife,'" explained Mike Ferguson.[10] *The Roach*, a long-defunct Hawaiian underground newspaper, reported in 1969 that "The drug scene on the North Shore seems to be drying up as the operations of the syndicate get increasingly ruthless," and went on to tell the story of four friends from Huntington Beach who brought in a quantity of pot and LSD from Southern California. "One recent evening, around 8:30, three oversized locals entered the house and demanded that the surfers give up the goods, which they denied knowing about," wrote *The Roach*. "So, in a highly professional manner, one of the three thugs pointed his .38 Special, 6-inch barrel gun, complete with silencer, at the sleeping nineteen-year-old boy, and fired. There was no noise, no wasted motion, no playing around or second chances. They rounded up 22 kilos of grass, 600 hits of acid, and 700 dollars in cash." The robbers dropped a half brick of marijuana in the front yard, enough for the Honolulu Police Department to arrest the survivors for possession of narcotics. "The case now, like so many others, is left unsolved and in the greasy palms of the HPD." When one faction of the Brotherhood of Eternal Love, an organization of psychedelic drug users and distributors based in Southern California, moved to Oahu's North Shore, their reception, according to the *Honolulu Advertiser,* "was considerably less than cordial."[11]

The big syndicates did not bother Terry Dawson, as long as they were the only ones who got his pot. When Dawson told Baxter that he was selling part of the load to hippie friends, Baxter told him that it was not for sale, his syndicate already owned it, and delivered the first $10,000 installment that night. When word reached a freelance North Shore thug that Terry Dawson, not Ralph Baxter, was the source of the incredible new pot, the thug showed up at Dawson's house at Kawela Bay and told him that in order to be safe from predators like himself, he would have to pay for protection. Although the smuggler politely declined the offer, he knew this was just the beginning and set up a fire zone in his front yard, complete with trip wires and simulation grenades stolen from the army's nearby training area at Kahuku. Dawson had picked up some

Hash slabs, North Shore of Oahu. Photo: Jeff Divine

tradecraft from the commandos who frequented his tug on the Mekong and had even shipped home an AK-47. He took the Kalashnikov out of storage, loaded his high-capacity magazines, donned his black Ho Chi Minh pajamas, and waited in a tree house across from his house. Sometime around midnight, a beat-up Chevy van pulled up and five local heavies approached the only lit window en masse. When Dawson pulled the wire on the simulation grenade and strafed the van with a short burst from his AK, the panicked robbers tripped over each other in a Keystone Kops frenzy trying to get back into the van. The whole physical comedy was strobe-lit by sparks, ricochets, and tracers.[12]

A surprising amount of Dawson's "Golden Voice" went to Maui, which by the late 1960s was the seat of Hawaiian and even international counterculture royalty whose leaders, like Timothy Leary, saw surfers as a more advanced species of mankind. To Leary, the act of riding a wave was the ultimate expression of his "be here now," live in the present philosophy. Jimi Hendrix's manager, Michael Jeffries, was impressed by the "cosmic surfers" he met on Maui. "It is not the same as everyone thinks it is. It's not the bikini beach party where the surfers are just lying around the beach drinking beer, bumming around with the evening orgies," he explained. "They've been through the changes ahead of everyone else: they've been through yoga, Zen, pure food—way before."[13]

Surfer Magazine editor Drew Kampion best described the role surfers played in shaping the 1960s counterculture: "Now the world's got amnesia. But the weirdness and relevance of the 60s had quite a lot to do with surfing; surfing somehow contained and reflected all the bizarre and contradictory facets of that time." After starring in *Endless Summer*, Mike Hynson was one of the most famous surfers in the world. But by 1969, Hynson had traded his navy blue blazer for love beads and smuggled his first load of Nepalese hash. The once dapper, clean-cut surfer had metamorphosed into "the Maharishi"—a super fit, surfer hippie aesthete who now practiced surfing as a form of ritual meditation. His wife, Bambi Merryweather, was a 1960s "It girl" who modeled for the Ford Agency and was a regular at Andy Warhol's factory. Her upbringing was anything but radical: not only was Merryweather the daughter of an Arizona state senator, she was also the goddaughter of conservative icon Senator Barry Goldwater, Jr.[14]

Presurf smoke, North Shore of Oahu. Photo: Jeff Divine

Why were so many privileged young American baby boomers deserting the comfortable paths that their parents had so carefully laid out in front of them? No generation's future seemed brighter. While Europe and the Soviet Union were digging out of World War II's rubble, the United States experienced a flood of material prosperity unlike anything in human history. With only 6 percent of the world's population, by 1948 Americans owned 80 percent of the earth's new cars and consumed 62 percent of its oil. With cars, houses, and college educations now middle-class staples, more babies were born in the United States in the five years between 1948 and 1953 than in the past three decades combined. By 1960, the most prosperous year in American history, the United States became the first society in the history of the world to have more college students than farmers.[15]

Unlike his German immigrant parents, who had survived depressions and two world wars, California-born baby boomer Mike Ritter knew only stability and prosperity. After serving in World War II, his father, Julian, returned to California, resumed his painting career, and started a family; his daughter, Christine, was born in 1947 and his son, Mike, in 1948.[16] The Ritters lived in a beachside section of Santa Barbara called "the Mesa." To the east was a view of the city and coastal mountains; to the west, the Pacific Ocean and the Channel Islands. What made Ritter's life so special was the hundred-meter stretch of nondescript beach down the hill from his house that became his playground, clubhouse, secret spot, and above all, the force that held him and his friends together from childhood until the end of high school. "I couldn't believe how lucky I was to be born American, to live in California, right next to the beach. We were special," said Ritter.

In order to get to the beach, one walked down a narrow, loose shale trail that was considered dangerous by many. Because there were plenty of beaches that were easier to reach, "the Mesa" was usually deserted, and that was fine with the boys who lived there. Not only did they run up and down the cliff like billy goats, they spent more of their waking hours at "The Lane" than at home. Although the young Californians caught surf perch in the foamy white water and skin-dived in the kelp beds, most of their energy went to mastering the difficult sport of surfing. Always the last chosen for teams in sports, Ritter no longer cared because he was a surfer. To the young gremmies, their sun-bleached hair and the calloused knots that grew on their knees and the tops of their feet were badges of pride, similar to a wrestler's cauliflower ears. "Anyone who lived inland was missing out and somehow just plain lame in our estimation. Surfers were our school's elite, even though we were outnumbered by 'greasers,'" said Ritter. "Anyone who lived more than a quick drive to the beach was a ho-dad or a greaser. East Coast guys were just plain geeks. It was good to be part of an elite."

During the summer mornings, when the coast was usually cloaked in thick fog, the first surfer on the beach had to make the fire. Although scavenging the driftwood was easy enough, it took skill to light the damp wood. Once warm, the boys braved the chilly water and returned shivering to the fire. Typically, by lunchtime the fog would burn off and be replaced by hot summer sun; for months their lips were chapped and their noses peeling. Many afternoons, warm land breezes that smelled of sage and chaparral, called "Santa Anas," blew in from the east and raked the ocean smooth. Some nights the young surfers camped on the sand, where they sipped their first beers and talked about girls and the future. They fell asleep to the foghorn's low moan and were awakened by barking seals and squabbling seagulls.

In high school, Mike Ritter considered marijuana a life-threatening substance. During his junior year, 1965, he visited the local police station to conduct research for a report on drugs. An officer briefed him and gave the teenager a stack of antidrug leaflets. The one about pot pictured sunken-cheeked social rejects smoking strange-looking cigarettes with captions that described their degenerate behavior. When Ritter learned that one of the stars of his swim team smoked it, he feared for his teammate's life. In addition to reading, writing, and arithmetic, Ritter learned in school about the free world, its arch-enemy, communism, and how victory in the Cold War depended on him. Preparing for an atomic attack was an important part of the curriculum in California schools during the 1950s and 1960s. "I can't say how others of my generation were affected by the bomb, but my tenth-grade history teacher's animated stories about cities blown away and people disintegrating terrified me. Fear sometimes woke me from sleep at night. Where in the world would I be safe?"[17]

Although baby boomers like Ritter were afraid of the atom bomb, nothing did more to shake their confidence in America than the Vietnam War. Underneath the veneer of tranquility and prosperity, discontent was coalescing around the rapidly escalating conflict. Though there were only 4,000 U.S. soldiers in Vietnam in 1962, by 1965 that number had climbed to 125,000, and by 1967 most young American men faced a draft and the prospect of combat in the rice paddies of Southeast Asia. The war shed a stark light on the contradictions between the nation he had learned about in school and the one he saw on the evening news. Like many young, upper-middle-class Americans, Ritter believed that the country had gone astray and was on a fear-driven path to self-destruction. The refusal to go to war turned many draft dodgers into outlaws. Another California surfer's suspicions about the Vietnam War were confirmed after a friend from his graduating high school class joined the army instead of going surfing with his friends. When he returned home in a casket six months later, the surfer attended the funeral, and the honor guards' rifle shots punctuated his decision to dodge the draft no matter the consequences.[18]

Many believed that the establishment had forfeited its moral authority and even its right to govern. "We wanted our nation to seek the moral high ground," said Mike Ritter. "We were convinced we were part of an imminent change of great proportions." For a generation that had been taught to condemn the spineless Germans for failing to stand up to Hitler, many felt honor bound to oppose America's role in the Vietnam War. "After all, isn't this what we had been taught was the right thing for a moral people to do? You're goddamned right it was! Eventually it became clear that our naiveté was immense and our education incomplete. In fact, our education was only beginning," wrote California baby boomer Art Robles*.

Mike Ritter temporarily avoided the draft by enrolling in the brand new University of California at Santa Cruz. The summer before he left for college, he spent most of his time surfing the pristine waves of the Bixby Ranch in a swan song to California surfing. Located on the coastline north and south of Point Conception, the Hollister and Bixby ranches had been privately owned for more than a century, and being there was like stepping back to Chumash Indian times. Not only were the waves protected by no trespassing signs, the rules were enforced by gun-toting cowboys who hated surfers. Only members of the Santa Barbara Surf Club and Santa Barbara Sportsman's Club were allowed onto the Hollister Ranch, and from there they could sneak onto Bixby Ranch to reach Cojo Point, one of the world's best summertime waves. For better or worse, this experience would stay with him for most of his life: "I learned that by breaking the rules, we achieved an otherwise impossible dream that produced some of the most glorious memories of my youth." Toward the end of the summer, after another day of empty, perfect waves, Ritter grew sad because he knew this paradise was not going to last. He had already seen superhighways cut through his favorite fields, obliterating meandering creeks and stands of old oaks that he had once climbed. By the 1960s, California's beaches were being overrun, and Ritter knew that if he wanted to surf uncrowded waves, he would have to travel the world to find them.[19]

Mike Ritter arrived at Santa Cruz to begin his freshman year in September 1966. His new roommate, Buzz Jones, an older transfer student from Los Angeles, was by far the hippest guy he had ever met. When Buzz opened his attaché case, he revealed a large bag of marijuana, a Meerschaum pipe, rolling papers, and various implements. Next, he adeptly rolled a joint and nonchalantly invited his roommate to join him in a nearby stand of redwoods. After they smoked, Ritter felt light and fuzzy and couldn't stop laughing. The sensation was nothing like he "had imagined from those tawdry police pamphlets." Within days, Buzz, Ritter, and a handful of others were the first stoners at UCSC. Although Ritter tried to limit his smoking to weekends so that it wouldn't interfere with his studies, he added a midweek smoke and before long, was getting high every day.

In addition to laughs, the pot smokers shared underground newspapers and discussed the antiwar movement and Eastern philosophy. Marijuana was now a flag of rebellion, a sacrament to be shared with the initiated, and a litmus test to see if someone was "cool." Ritter considered joining the antiwar movement until he went to a rally and met members of Students for a Democratic Society (SDS). They reminded him of "the geeks who participated in student government back in junior high school." Although he was against the Vietnam War, he likened the antiwar rally to a school dance: "these were privileged kids, after all, and none of us would have to go to war if we played our cards right. It's all very well to say you are against the war. But if you weren't faced with the imperative to make a choice, you could really continue your life as always. There was no fighting in America, after all."[20]

Mike Ritter could barely believe it when flyers appeared on university bulletin boards announcing that counterculture icons Timothy

Leary, Richard Alpert, Allen Ginsburg, Gary Snyder, and Alan Watts were coming to campus to speak. The university buzzed for weeks with excited anticipation, and on that auspicious day, Ritter secured a front-row seat on a picturesque knoll. He listened to each man talk about the importance of "doing your own thing" and was captivated by their words because they affirmed what he already believed. When the last speaker, former Harvard professor Timothy Leary, took the stage and implored the students "to turn on, tune in, and drop out," it struck Ritter like a call to arms. Because the traditional sources of wisdom—parents, priests, professors—were falling so far short in the eyes of young Americans, they began to look elsewhere for answers. Nothing was too "far out" for the counterculture, as long it was not part of Western culture.

The roots of the 1960s "Cosmic Consciousness" can be traced to American religious revival movements, and some have compared it to the First Great Awakening (1740s) and the Second Great Awakening (1825–1850). The counterculture had extremely deep roots in the Golden State. Whether Theosophy, Christian Science, the White Aryan Resistance, Aquarianism, Naturism, surfing, or Scientology, California has always tolerated countercultural movements far outside the American mainstream. The hippies of the 1960s were pale imitations of their forefathers, the California Nature Boys.[21] Before he emigrated to America in 1906 to avoid military service, Bill Pester was part of a German utopian back-to-nature movement (*Lebensreform, Naturmensch, Wandervogel*) that advocated pacifism, vegetarianism, raw foods, physical fitness, nudism, natural medicine, abstinence from alcohol, sexual liberation, communitarianism, women's liberation, and animal rights. Pester built a palm-frond hut in the San Jacinto Mountains near Palm Springs, where he made walking sticks, sold postcards with health tips, and charged people to look through his telescope while he taught them about astronomy. Almost totally self-sufficient, the German immigrant so impressed the local Cahuilla Indians that they adopted him as one of their own.[22]

German professor Arnold Ehret arrived in California in 1914 and provided the Nature Boys with the intellectual underpinnings of their dietary beliefs in his books *Rational Fasting* (1914) and *Mucus-less Diet* (1922). When husband and wife John and Vera Richter opened a raw-foods cafeteria called the Eutropheon in 1917, it gave the Nature Boys a place to work and congregate. Although they wandered throughout the southland, more often than not, the hippie forefathers could be found living in the caves of Tahquitz Canyon near Palm Springs. Eden Ahbez, a piano player at the Eutropheon, would become world famous after Nat King Cole recorded his song "Nature Boy" in 1948 and it became a number one hit for eight weeks. Usually dressed in diaphanous white robes, Abenz camped with his family under the Hollywood sign and claimed to live on only three dollars a week. Nature Boy, fitness pioneer, author, and actor Robert "Gypsy Boots" Bootzin owned a well-known health food store called The Health Hut on Beverly Boulevard. Gypsy Boots not only performed at the Monterey Pop Festival, he was the link between the Nature Boys and the hippies.[23] By far the biggest difference between the hippies and their forefathers was that the Nature Boys did not use drugs to find satori.

Well into his freshman year, Mike Ritter still had not tried LSD. So when one of his closest friends returned from a weekend trip to San Francisco with a handful of gelatin capsules filled with a purple powder, supposedly made by the legendary LSD chemist Augustus Owsley Stanley III, the eighteen-year-old felt the same quivering in his stomach he did before paddling out in big surf. They took the acid on a Friday night and the trip lasted all night; after feeling extremes of near panic and wondrous ecstasy, just before dawn, as he was coming down, the rising bright-orange morning sun mirrored his sense of rebirth. Ritter believed that this experience was "equal to and every bit as valid as the spiritual visions I read about in the scriptures of Eastern religions."[24]

It is not an exaggeration to say that for a short time, LSD providers were considered apostles. *LIFE* magazine's Lawrence Schiller was astute to observe in a 1966 article: "LSD salesmen often have the air of men engaged in holy work, and they operate with a messianic conviction that is completely unknown in the rest of the drug world." Augustus Owsley Stanley III and the other big 1960s acid dealers charged very little, given their virtual monopoly after the drug was criminalized in 1966.[25] During the 1960s, many in the counterculture saw psychedelic drugs as the sacraments of a new religion and believed that LSD provided the key to an "evolutionary expansion in consciousness which would save humanity and revitalize spirituality." Acid introduced young Americans to a new reality unbound by the limits of the material world that the World War II generation had worked so hard to establish. LSD took them on a modern version of the shaman's magical journey and if nothing else, altered their consciousness.[26] Many did not consider smuggling and selling drugs like marijuana, hashish, and LSD crimes. These were not stereotypical "drug pushers," explained Palos Verdes, California Rev. Melvin Knight, Jr. In a 1968 *Time* magazine article, he described the new dealers as "Billy the Kid drug heroes. . . . They're intelligent, good looking. Good at sports, popular around school. They have all the characteristics of the old style campus hero, but they also take and perhaps push drugs."[27]

Mike Ritter had heard about a group of young Southern Californians who called themselves the Brotherhood of Eternal Love and distributed LSD almost as a nonprofit endeavor. "Righteous dealing" became the Brotherhood's mantra; they were unique because they did not exploit their market advantage and made exponentially less money than they could have, given how massive their distribution efforts were. "We went from joints, to lids, to kilos, to cars, to planes, to boats. Every time you do one, you want to do it bigger," explained one original Brotherhood member. "We were impressed—the Brotherhood had boldly taken the very action that we only talked about," said Ritter.[28]

Brotherhood of Eternal Love leader John Griggs followed Timothy Leary's advice and formed a religion that used LSD as a sacrament, similar to how some American Indians used peyote. Weeks before the drug was criminalized in 1966, the Brotherhood registered as a church with the state of California. According to their papers of incorporation, their church was an "earthly instrument of God's will" founded to "bring to the world a greater awareness of God through the teachings of Jesus Christ, Buddha, Ramakrishna, Babaji, Paramahansa Yogananda, Mahatma Gandhi, and all the true prophets and apostles of God, and to spread the love and wisdom of these great teachers to all men." The group would finance their lifestyle by smuggling marijuana and hashish and manufacturing more LSD than anyone else during the 1960s. If it hadn't been for the drugs, the early Brotherhood would have been a less disciplined version of the California Nature Boys, or early American utopians like John Humphrey Noyes and his Oneida Community in New York in the 1840s.[29]

Before Griggs became the Brotherhood's spiritual leader, he was a streetwise former Anaheim greaser. Unlike many in the New Left who felt "inauthentic" due to their bourgeois or red diaper roots, Griggs was never burdened by such doubts. Although the beatific-looking blonde was only 5'6" and weighed a scant 140 pounds, he was a former high school wrestling champion and a fearless small-time hoodlum and junkie whose car club, "The Street Sweepers," was known throughout Orange County "as authentic badasses." "Johnnie, for all his smallness, was an iron man, and possessed of an endless amount of energy," wrote his friend Dion Wright.[30] Although Griggs had smoked pot and even shot speed and heroin, he could not get his hands on the acid they had heard so much about. When he heard about an LSD party in Hollywood, "he and Black Bart and Mad Dog burst in upon a social occasion in the man's house, ski-masked and waving pistols. The man was relieved when he found out that all they wanted was the LSD." After they took huge doses in the California desert, Griggs, like many during the 1960s, had a transformational experience, and by sunrise the car club hood was a psychedelic missionary preaching acid salvation. "Whatever John's religious and spiritual roots may have been, they kicked into overdrive. He came back into this plain of objectivity with a single conviction: 'It's God! It's all God!'" wrote Dion Wright. "The bedrock realization never left him, although his subsequent interpretations of how to deal with it were not always sound."[31]

Griggs and his friends did not take LSD "to party," but to find themselves and to introduce the drug to others in guided, controlled, group trips in remote wilderness locations. One person compared the group's use of hallucinogenic drugs to deep meditation. A frequent location was the Nature Boys' favorite haunt, Tahquitz Canyon. Original Brotherhood member Glen Lynd believed that LSD enabled him and his friends to see God and communicate on a higher plane of wordless, transcendent consciousness.

Griggs and a handful of young couples decided to form "a family." They would buy a tract of self-sufficient land and live communally. After their first house, in Orange County's Modjeska Canyon, burned in a fire, the group moved into a series of houses behind Laguna Beach on a dirt road called Woodland Drive. Although some worked as gardeners for the town, others began to finance their alternative lifestyle by smuggling and distributing marijuana, hashish, and LSD. One Brotherhood member drove two big loads of marijuana from California to New York in one month in late 1967–68 and earned close to $100,000. The Brotherhood shipped their first load of Afghan hash to California in the engine compartment of a VW van in late 1967. They began to specialize in packing hash into the bodies and engine compartments of Volkswagen campers, Land Rovers, and other vehicles they shipped from Europe and the Middle East to the United States. Soon the group owned a ranch in the California high desert and a hippie general store on the Pacific Coast Highway in Laguna called Mystic Arts World.[32]

To be trusted totally by the Brotherhood, you had to pass a daunting test that no true Bro could avoid: the acid test. Brotherhood members prided themselves on their ability "to handle" massive doses of pure LSD. "It was a type of initiation into, you could almost say, a fraternity of dealing where you could trust a person or not," said one smuggler who worked at the Brotherhood's store. "To know how they would behave when their ego was stripped away. Who was the real person underneath the ego?" "High-dosing" was a mark of mettle; some survived without a scar, while others never came down. One smuggler recalled a day at the beach when a five-gallon jug of apple juice laced with fifty hits of acid was passed around. "I can remember seeing this one guy guzzle the last quarter of a gallon of organic apple juice and seeing the residue of the bright orange chunks of sunshine acid that were at the bottom of the jug swirling down, like a toilet bowl emptying into his throat. This particular guy showed up the next day at the beach with his head shaved and kind of freaked out, and he may never have been the same."[33]

The Brotherhood was a classic example of the nonhierarchical, network marketing that would come to characterize the boutique marijuana industry. Their Laguna Beach compound quickly grew into a psychedelic drug co-op where LSD and marijuana could be purchased and smugglers could dump weight and get paid a fair price fast. Their loose structure worked like a farmer's cooperative. For example, a person who wanted to do a smuggling run might approach a Brother with his plan: "'I got $20,000, I am gonna buy some hash.' 'Okay, c'mon over, I'll load you up,'" explained one former associate. "They would take a percentage of it. They would tell people how to do it." Smugglers drove from Mexico straight to Woodland Drive and sold their entire load. "You don't want to be selling it in your backyard," said one smuggler. "You take it to Laguna and let them take the heat." Many who bought and sold drugs with the Brotherhood believed it was simply a shared set of values. "There were no papers or dues or anything, nobody cut his finger and passed blood around, but whenever we saw somebody who was into dope and acid and surfing, we said there was one of our brothers."[34]

Scraggly dogs and hippies on bicycles patrolled the Brotherhood's compound. The houses backed up against a cave-pocked hillside, and as a result, police could not easily observe their activities. "There was a system where the guys that lived in the front houses could easily get hold of the guys in the back houses if they saw [local police detective] Neil Purcell's marked mobile driving down. It was real easy to see," said one former Laguna Beach resident. "There's a police car or somebody we don't know, and if something big was going on like a capping party or something like that, you would want to let everybody know." There were numerous escape trails, and the girls who lived in the canyon acted as guides and helped people escape.[35]

When one surfer smuggler walked into a house on Woodland Drive carrying two pink cake boxes filled with his finest seedless Oaxachan colas, he felt as if he'd entered King Arthur's Court of Hippie Royalty. The house was furnished with only Afghan rugs and pillows, the Learys and all of the Brotherhood guys gathered around a stand-up hookah (water pipe) while young, sun-bleached Southern California beauties came in and out of the room with fresh water for the pipe and patties of the finest Afghan hash they had just heated over the stove and crumbled. According to one smuggler, Laguna Beach was "a big party whether you were in the lotus position or not. We were all just the same kind of Indians. All in the same place having a wonderful time."[36]

If the Brotherhood of Eternal Love had a high priest, it was Timothy Leary. The counterculture icon argued that this group of "Golden Bootleggers" sought nothing less than the "mind-blowing liberation of their fellow man." Leary pointed out an important socioeconomic truth about dealing psychedelic drugs: "Here we have an enormous, billion-dollar industry going on in the United States, all of which is essentially run by amateurs." He even interviewed a Brotherhood member for the *East Village Other* newspaper and asked him why they dealt marijuana and LSD. "We deal because that is our thing. We believe that dope is the hope of the human race, it is a way to make people free and happy," the Brotherhood member replied. "We wouldn't feel good just sitting here smoking the dope we have and saving our souls, knowing that there are thirty million kids that need dope to center themselves." The smuggler scoffed at the police and their efforts to catch him: "We are smarter and wiser than the FBI, the CIA and the Narcotics Bureau put together. We

World champion surfer David Nuuhiwa with second-generation Brotherhood member John Gale. Photo: Jeff Divine

have to be. We just can't admit defeat just because they have more and more equipment against us."[37]

Even the FBI would concede that they had never seen a criminal organization quite like the Brotherhood: "For many years, the concept of organized crime in drugs has always meant the Mafia, or the *Cosa Nostra*, or the *Union Corse*—traditional and reasonably well-identified criminal groups with specific ethnic connotations. The Brotherhood of Eternal Love represents one of the new, recently emerged forms of organized crime totally different from our past notions in terms of membership, motivations, lifestyles, and drugs of preference." While privately Leary was condescending toward this group of uneducated "white lumpen," but given their generosity toward him, he happily fed their delusions of grandeur: "I have been in India, Japan, all through the Middle East and Europe. I have talked to swamis, the Rishis, the Maharishis, and I can say flatly that the holiest, handsomest, healthiest, horniest, humorest, most saintly group of men that I have met in my life are the righteous dope dealers."[38]

However, not everyone was impressed by the Brotherhood of Eternal Love. Many European hippies and surfers who had been scamming before them resented their arrogance because it drew heat. "They were totally uneducated people, total numb nuts," said one of the first surfers to smuggle hash from Afghanistan. "Nobody said shit, nobody knew anything until all those fucking Brotherhood guys. 'Oh, we're free, we can do anything we want. We're Ommmed out! Got acid in my mind!' They fucked it all up! They taught Customs everything on all their mistakes. Mistake after mistake, man!" By early 1968, smugglers were growing wary of Laguna Canyon because young hippies from all over California flocked to the area to buy drugs. Many Laguna Beach smugglers avoided the canyon because the Brotherhood had gotten too high profile, or as one smuggler explained, "they got themselves into trouble."[39]

2

THE HIPPIE TRAIL

In 1968, drug arrests were up 60 percent in the United States and a shocking 324 percent in California. With law enforcement now cracking down on pot, more and more upper-middle-class college students were getting busted. The Friday after his last final exam, Mike Ritter and his two best friends drove down to the beach to get away from their studies for the afternoon. After a few hits of marijuana, they took off running down the beach and were sweating and breathing hard by the time they got back to the car. Suddenly, a police officer popped out of the bushes and walked over to the car. He pointed to the marijuana seeds visible on the car's floor, opened the door, and pulled their stash out from under the seat. The students were arrested, charged with marijuana possession, and spent the weekend in cells at the Santa Cruz police station. In the end, their lawyer proved that the search was illegal, the case was dismissed, and Ritter "strutted about campus like a war hero."[1]

Returning to Santa Barbara for summer vacation, Mike Ritter saw packs of young, long-haired hitchhikers on the side of the road where

Highway 101 intersected downtown. Many of his friends were setting out "on the road" and coming back with stories about hippie communes like "the Hog Farm" and "New Buffalo." Some were venturing to more exotic destinations like Afghanistan, Nepal, and Laos, where cannabis products were smoked openly.[2] Many young Americans like him were convinced that life on the road would be infinitely more valuable than college. Just as he was set to begin his sophomore semester, Ritter bought a ticket to Europe and began a long, overland pilgrimage to Afghanistan on the Hippie Trail. "It felt right in step with my life, a natural progression, as if popular thought was getting closer to my own," he said.[3] However, much of mainstream America did not share Mike Ritter's or the counterculture's view of America's future.

Although the Brotherhood had initially been close to untouchable, their drug-induced tragedies were mounting and drawing the attention of the authorities. One faction of the group did not support leader John Griggs's decision to invite Timothy Leary and his entourage to move to California and live as their guest. Leary was arrested on July 14, 1969 after seventeen-year-old Charlene Almeida drowned in a pond at the Brotherhood's ranch and an autopsy found large quantities of LSD in her system. However, the most significant blow to the Brotherhood of Eternal Love came weeks later, when Griggs overdosed on synthetic psilocybin in front of his wife and sons in their tepee at their ranch and died at Hemet Valley Community Hospital a few hours later. While a mutated form of the Brotherhood of Eternal Love would survive under new, more criminal leadership, to some, Griggs's death marked the end of the group's idealism and utopianism. "It was the end of the era as far as I'm concerned," wrote Dion Wright. "He was the true believer. When he died, the chance of his vision becoming reality was gone."[4]

By 1969, California's counterculture was imploding and the Manson murders marked its end. What once appeared to be youthful exuberance was fast turning into a second Children's Crusade. When Hawaiian smuggler Terry Dawson* visited Haight-Ashbury after a long absence, he was horrified to find "fatherless children hung on the tattered skirts of welfare mamas while the 'Grateful Dead' muttered inane truths in endless, meaningless songs and everyone smiled with hollow eyes and aumed along in the musky smell of perspiration." Above all, the smuggler believed that drugs had duped the young, who were wandering around "in a phantasmal, colored world of make believe where nothing mattered, free love reigned, and work and order were out of date."[5]

Brotherhood members were scattering far and wide—from Oregon to Hawaii to Afghanistan. A second-generation California smuggler best summarized their influence on the next generation of American marijuana smugglers: "In reality, the Brotherhood was a bunch of loosely associated guys that did small loads compared to today; they started everything out. But they taught us all a good lesson."[6] The early, Brotherhood-inspired surfer scammers were captured for posterity in a pseudo documentary film produced by Warner Brothers called *Rainbow Bridge*. Shot in Maui and featuring one of Jimi Hendrix's final concerts, the film is a remarkable snapshot of the counterculture's elite grappling with the death of the 1960s. In the most relevant scene, surfers Les Potts and Mike Hynson are sitting inside their surfboard-strewn house in Maui when a bearded friend carrying a Pan Am flight bag and an elaborately airbrushed surfboard enters the room. The traveler describes his grueling, hour-long interrogation by U.S. Customs in Honolulu and dismisses it with a shrug, as if protected by some unseen force: "That's why the Dao brought us here at this time. Something for us," says the traveler as he hands Potts a knife, pulls out a joint, and says, "Ganja from Vietnam," as he lights it. Potts cuts a square panel from the bottom of the surfboard, pulls out a big baggie, dumps what looks like loose dirt onto the bottom of the board, and says, "Afghanistan, Primo Pollen." The trio proceed to smoke themselves into a coughing stupor, and the bearded smuggler even offers a hit to a poster of Richard Nixon.[7]

The 1968 presidential election would serve as a referendum on both the counterculture and the increasingly anarchic antiwar movement. If nothing else, the American body politic had lost patience with both. Richard Nixon delivered his most memorable presidential campaign speech at Anaheim Stadium on September 16, 1968. After Pat Boone warmed up the huge, hometown crowd and Nixon took the stage to thunderous applause, the California native compared drugs to "the plagues and epidemics of former years" and vowed to take action against the narcotics that were "decimating a generation of Americans."[8] Above all, Nixon hated pot; to him it represented everything that was wrong with America. "Marijuana was part of the larger tapestry," his aide John Erlichman explained. "The people who were demonstrating against what he was doing in Vietnam, the wearing of long hair, and the smoking of dope were all part of a picture. These were people he had no use for."[9] After the California Republican was elected president, the Brotherhood of Eternal Love and other hippie smugglers soon found themselves in the crosshairs of law enforcement.

After Richard Nixon was sworn in as president in January 1969, he wasted no time and declared a "war on drugs," establishing a White House task force on narcotics, marijuana, and dangerous drugs. They concluded in their June 1969 report that most of the marijuana in the United States came across the southern border and pressed the Mexican government to take action. Although U.S. Customs had seized only 393 pounds of pot at the Tijuana border in 1961, seven years later that number was up to 37,679 pounds and by 1969, marijuana was Mexico's third biggest export ($100,000,000 annually). "Next to football," complained one customs official, "white-collar smuggling is becoming the national sport." When the Mexican government proved unresponsive to Nixon's demand that they crack down on pot, the United States launched a surprise border crackdown called "Operation Intercept."

Traffic along the 3,200-kilometer long border crawled to a halt on September 29, 1969, as cars were carefully searched and suspicious persons strip-searched. Not everyone in the Nixon administration thought drawing the line in the war on drugs at marijuana was a good idea. The Budget Bureau considered it a dangerous move because it "failed to consider the place of marihuana [sic] in the total drug picture." While successful in temporarily slowing the flow of commercial Mexican marijuana, Operation Intercept had a massive blowback. It motivated Americans to utilize the knowledge and seeds they had obtained overseas and begin growing their own high-potency *sinsemilla* (Spanish for "seedless") in Northern California, Oregon, and Hawaii. In California, the marijuana industry would quickly eclipse the wine industry; within a decade, pot would become the state's most valuable cash crop.[10]

Nixon's crackdown also pushed smugglers to set up operations from farther-flung Hippie Trail outposts. A modern-day Silk Road, the Hippie Hash Trail started in Europe and wound through Morocco, Turkey, Lebanon, Iran, Afghanistan, Pakistan, India, Kathmandu, Nepal, Thailand, and Laos—all places where marijuana, and especially hashish, were plentiful. "In those days, one could catch a hippie bus from either London or Amsterdam for around 100 British pounds or less," wrote hippie smuggler Joe Pietri. "The bus would travel overland through western Europe, and then on to Greece, Turkey, Iran, Afghanistan, Pakistan, India, and finally to the end of the drug trail, at Kathmandu, Nepal. For $10 U.S. per kilo one could purchase Afghan cream hashish in Kabul, the finest Chitrali hashish in Pakistan or the best Nepali fingers." One of the things that made the Hippie Trail so attractive to the young travelers was that "the road to Kathmandu is paved with cannabis." By the time overland travelers reached India, they were 6,400 kilometers deep into Asia and had entered a world guided by different rules: cows got the right-of-way in traffic; barefoot, matted-haired *sadhus* carried Neptune staffs, and cannabis use was part of the culture. In short order, Mike Ritter traded Protestant Christianity for a mishmash of LSD-inspired Eastern transcendentalism and believed that he was part of a massive social change.

Although Islamic law prohibits drinking alcohol, smoking and eating hashish is perfectly acceptable. Hash is to marijuana what brandy is to wine. The powder or putty is made from the glandular trichromes that coat the bracts and the leaflets of the female marijuana flowers (buds) and contain the most THC, one of the main psychoactive ingredients in marijuana. Of all the branches of Islam, the Sufis are the best known for using hash for religious insight. Some travelers sought out locations mentioned in ancient Sufi tales.[11]

After weeks of overland travel, Ritter finally reached the home of the Afghan consul in Masshad, Iran, to get his visa. A cordial assistant ushered him into an office where a tall, handsome man, who looked like Omar Sharif, greeted him with a smile and asked, "What do you know of Afghanistan? We have the finest sheepskin robes and gloves in the world." He added nonchalantly, "Afghanistan produces the best hash in the world." A bus ride took the Californian deep into the rocky landscape, and after hours of driving, a town materialized. The bus stopped and Ritter walked into a teahouse where everybody had a piece of hash better than anything he had ever seen. Unlike the prying, sometimes-hostile people in neighboring countries, not only were Afghans "cool," they were some of the world's great connoisseurs of hashish.

Hash is to Afghanistan what wine is to France, and if Afghanistan had a Bordeaux region, it would be the northern towns such as Balkh and

Mazar-I-Sharif, where they have been expertly making hashish for centuries. If you wanted to buy fine "Number One" Afghani hash in remote places like Balkh, there was no getting around smoking from the stand-up hookah. After hot coals were placed on top of a tennis ball-sized lump of hashish, the senior smoker lit the pipe amid chants to Baba Ku, the folk legend who supposedly introduced hashish to the region. If a flame jumped from the bowl and burned like a candle, the smoker was treated with respect. "That's a mark of your mettle; can you make that thing burn like a candle, when you hit it? They didn't sell you anything if you didn't go through that trip with them. They didn't trust anybody who didn't," recalled one smuggler.[12]

One California scammer who visited the chai shops in Mazar-I-Sherif and smoked the hubbly-bubbly (stand-up hookah pipe) like a pro won the trust of the locals. They took him to the countryside to see the ganja farms and to meet Balkh's master hashish maker. *Shirac*, the Pashtu word for "sticky," is used to describe this purest unpressed resin, and, like wine, some years the hashish is better than others due to weather. Unlike in India and Nepal, where the resin is rubbed off the plants by hand, the Afghanis let the resin globules on the plants harden before harvesting them in the fall, when the weather is dry and cold. After the plants are pulled from the ground, they are brought into the courtyard of the village's walled compound to dry and are only exposed to the early morning sun. When the plants are ready, they are taken to a back room where the floors are covered with rugs.

Although much of the modern Afghan hash was made by hand with sieves, traditional hashmakers strip the buds off the plants and place about 20 kilos on a rug that is rolled up and then walked on by barefoot men. Once the buds are crushed, the carpet is unrolled, lifted to waist level, and gently shaken as a man with a stick taps the sides so the pot falls into the center. The crushed pot is removed and the remaining resin is dumped into a large clay bowl that is tightly covered with a homemade cotton cloth and shaken to remove the dust and remaining plant matter (*barc*). Finally, a small quantity of resin is placed in a silk turban, which is tied shut like a sack and shaken vigorously; the agitation forces the remaining chaff into the cloth. It took 20 to 30 kilos of prime buds to produce 1 kilo of beige-gray powder the texture of flour—*shirac*—the purest resin from the ripest marijuana plants.[13]

Afghanistan lived up to the wildest fantasies of the hippies, and by the late 1960s, it was such a major destination for smugglers and the export trade was so well established that children in Kandahar sold necklaces of hashish beads, hashish-filled belts, and hashish-heeled shoes. By 1970, the Brotherhood of Eternal Love was exporting more hash than anyone else.[14] The Tokhi brothers ran a small hotel and rug shop that had been supplying European and American smugglers with hash long before the Brotherhood entered the market. Their operations expanded greatly once the Brotherhood provided them with an international export arm. Inside their walled Kandahar compound, mechanics welded false bottoms onto vehicles, filled them with hash, then undercoated and repainted them. "Ayatullah ran the town. He paid the military off who you had to pay off," recalled one smuggler. Rip-offs and checkpoints were less of a worry because the Brotherhood's fixers also paid off government officials.[15]

After Ritter smoked hash to his heart's content in Afghanistan, he was eager to get to India. His fantasy was to vanish inside a northern Indian monastery and reappear years later as an enlightened man. As his bus was about to leave the terminus in Kabul, the American glanced at a group of Afghanis selling snacks and locked eyes with a teenaged boy. With a large smile on his face and without averting his gaze, the boy picked an orange from his basket and handed it to the American through the window. For Ritter, this small gift was a lasting memory of Afghan hospitality. His bus left the winter snow of Afghanistan, descended into the lush green valley of Jalalabad, wound through the Khyber Pass, and reached Pakistan the next day. The cool, clean mountain breezes had been replaced by the thick, pungent air of the Indian subcontinent. Also gone was the aristocratic "mind-your-own-business" Afghani attitude, replaced by endless questions and hundreds of hands reaching out to touch him.

The bus dropped Ritter at the Pakistan border; he rode in a donkey cart across no-man's land to an army tent on the Indian side. "Welcome to India," said a plump soldier with a cherubic face and waxed mustache in the style of the British Raj. "What is your purpose in coming here?" The American wanted to say enlightenment, but before he could reply, more rapid-fire questions followed: "Where do you hail from? Has your father given you leave to go? What is your alma mater?" Although the Indian official could not make sense of the long-haired foreigner, he stamped his passport, and Ritter made his way to Rishikesh, an Indian holy city on the Ganges River in the foothills of the Himalayas, home to the Maharishi Mahesh Yoga. One of the Beatles had just left, but Mike Love, the pseudo-surfer crooner from The Beach Boys, was still in residence. After only a week Mike Ritter was horribly sick from dysentery that he got from eating banana-leaf snacks on the street. "My weight dropped from a thin 140 pounds to an emaciated 120 pounds; my health fluctuated between times of continuous diarrhea to several days of constipation," he said. Fed up with the poverty, the beggars, and the overpowering press of humanity, Ritter abandoned his quest for enlightenment and bought a ticket on Thai Airways from Calcutta to Bangkok.

Although only two hours by air, Thailand was a world away. Unlike Vietnam, Cambodia, and Laos, the Kingdom of Thailand has never been occupied by a foreign army. As a result, the Thai people have retained a unique, independent, and refined culture. Their outnumbered kings rode into combat atop battle-dressed, yellow-eyed albino elephants, staved off foreign invaders for centuries and led Dionysian lives untempered by the prim dictates of Christianity; even one of their most Westernized kings, Mongkut of *The King and I* fame, had 82 children from 39 wives. It is impossible to understand Thailand without considering both their constitutional monarchy and Theravada Buddhism; the Thai king's title is "Head of State, Head of the Armed Forces, the Upholder of the Buddhist Religion and the Defender of All Faiths." It is rare for Westerners to see Thais disagreeing in public, outward displays of emotion are frowned upon, and a good sense of humor is prized. Feeling good, *sabai*, and having fun, *sanook*, are extremely important because Thais believe that life is something to be enjoyed, not endured.[16]

After landing at Don Muang Airport, Ritter took a public bus into the city. Located on the left bank of the Chao Phya River, Krungtep, known to Westerners as Bangkok, is referred to by Thais as "the City of Gods." The 30-kilometer ride took over an hour. Ritter was amazed by the Buddhist temples and felt happy to be in this new country, fantasizing about what it would be like to spend some time there.[17] By the time he reached Hua Lumpong Railway Station, the sun had set and the city had come to life. Dwarfed by his oversized backpack, the young American marched down the busy street. He was overwhelmed by colors, cheerful faces, laughter, and inviting aromas. Long tail boats whisked passengers around the canals like New York City buses, while smaller boats went house to house selling everything from hot noodle soup to ice cream to hardware. Not only did the narrow streets teem with life, but everywhere Ritter looked, he saw beautiful, smiling black-haired women. "The sparkly Thai girls were so friendly and had a sexual nonchalance that was totally foreign to me."[18]

Mike Ritter checked into the Thai Song Greet Hotel, where a young English traveler asked if he was interested in buying some Pakistani hash. The Californian bought four large slabs that looked like Hershey chocolate bars and weighed over a kilo all together. When Ritter took a trip to Chiang Mai in the far north, he was overwhelmed by the beauty of the countryside; everywhere he looked there were lovely, well-tended gardens and wondrous temples with tinkling glass ornaments dangling from spires. The American stayed with a farmer and his wife, and before bed they brought him sweetened milk, cookies, and a mosquito net. Even before he had smoked a Thai stick, Mike Ritter was totally smitten by Thailand and the warmth of its people.

Ritter heard that jobs on freighters transporting war materials between the United States and Vietnam were easy to get due to a shortage of trained seamen, so he flew to Japan. With little formality, a man at the U.S. consulate in Yokohama told him to report to the *Robin S. Gray*, a World War II vintage ship redeployed from mothball storage. The nineteen-year-old was assigned to the engine room, where he worked as a "wiper," chipping rust, checking oil levels, polishing pumps, and cleaning the toilets. The ship was empty except for the battle-wrecked tanks and shot-up armored personnel carriers strapped to the deck. During his off-duty hours, the draft dodger liked to wander among them "imagining the horrors of combat that I had avoided." In the mess hall, seasoned sailors recalled massive storms and voyages to exotic ports around the world. After transiting the Panama Canal, Ritter signed off in Mobile, Alabama. More valuable than his $400 in pay was the kilo of hash in the bottom of a peanut butter jar in his footlocker.

Although Mike Ritter cleared customs without a problem, the DEA's predecessor, the Bureau of Narcotics and Dangerous Drugs (BNDD), was gaining ground on amateur hippie smugglers. By June 1970, 513 Americans were held in foreign jails in 37 countries. John Cusak, the chief U.S. narcotics agent for Europe and the Middle East, admitted that most of them were not professional smugglers. "They have no records. They are users, and many of them are 'missionaries.' They want to turn others on—and if there's a profit in it, so much the better." The Nixon administration continued to escalate its offensive against marijuana; in 1970 Congress passed the Comprehensive Drug Abuse and Control Act, which placed pot in the same criminal category as heroin (Schedule 1) and declared it addictive, dangerous, and without medical value. That same year, the Nixon administration appointed Ray Shafer, a Republican former governor of Pennsylvania, to head a commission that would study marijuana and issue a report.[19]

The President was also beefing up the Bureau of Narcotics and Dangerous Drugs by recruiting Vietnam veterans like marine captain Jim Conklin to fight the war on drugs. The son of an FBI agent, Conklin had graduated from the small Catholic college St. Bonaventure in 1965 with a philosophy degree, then joined the marines and served in Vietnam as an infantry officer. Afterward, he worked civilian jobs but was dissatisfied: "I just didn't like being a businessman. It just didn't have any appeal to me." One of his friends from the Marine Corps told him that the BNDD in New York City was looking for ex-military officers, so he applied and was hired. "It was an unusual time," he said. "When I came on with BNDD was a time when drugs were used by everybody, all the common people, all my friends from New York, the guys I knew in college. You'd go to a party in New York City, everybody would be using drugs."

While the BNDD agent considered marijuana a crutch that was bad for American society, he turned a blind eye. "It wasn't just what the youth were using—the politicians were using it. The courts were permissive; everybody was very permissive toward the use of it. They didn't want people to go to jail for it because so many people were involved, and I think that caused it to spread a lot."[20] However, hippie pot smugglers like Mike Ritter were far more worried about the draft than law enforcement. When the Californian finally returned home from his international odyssey, a notice was waiting for his draft physical induction; even worse, the FBI had called, checking on his whereabouts.

Since Ritter had missed his first physical appointment, he was already a suspected draft dodger. If he passed his induction physical, he was headed straight to boot camp. He had learned ways to fail the examination from other surfers: one guy ate a pound of sugar the night before his physical and his blood sugar was so high the doctors thought he was a diabetic; another took LSD, wore a flowing white robe, babbled like a phony holy man, and was labeled crazy and rejected. Ritter knew that he wouldn't be able to pull off anything that obvious in Los Angeles, where they were wise to these kinds of games, so he moved to Spokane, Washington, and immediately began to see a psychiatrist.

When he went in for his physical and was given a written test, he answered only a handful of questions. The lieutenant administering the test threatened all of the recruits about intentionally failing but was talking to Ritter. All the others were "straight kids from redneck families, diligently working as if they were taking an SAT." Finally an officer took Ritter aside and gave him a reading test with flash cards and simple words like "chair," "car," and "gun." "I was on a roll now," said Ritter, "and continued to fail every test I could: the vision test, the color-blind test, and the hearing test. They kept retesting me until I was the last one remaining in the examination room." They took him to the army psychiatrist: "I think they knew what I was doing, but probably let me get away with it because they didn't want one bad apple to spoil their barrel." When the army declared him 4-F, unfit for military service, he walked out with a sense of triumph: "It was a bright blue sunny day, and my draft worries were over." What Ritter didn't realize until many years later "was that by beating the draft the way I did, I moved closer to the outlaw I became."

As much as Mike Ritter liked Afghanistan and India, he longed for the sea and the surf. Word was spreading that Bali had world-class waves, and when a friend showed up with a pile of stolen, blank airline tickets, it felt preordained, so he bought a stack and wrote himself a ticket to Indonesia. One of the world's most exotic tourist destinations during the 1920s and 1930s, Bali had been off the map for decades because of the Japanese occupation during World War II, the subsequent fight for independence, and the bloody coup of 1965–66. Ship passengers once disembarked on the north side of the island in Singaraja, and several European artists helped establish a colony at Ubud, a few kilometers north of the capital, where the rice paddy terraces rose like staircases to the volcanoes in the center of the island. By the time an international airport was constructed in 1969, hardy travelers had begun to return. Cheap as it was, travelers in Indonesia required a little more money than the average hippie in India or Afghanistan.

On the west side of Bali's southern peninsula, white sand beaches stretch for many kilometers. Initially, with the exception of the Kuta Beach

Hotel, there was no place to rent a room in Kuta. Enterprising Balinese, noting the rising number of travelers, turned their family compounds into *losmen*, the Indonesian equivalent of the European *pension*.[21] Mike Ritter flew from Jakarta, Java to Bali and was immediately overwhelmed by the smells of incense, frangipani, and the smoke from coconut-husk fires, not to mention the gamelan sounds of gongs and bells.

A 1950s Chevy sedan taxi, held together with baling wire and only slightly faster than a bicycle, drove the American from the airport to Kuta. The main road was just two sand tracks with thatch-roofed Balinese huts on each side. Tall coconut trees fronted the seaside and diminutive Balinese cattle grazed on the soft grass, their wooden cowbells clonking in the breeze. Out of their dung, following a rain, the fabled magic mushrooms sprouted.

The Balinese religion is a unique blend of Hinduism, animism, and ancestor worship; while their gods live in the mountains, their demons and evil spirits live in the sea. Few Balinese live near the beach, and most houses are built so that their windows and front doors face away from the ocean.[22] The taxi dropped Ritter off at the Garden *losmen*, a compound belonging to an extended Balinese family who had moved into one room and rented their bedrooms to tourists. For less than fifty cents a night, Ritter got a room and meals from the family kitchen, where the Balinese women still wore sarongs and went topless.[23] In an effort "to modernize," the Indonesian government encouraged women to cover their breasts with pointy, wire-reinforced bras they wore as bikini tops. Public electricity had not reached Kuta, and even camping lanterns were scarce, so most Balinese used old-fashioned coconut oil lamps. The lack of electricity meant that the nights were quiet. There were very few cars or motorcycles, and even bicycles were considered signs of prosperity. Most Balinese walked, and when they traveled farther than their feet could carry them, it was in run-down, old yellow school buses purchased cheaply or donated by first world countries. Only a privileged few had private phones, and if you needed to make an overseas call, you went to the main exchange in Denpasar to wait an hour for a bad connection.

What was most attractive to Ritter about Bali was the surf of the Bukit Peninsula. From April through October, offshore winds groom the big swells generated in the Roaring Forties. Towering cliffs drop down to narrow, rocky beaches, and at high tide waves smash against the jagged lava at the base of the cliffs, while at low tide the whole reef is exposed. At the end of the peninsula, almost suspended over the water, sits the temple of Uluwatu. Troops of monkeys, protected by Hindu beliefs, live in the temple and along the steep cliffs, giving the area a *Wizard of Oz* feel. Below it sits the crown jewel of Balinese surfing, a left-hand reef break. Lines of swell, as even as wide-wale corduroy, stretched all the way to Legian, with turtles swimming through the faces of unbroken waves and the fishermen from the nearby village of Jimbaran chasing them in dugout outrigger canoes with homemade harpoons in hand.

Mike Ritter had grown up reading books about the South Pacific and the *Tales of Sinbad the Sailor*, and Bali lived up to all of them. Just as the Swiss artist Theo Meier said of his first impression of the island in the 1930s, "the delirium laid hold of me which even today has not subsided." Bali was idyllic; not only was there perfect surf, there was also abundant hash because it was now a regular stop on the Hippie Trail. Some of the surfers from California and Australia Ritter met had already made good returns on smuggling runs and Ritter thought "they were the most impressive guys on the beach." He envied what they had accomplished and began thinking about doing a scam himself. Almost immediately the Californian's main goal in life was to live in Bali and explore the Indonesian archipelago until the day he died. "I toyed with ideas about setting off to do a scam myself; however, mostly I surfed and soaked in Bali," said Ritter. "Smuggling marijuana would become a means to that end."

One experienced scammer who showed up in Bali was the Brotherhood's David Hall. A little older than everyone else, Hall looked like a young Lucky Luciano, and he was a skilled social operator. While his beautiful black-haired, olive-skinned wife prepared huge meals for everyone, he probed people about their latest scams. "He would try to get involved in other people's scams for the payoff without really sticking his neck out," said Ritter. "Still, I liked the guy. He was another one that was just loads of fun."

Another scammer who followed the Hippie Trail to Bali was "Afghan Ted." While in Afghanistan, the German citizen embraced the Pashtu culture with such zeal that when he left the country in his Mercedes ambulance, he had two wives and two Afghan fighting dogs. "Ted was about my size, but tough," said Ritter, "always driving his motorcycle too fast, tight turns; he was looking for trouble. He didn't mind getting in fights and kind of enjoyed getting bruised or even cut up. Sort of like the attitudes of the fighters in the book *Fight Club*." Others were more ominous, like the big, muscular American scammer who came from Kathmandu and always seemed on the verge of violence. Some suspected that his mental instability was the result of a motorcycle accident in Malaysia that left him with a permanent dent in his skull. "He never went to a doctor to do anything about it and had a nervous habit of reaching up and touching the dent in a soft, almost loving way, as if that effort would heal the dent. Or maybe his body was trying to tell him to get some help."[24]

After a few months of surfing and exploring the island, Mike Ritter flew back to California and tried to start an export business that sold Indonesian wares. After working a few weeks as a salesman, he dumped his inventory at cost, built two hollow surfboards to fill with hash, and returned to Kuta. While he was gone, more nonsurfing "Magical Mystery Tour" hippies had arrived. One morning Ritter saw a tall, handsome American at his *losmen*. He was blind and traveled in a VW van with the two beautiful women who took care of him. "They liked to bathe naked in the outdoor shower. The Balinese would get so upset at his indifference to modesty, but they were too polite to say anything." Ritter met another American who owned a nightclub in New York City and was in Asia buying opium pipes and learning how to use them because he wanted to open a full-service opium den in Manhattan.

By far the strangest person he met in Kuta was a rich American blueblood with long, matted hair and wild eyes. "Bogie" was from a prominent East Coast family and had been in and out of trouble most of his life. After he stole a police motorcycle and got caught, the prosecutor agreed to drop the charges if he left town and never came back. Bogie was, if nothing else, accident prone; while trekking in Nepal, he fell into a roaring river and was swept far downstream, but miraculously, not even the icy water could kill him. Although he didn't need the money, Bogie liked the romantic idea of being a marijuana smuggler, so he bought a small trimaran called the *Madrigal* and outfitted it in Singapore, where he rented a Mercedes, ate only the finest food, smoked opium, and dated a beautiful Chinese girl. Most nights he could be found at the Bugis Street night market, buying durian fruit before looking for the skinniest cyclo driver he could find to take him to the nearest opium den for a few pipes before bed.

Once the *Madrigal* was ready, Bogie and an Australian friend sailed to Sumatra and picked up a load of pot in Aceh. En route to Western Australia, the weather got so foul that they headed back to Indonesia. Initially, they planned to stash the pot on a stretch of deserted coast near Java's Grajagan Peninsula, but the wannabe smuggler lost his nerve, jettisoned the weed and headed back to Bali. Bogie had been fasting during the voyage and began hallucinating from dehydration and hunger. Although his dried fruit was now moldy, he ate it anyway, and as he later explained to Ritter, "Suddenly he heard a 'crack,' like the sound of a branch breaking inside his head," and his memory was gone. When Ritter first met Bogie, he had partial amnesia; episodes from his life would pop into his mind like a flash and he would frantically scribble them down on scraps of paper that he kept in a dirty shoulder bag. Once after they had just finished a huge pizza and the table was cleared, Bogie asked, "'What's there to eat?' He didn't remember that they had just finished a huge meal and he was ready to start another."[25]

3

KUTA BEACH

Ironically, the most unusual character to show up in Kuta that year was neither a surfer scammer nor a Magical Mystery Tour hippie, but a decorated Vietnam veteran. By the time he left Vietnam in 1967, Bob Martin had earned a Bronze Star with Combat V for rescuing a pinned-down platoon and the South Vietnamese Cross of Gallantry for capturing a North Vietnamese officer. When he rolled into Kuta with his beautiful, California-blonde girlfriend, he had recently completed his first scam and was thinking about doing another. Mike Ritter was immediately impressed by the strong, silent veteran.

After Bob Martin returned from Vietnam, he threw his military duffle bag in a ditch at Andrews Air Force Base and returned home to Santa Cruz, where he began making up for lost time. Not only were drugs everywhere, many of his friends had successfully completed pot scams. The transition from combat to smuggling was easy. Martin considered doing a hash oil scam, but lying to a customs inspector wasn't his style; he didn't want to con anyone. "That's what turned me off. I didn't like that method. If you have to fool somebody, you have to go to a point where you're not in control, you're just rolling the dice." He wanted to rely on the same tradecraft that had kept him alive in Vietnam: he planned to sail right past law enforcement in the middle of the night. For $2,500 he bought a boat in Majorca; the *Tiki* was a 6-meter, bilge-keeled, gunter-gaff rigged sailboat with a mast full of bamboo parrels, rings that slid freely on the mast, a tiny cabin, and a one-cylinder Lister diesel engine that had to be started by hand. "The boat had a tiller to steer, and you had to drive from the leeward side because the cockpit was so small."

Martin and a friend sailed to Morocco and went overland to the Rif Mountains near Ketama to buy their hash. Much of the area was not reachable by car and under the political control of the Berber tribe.[1] They successfully loaded 15 kilos of hash on their boat and set sail for the Caribbean. Just off the coast, a big storm hit, and the smugglers spent a few scary nights going up and down in the massive swells. Although the sailboat only went 3.5 knots no matter what the wind speed, the *Tiki* was quite seaworthy. The smuggler compared sailing a small boat to traveling overland in India. "There is a thing that happens in a small boat at sea—you lose it. There's a point where things don't make sense, where you hate everything. It's like a bad psychedelic experience. You have to deal with yourself and who you are and you come out the other side," he said. "People have this idea about going to sea. 'Ah, the wind in your face, ah, glorious!' Well, when you're at sea, it's funky. You're always salty. You're hungry."

Their days revolved around lunchtime sextant shots, BBC World Service reports, and their rapidly dwindling food supplies. After a week, their Moroccan flatbread sported every color of mold in the rainbow. "You had to use a sharp-bladed knife and hold it to cut it. And break little chunks and put it in the broth. It tasted really solid, just like a piece of steak." The smugglers caught a few big mahi mahi, ate every part of the fish, and even made broth with the bones. During their last week, their daily rations were down to a can of peas, four glasses of water, and a spoonful of chia seeds with honey. When they caught their first glimpse of Barbados, they were ecstatic. The *Tiki* dropped anchor in a cove in St. Lucia; Martin rowed their dingy to a bar on the beach, bought a cold beer, and met a local who wanted to buy all the hash. The next day his new friend drove him to the post office run by his cousin. The smuggler nearly had a heart attack when the local dropped the block of hash on the postal scale and said to his cousin, "Hey mon, weigh this thing for me." After Martin was paid in full, he was eager to do another scam.[2]

None of the scammers Ritter met in Bali that year impressed him more than James "Abdul" Monroe*, who was "flamboyant, goofy, and so bold." With his long, wild hair and dark olive skin, he stood out from the others. "He was always teasing and cracking jokes, like when he offered you a joint. If you refused he'd ask, 'What's the matter? Afraid to get high?' Or about spending money, 'Spend money have fun, save it have none.'" Although Abdul was just a novice surfer, he would take off on huge waves and get pounded. He loved to gamble, and for a time, that would serve him well as a smuggler. "He'd bet on everything—cards, backgammon, golf, tennis, and won more often than not," said Ritter. "I think that's one reason he became such a successful scammer." Definitely not another blond-haired Adonis, the hawk-nosed Californian had a Syrian mother, and after a week in the sun his skin got so dark that he looked like a seafaring Arab, hence the nickname "Abdul." His father was a former World War II fighter pilot, a well-respected Southern California businessman, and a staunch Orange County Republican who wanted his eldest son to take over his business. James grew up "working in his sweatshop," learning the business from the bottom up. At times he had three jobs at once; he drove a tow truck, worked at a warehouse, and sorted inventory for an auctioneer.

Like many baby boomers, the smuggler believes that the strictness of his upbringing made the counterculture especially attractive, because his whole life had been planned without his consent. When Monroe was fifteen, he and a friend smoked their first joint. Most of his friends were drinkers and hated people who smoked marijuana. "I remember not even wanting to tell them about it because they would beat you up. They'd want to go out after they got drunk and look for some potheads and stuff. And I'd be with them, but they didn't know that I liked pot too. So it wasn't that accepted; people didn't like it." After high school, Monroe grew his hair, began smoking pot regularly, and moved into a house with like-minded friends, and they started to deal Mexican weed. "I didn't want to spend my money just to get high, just to supply myself. So I started looking at it like a businessman."

Although he was soon tripling his money, the young pot dealer was incredibly careless and got busted. His parents were notified, and in the visiting room at L.A. County Jail, his father gave him an ultimatum: "I've got the bail money right here in my pocket, but the rules are: you move back home, you cut all your hair off, you're grounded for at least a month or until we decide. No more contact with your old friends." Each day he and his father drove to work together in sullen silence. After a few months, Abdul had saved $500. He tried to buy a few kilos of pot, but the deal went bad and he lost all his money. His father asked him where his money had gone and if he'd tried to buy pot. When Abdul admitted how he had spent it, his dad said, "Okay, you're out of this house. You have no car, you're not a member of this family anymore. If you ever try to come back here, if I hear of you giving drugs to any of my other kids, I'm coming after you with a gun and [will] kill you."[3]

The nineteen-year old moved into a beach house in South Laguna Beach with his old high school friend Jim Lawton*, where they dealt pot and hash. They were less interested in making money than in supporting their hippie lifestyle; once they made enough to last a month, they did not worry about money again until it was gone. Although he was a bit player, Abdul could always get hash from the Brotherhood because he was trust-worthy and abided by the unwritten rules. "I never fucking came back with bad stories about what happened. I always paid them off, so I could always get a kilo." After more than a year with no contact from his family, Monroe's father called out of the blue. Even stranger, he sounded unusually happy. When he informed his son that his draft notice had arrived, it all made sense: "My dad was so stoked. He goes, 'Now what are you going to do? They got you. They're going make a man out of you. You're going be in the army and they're going make a man out of you and you can't do anything.' I said, 'Oh yeah? I'm a drug addict. I've been busted twice. They're not gonna take me. Plus, I'll tell them anything. I'll tell them I'm a faggot if I have to.' He goes, 'You do that, you'll never be able to get a job. That'll be on your record for the rest of your life.'"

During the week before his preinduction physical, Abdul took LSD every day, put a pair of jeans in the backyard, pissed on them every day, and made track marks up and down his arms with a sewing needle. He walked into the induction center in his piss-baked jeans, soaring on LSD, wearing cowboy boots and a T-shirt. He made sure not to wear underwear because he knew that within minutes of his arrival, he would be told to strip down to his shorts and shoes. It was all going according to plan:

Monroe was now parading around the induction center naked except for his cowboy boots, babbling incoherently. Suddenly a screaming sergeant grabbed him and dragged him to the army psychiatrist's office. Abdul had studied the symptoms of paranoid schizophrenia and responded to the shrink's questions with questions, scratched himself, looked around the room; by the end, he wasn't even answering questions. Given his bravura performance, Abdul figured he was home free until the doctor said, "You know, your father thinks the military would be the best thing for you, straighten your life out and make a man out of you." His blood ran cold when all the army officers in the office began laughing uproariously and one said, "Just go down the hall here and clear up your civil offenses. Because of your scores, by the way, you're front-line material. We'll see you in twenty days." Abdul was walking down the hall in shock when suddenly a bathroom door opened and he saw daylight. The induction center shared a common bathroom with a Bank of America. Without a second's hesitation, he stuffed his files under his jacket and escaped from the building, and within an hour, his files were ashes in his yard.

Arrested half a dozen times and now a draft dodger, the young Californian was facing five years of hard time in state prison when he turned to the Brotherhood of Eternal Love for a new identity. "The Brotherhood people were connected with the Weathermen, so for five hundred bucks I got a birth certificate from Ohio, a license from Nevada, and a draft card." Abdul went to the federal building in L.A., showed them his plane ticket to India, and requested express service. "They gave me a passport under the name James Robert Monroe the next day."

Before he left, Abdul went to his parents' house and tried to make peace. The probation department had been calling, and his parents begged him to turn himself in. His father scoffed when he said he was leaving the country: "You'll never get a passport!" Abdul pulled out his new passport, handed them his address in India, and thanked them. "Look, you guys raised me as good as you could, as good as you thought. I'm sure you tried your best, but things are happening now. It's not like you want it. I'm splitting." Days later, Monroe was walking around in Delhi, barefoot and camping in the Astrological Park. Because he had cut off all his hair when he left the States, the other hippies didn't trust him. "I was overdoing the fugitive thing—you know, dressing like a nerd and a real straight haircut. People just wouldn't accept me. The ones I wanted to accept me, you know, turned their backs on me because I wasn't like them."

Abdul decided to copy a friend who was smuggling Nepalese hash inside cages containing live Lhasa Apso dogs. The hash was hidden between layers of plywood. "I knew the scam had worked every time. They would send other stuff too—furniture, anything that required a crate—but live freight was the quickest." When Monroe traveled to Kathmandu, he was amazed by the English advertisements for hash and ganja on the street. D. D. Sharma's Eden Inn had an officelike showroom where jars of different types of hash, hash cookies, and marijuana lined the walls and a sign read: "We ship ANYTHING ANYWHERE ANYTIME."[4] Nepalese marijuana plants, grown in the lower Himalayas, often reach five meters and are harvested live. Skilled workers rub buds between their palms, scrape the resin off with knives, and hand press it into balls that are placed in plastic bags to sweat and soften in the sun. Once soft, the hash is pounded into a patty and then hand shaped into a perfectly symmetrical billiard ball. First-quality Royal Nepalese "temple balls" had to meet the highest standards. They could have no white pin dots of mold on either the inside or the outside. While the ball was pliable, it was never gooey or sticky and had a perfect, uncracked dark-brown skin that sealed the hash.[5]

Abdul bought hash and set up a lab that consisted of two-liter flasks and an electric burner. He placed the hash in a bucket of ethanol until it dissolved and then strained it through a filter. The process was extremely dangerous because he had to heat the remaining solvent until it evaporated through a coiled tubing contraption that resembled a moonshine still. After he repeated the cycle a few more times, an extremely viscous, concentrated cannabis extract remained. Abdul had a carpenter build the first two dog cages, and bought a VW bus from a member of the Brotherhood that he drove from Kathmandu to Delhi.

In Delhi, he met a hippie girl and paid her to send the cages off. "I had her go to the beauty salon and bought her a dress and just handed the cages to her. I told her I was working for these dog show people in the States and this was a rare breed that was real desirable in America." Twenty-four hours later, the dogs and the oil had cleared customs and were safely in Seattle, thanks to Pan-American Clipper Cargo.[6] While he was in Delhi, the same fugitive Brotherhood member who had sold Abdul his VW van told him about Bali's beautiful beaches and perfect waves. "After being in India and the mountains for the last year and a half or so, I really wanted to get back to a beach area. We all just wanted to get to the beach." In order to pay for his surfing safari, Abdul returned to Kathmandu and reduced more than 45 kilos of hash into 12 kilos of oil that he successfully shipped to Seattle. Then he flew to Vancouver, took a bus across the border, and made his way to California to sell the oil by the milliliter. The nervous fugitive made $90,000 in a few weeks, then bought a quiver of surfboards and a plane ticket to Bali.

When Abdul arrived, he found a group of surfers from California already there. "I was surprised to see that everybody was pretty much doing the same kind of little thing—different scams, but everybody was involved in hash, weed, and hash oil." It did not take him long to make friends with California surfers Mike Ritter, Bob Jones, and Ray Lee. "We were all lonely guys with surfboards," said Abdul. At the time, Bali was a place where people hung out between scams and compared notes. The surfer scammers were free with their talk—everybody still trusted one another. "There was no weirdness yet, no snitching and backstabbing," recalled Abdul. "People at that time actually had a code of mutual respect. Plus we were all pretty much like hippie mentality."[7]

Although they looked similar, there was a significant difference between Bali's hippies and the surfers: no matter how many drugs the surfers took at night, each day they climbed down the three-kilometer trail to Uluwatu and paddled out into dangerous surf. The surfers were all skinny and wiry, strong and fit from hours in the water; most were vegetarians who smoked pot but did not drink. The era was best captured in the classic surfing film *Morning of the Earth*, where in one scene, surfers shared a conical clay pipe called a chillum with a group of Balinese men in the cave at Uluwatu. By 1971 a new genre of surf cinema celebrated marijuana use and the iconic, international man of surfing mystery—the "soul surfer." Even surf stars like former world champion Nat Young were hippies, "heavily involved in meditation, astrology, health foods," wrote Young. "Taking psychedelic drugs and smoking marijuana became the norm."[8]

Abdul liked Bali so much that he decided to buy land near Kuta through a Balinese friend. When another American expat named Mike Boyum found out, he told Abdul he would not get his building permit unless he "loaned" him $5,000. The son of a career navy pilot, Mike Boyum moved to Bali in 1969. Although the super-fit military brat was a small-time, second-rate scammer, he was a hustler of the highest order whose greatest gift was his ability to seduce everyone from pubescent girls on vacation with their parents to defense attachés at diplomatic receptions to professional surfers on the hunt for perfect waves. Abdul gave Boyum the money, got his permit, and built a stilt house with a thatch roof and bamboo walls. But he was very wary of his new neighbor. "What a strange guy, probably the weirdest guy I've met in my life."

A classic autodidact, Boyum would become obsessed with subjects and activities and attempt to master them in short order—everything from extreme physical fitness to magic mushrooms to surfing. After meeting a group of musicians in Bali, Boyum convinced them to form a band that he would promote and named it Prophesy. They toured Indonesia and built a substantial following, until the day they failed to show up for a sold-out concert and thousands of their fans rioted. Although the Indonesian government briefly blacklisted Boyum, he paid the necessary bribes and was allowed back into Bali.

When Mike Ritter learned of Mike Boyum's passion for durian fruit from a former Peace Corps worker, he sought him out. Ritter had been experimenting with a fruitarian diet, and the foul-smelling fruit with a creamy, nutty interior was one of his favorites. Ritter went to his house in Kuta and introduced himself, and Boyum handed him a couple of small durians from a large basket on his porch. "They were not number one quality fruit, as I found out later when I opened them," said Ritter, "but I was thankful nonetheless. Mike was such a charmer when he wanted to be." Although he had great charisma, Boyum's brother Bill believed that his true genius lay "in delving into a person's dreams and aspirations. Since almost all of us were surfers, he could show how his interpretation of 'living the dream' was the ultimate manifestation of the surfing life." Like Ritter and Abdul, the two brothers lost all interest in college and normal jobs when they realized they could scam and surf. "Smuggling Black Afghan hashish seemed tame in the context of Vietnam," wrote Bill Boyum. Although his older brother rationalized it by claiming that they were "enlightening the masses to a reality that would value life more," smuggling was a means "to free us up for a life of endless surfing. I was 21 and the future appeared exciting for me. We had obliterated any doubts by smoking hashish."[9]

Mike Boyum's house became a landmark after Errol Flynn's son, Sean, stayed there before his final, fatal trip to Cambodia. Boyum's strong and faithful houseboy from the east side of the island worked under a thin nervous man who was in charge of the house. Both servants honored the American's requests, no matter how bizarre, with straight faces. Imagine what they thought when they were told to collect dry cow dung and water it. "Mike Boyum would consume vast amounts of these hallucinogenic mushrooms, greater quantities than anyone I ever saw," said Mike Ritter. "He would blend seventy or more into a fruit smoothie."

The mushrooms would take one to two hours to come on, just enough time to climb down the cliff at Uluwatu. By the time Boyum got to the beach, he would be in the fetal position, writhing around in the sand with puddles of drool and puke near his head. An hour later, he would enter the second stage of his trip and spend the next few hours talking to spirits and running the zigzagging paths along the cliffs, stopping to fight with monkeys on the craggy rock outcroppings. Pro surfer Jeff Hakman remembered seeing the novice surfer out at Uluwatu, out of his mind on mushrooms. After he took off on a good-sized wave, he fell and vanished for two hours; then "suddenly he comes swimming along from the temple end of the reef, giggling away." Although he "had no style and even less grace," as a surfer, wrote Jeff Hakman, he "was scared of nothing."[10]

Ritter toyed with ideas about doing a scam in Bali, but mostly he surfed. Just as his money was running out, surfer scammer Bob Jones asked him if he would build him some false-bottomed suitcases. Ritter had worked at a boat factory in Santa Cruz and was a skilled fiberglass laminator. Jones was one of Bali's early surfing standouts, having surfed Oahu's North Shore extensively, he had the casual grace of an experienced big-wave rider. After driving a customized Land Rover camper from Europe to Afghanistan and exploring some of the country's most remote regions on a motorcycle, Jones, like Ritter and Abdul, was eager to get to Bali and go surfing. The scam, typical at the time, involved hiring young women to book around-the-world tours on Pan Am Airlines. They stopped in Karachi, where their suitcases were switched with hash oil-filled copies. "A crucial component for planning the flight schedules of the runners was their horoscopes that were examined by an astrologer to determine the most astrologically favorable days," said Ritter.[11]

Ritter, Boyum, and Jones first flew to Pakistan. Always a fanatic about his health, Boyum hired a taxi to drive them out to a stretch of deserted beach, where they ran for many kilometers on the sand. In Karachi, Ritter bought a "Flashman" book, the first in a series of novels about a cowardly British officer at the height of the British Empire who took every opportunity to escape danger and stepped on anyone in order to look good. "In this one the despicable but loveable hero makes his name during a campaign up the Khyber Pass after his horse accidentally stumbles toward the enemy instead of fleeing as its rider had intended," said Ritter. "It was a curiously timely book to read, given that we would be traversing the famous pass in the next few days." The trio traveled overland to Kabul, and bought unpressed hash, made the oil in Afghanistan, and successfully shipped it to Singapore.

Singapore had been a favorite of international traders since Sir Stamford Raffles of the British East India Company established it as a trade post in 1819 to help facilitate commerce with China, because it had a natural deepwater harbor. "The port of Singapore is a free port, and the trade thereof open to ships and vessels of every nation," announced Raffles, "free of duty, equally and alike to all." Before the British established a presence, pirates had ruled the Singapore Strait for as long as anyone could remember. After World War II, Singapore shed its colonial past without rancor and with an eye toward profit. While the remaining British lived on quiet streets in large estates with great lawns, enormous trees, and well-tended gardens, modern skyscrapers and huge shopping malls were quickly replacing the sedate remains of colonial rule as well as the solidly built two-story Chinese shops with ornate trim and the company names boldly embossed in Chinese characters. New hotels were popping up on Orchard Road to accommodate the influx of oil, timber, and mining industry executives. This city of merchants was so enamored with commerce that they awarded medals to the developers who built multilevel, air-conditioned shopping malls and filled them with the latest Japanese cameras, electronic gadgetry, Ray-Ban sunglasses, gold jewelry, and gemstones.[12]

Singapore would soon become an important port for Thai marijuana smugglers; not only was it close to Thailand, it was an efficient city with little crime or corruption and an easy place to outfit or repair a boat of any size. Charts, navigation gear, and anything else necessary for a trans-Pacific voyage could be purchased from Motion, Smith's store.

The city's diversity was most evident at the food stalls and the open-air night market at Buggis Street, where Indian, Chinese, Malay, and Arab food vendors sat side by side. Spice merchants lugged gunnysacks full of nutmeg, cinnamon, and cloves; aromas wafted out from the cool, dark shop interiors and yellow and reddish powders nearly spilled onto your feet as you walked by. Ritter stayed in the Chinese-owned Supreme Hotel on lower Orchard Road and walked a few blocks to his favorite restaurant on Serangoon Road, where Indian waiters ladled hot curries out of tiny silver buckets onto banana leaves. Although the Chinese durian sellers were amazed that foreigners like Ritter and Boyum could pick a good one, they were even more impressed by how much money the Americans were willing to spend.[13]

For a small fee, you could catch a "bumboat" at Clifford Pier to take you out to the ships in the harbor. Merchants on wooden *tongkang* boats unloaded their wares while larger freighters still carried derricks to hoist colorful crated cargo into their holds. Farther out were modern oil-supply ships, visiting warships from friendly nations, grand private yachts, and mysterious research vessels. Mike Ritter felt at home in the exotic city whose origins dated back to the time when the spice trade ruled the seas.

There were many similarities between the exotic marijuana trade during the 1970s and the exotic spice trade during the Age of Discovery (1400–1600). Both were incredibly dangerous and incredibly lucrative. By the time cloves and nutmeg reached Western markets during the seventeenth century, the markup from the original purchase was 2000 percent. Like spice production, the Thai marijuana season reflected the monsoons; the product was obtained by "unknown means and ferried by unknown hands, on streams flowing from another world, spices arrived from a place known only from Bible and fable, washing up in the souks of Cairo and Alexandria and thence to the markets of Europe like so much cosmic driftwood. Or, perhaps more to the point, like gold dust," wrote Jack Turner in his definitive study of the spice trade. "Wasn't marijuana another exotic spice, and weren't we the few brave adventurers to search it out?" asked Ritter.[14]

The three Americans bought fiberglass cloth and resin near Collyer Quay at the mouth of the Singapore River and got to work forming fiberglass shells, using the inside of a Samsonite suitcase as the mold. The idea was to create a false bottom to the suitcase, leaving a thin cavity between that and the actual outside, and pour hash oil into an opening concealed by the leg of the suitcase. One afternoon when Jones got out of his taxi at the hotel, he saw the finished fiberglass shells hanging out of Ritter's window, curing. They had trouble finding runners, so Ritter and Boyum decided to take the suitcases on Pan Am's Flight #2 that circled the globe from west to east. Although Ritter made it to Canada, the American's lightweight shirt and pants were totally unsuited to the cold Canadian winter and drew unwanted attention. Canadian officials allowed him to clear customs and leave the airport, but the Royal Canadian Mounted Police busted him at a nearby hotel. After deplaning in Los Angeles, Mike Boyum realized that he had left part of his stash on the plane and tried to sweet talk a stewardess into retrieving it. Instead she called the police, and after a brief foot chase he was also arrested.

Following his bust, Mike Ritter didn't want to contact his father and hoped to get out of prison on his own. However, when bail was set at $10,000, he knew his father was the only person who would help him. When he phoned from prison, "it was harder for me than for him; he wasn't angry or really very upset, but sounded businesslike, perhaps sensing the seriousness of my situation." Although Julian Ritter agreed to post bail, he let his son sit in jail for two weeks. To raise the money, he sold a violin that had been in the family for a century and one of his best nude paintings. When father and son were finally reunited after the tedious formalities of prison discharge, the elder Ritter's demeanor "was one of resigned disappointment. He realized there was not much he could say that would influence me to quit what I was doing, but nevertheless wished I would have a more normal life." On the flight back to Santa Barbara, the young smuggler had only two thoughts: repaying his father and resuming the fairy-tale life he had tasted in Bali.

Mike Ritter set up a production line at his father's house and began to manufacture false-bottom suitcases; each luggage set consisted of a 24" suitcase, a 26" suitcase, and a ladies' makeup case, all with fill holes for hash oil on the bottom. The big suitcases held four liters ($40,000 worth of oil). Ritter received $3,000 for every suitcase, and all of his runners made it through, allowing Ritter to repay his father and return to Bali.[15] He moved into Mike Boyum's house in Kuta, bought a dugout canoe for $75, and built new bamboo outriggers. He made a sail out of shirt cloth he bought from the Indian merchants in the main market. After sailing from east Bali around Uluwatu to Kuta, past so many of the surf spots that would one day become famous, Ritter realized that Uluwatu was only the tip of the iceberg when it came to Indonesia's surf potential. There were quiet whispers about an amazing surf discovery in Java. Bob Laverty, a wealthy young Southern Californian surfer who had left an executive position in his father's business to travel to the South Seas, had shown Abdul, Ritter, and a handful of trusted others a chart of the islands near Bali. After examining the shape and geographical orientation of the surf-rich Bukit peninsula, he pointed out that Java's Grajagan peninsula had the same outline, but was even larger.

Laverty made a solo recon trip to Java and returned with photographs of the most beautiful, perfect waves anyone had ever seen. The Californians and Aussies decided to mount an expedition from Bali. Although Ritter agreed that there had to be good surf there, life in Bali was so comfortable and he was so stoned that he missed the first trip.[16] Abdul, Ray Lee, and Bob Jones sailed a 6-meter Hobie Cat from Bali to Grajagan Bay while Laverty and others traveled overland, walked the final 20 kilometers on the beach, and were greeted by flawless, double overhead waves. As soon as they rushed out into the surf and were hundreds of meters from shore, monkeys raided their camp. After that they surfed in shifts and took turns guarding their food and water. After about a week, they were so surfed out they returned to Bali, stunned by their discovery.[17]

Shortly thereafter, Bob Laverty and a few others were out surfing Uluwatu. After they were cleaned up by a big set of waves, Laverty told the others he was heading to shore. Sometime later, one of the surfers saw his board floating in the lineup. When he tried to retrieve it, he saw that it was attached to Laverty's dead body. It appeared that he had been knocked out by his own surfboard. Although they managed to get him into the cave at Uluwatu, the American was way too heavy to carry up the rickety bamboo ladder. Because most of the surfers were smugglers who had overstayed their visas, they were reluctant to go to the authorities. Finally, Abdul contacted the police and informed them of Laverty's death. Some claim that when the police finally arrived to recover his body, a sea snake was wrapped around it. This was especially troubling to the superstitious Balinese, who believed that the mythic Indonesian Queen of the South Seas, *NyiRoro Kidul*, had taken him. When Laverty's father arrived in Bali to claim his son's remains, he cut his long red hair, shaved his beard, and dressed him in a tuxedo for the trip home.[18]

Although the surfers in Bali were shaken by their friend's death, they mounted a second expedition to Java. Mike Ritter, Bob Jones, and two others sailed Bogie's trimaran, the *Madrigal,* across the strait at night and reached the Grajagan peninsula just as the sun was rising. They gazed at the endless raw jungle before rounding the point into Grajagan Bay. Other than the giant Spanish mackerel that jumped from the water, the turtles that swam leisurely through the aquarium-clear waves, and the prized reef fish that glided over the coral, they were alone. They camped onshore and every evening, just before sunset, monkeys appeared on the beach for an evening stroll, chattering and carrying on. Their nonchalant behavior made it clear that they were the real locals. Although the surfers found signs of wild boar, they never saw the tigers they'd been warned about.

The waves Ritter surfed in Java were without question the most memorable of his life. He remembered watching one of the surfers, "standing straight up, deep in a tube, arms outstretched, and turning from side to side to show us how big in diameter the barrel was." The only other people they saw were a boatload of Javanese sailors from the island of Madura, whose residents were known throughout the archipelago as expert seamen. They anchored near the Americans and dove for shellfish right in the impact zone where the waves were breaking. Ritter took off on a big wave and when he looked down, he saw the face of a diver in a bright cloth cap looking up at him through hand-carved wooden goggles with lenses fashioned from window glass. The American was amazed by their ease in the treacherous surf, and the Madurese were equally amazed by the surfers. One night, the divers came to the beach camp and could not contain their excitement. They pointed to the surfboards and asked, "Where did you buy those rockets [*Dimana beli rocket itu*]?"

While the Californians and the Aussies wanted to keep the secret to themselves and the cameras out, Mike Boyum had other ideas; he planned to corner the market by turning the bay into his private surfing sanctuary. In short order, he managed to navigate the Indonesian bureaucracy and obtain the necessary permits to build traditional stilt huts, safely above the jungle cats that prowled in the night. After the discovery of Grajagan, both Ritter and Boyum decided once and for all that smuggling was going to provide them with the financial means to pursue "the surfing lifestyle."[19]

While Ritter and Boyum continued to travel to Kabul and sent off loads of Afghani hash oil, the Nixon administration had been pressuring the Afghan king to crack down on hash smugglers. On one of the trips to Afghanistan, they stopped in Bangkok and stayed in the brand new Indra Hotel, ate at hotel buffets, watched Charles Bronson movies, and bought durian at the markets. After Ritter smoked fresh Thai sticks, his Siamese seduction was complete. Only a short while later, the political situation in Afghanistan made it nearly impossible for foreigners in the hash business, so "we naturally gravitated to Thailand."

4

THAI STICKS

The seedless *cannabis sativa* buds were tied neatly and uniformly to a small hemp stick with a thread of hemp fiber or fishing line. Fresh Thai sticks had a spicy, thick, pungent aroma, like camphor with a hint of cinnamon. There was nothing dainty or sweet about them, and the intoxication was similarly powerful. One smuggler remembered taking a couple of big hits and waking up with a barely smoked joint still in his hand. "It was the most exotic thing anyone had ever seen. Everyone had to have it," said Mike Ritter. "A rough test used in Thailand to determine quality was to press a Thai stick against the wall; if it stuck and didn't fall to the floor, it passed." Even *High Times* magazine, the journal of record for pot connoisseurs, would later write: "Years before sophisticated *sinsemilla* techniques were incorporated into the crop management of U.S. growers, the Thais were, without effort, turning out a superior product."[1]

While Nepalese Temple Balls, Afghan Primo Hash and Papa Grande's *Colitas* were valuable, if you had real Thai sticks (reverently known as Buddha Sticks), you named the price—consumers happily paid 10 times more than anyone had ever paid for marijuana before. What sold for $3 per

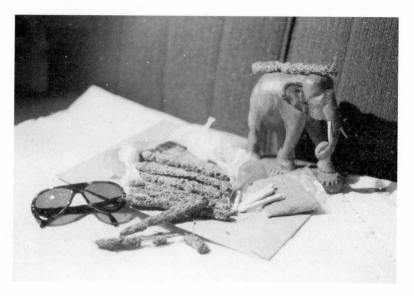

Thai sticks. Photo: Michael S. Ferguson

kilo at the farm in Udorn fetched $2,200 in any city in the United States. Those who smuggled Thai sticks presold them like fine wine to the counterculture's cognoscenti. "It never hit the streets—this stuff was sucked up by rock and roll, doctors, lawyers, entertainers, and Indian chiefs," recalled one smuggler. Customs inspector Robert Clements called one shipment of Thai pot he seized in 1969 "the finest marijuana I've seen in my fifteen years as an agent"; another DEA agent called it "the Cuban cigar of the marijuana world."[2] Given how limited a commodity this prime quality, perfectly dried and packaged Thai and Laotian pot was, it was a seller's market with no end in sight. Unlike other drugs whose distribution was tightly controlled at the upper levels by syndicates, the Thai marijuana trade was controlled only by the economic law of supply and demand.

Due to geography and soldiers transiting to and from the Vietnam War, Hawaiians dominated the Southeast Asian marijuana trade during the early 1970s, and nobody had a bigger head start than Terry Dawson*, whose "Golden Voice" was now some of the most sought-after pot in the world. He quickly grew familiar with how the American military infrastructure worked. Many of his military coconspirators were amazed that Dawson, like the vast majority of hippie scammers, refused to smuggle heroin. One military coconspirator offered to take his pot out by helicopter if he would take a small load of China White "for some real profit." Marijuana was bulky and difficult to smuggle—one ton of packaged pot took up nearly 100 cubic meters—whereas one kilo of smack would fit inside a briefcase. When Dawson tried to tell him about "sacramental drugs," it fell on deaf ears. "Karma to Tiny was an unfamiliar card game, and moral fiber was something you put milk on for breakfast. That's why they always kept hammering on us for heroin, because its small, yeah, but it's death money, blood."[3]

Dawson returned to Thailand to ship his largest load yet—one ton. He took a taxi from Bangkok up past Udorn to the Thai town of Si Chiang Mi on the Mekong River, directly across from Vientiane, Laos. His suitcase was filled with fiberglass cloth, resin, brown paper, and cash. Dawson was sneaking into a country at war and had to evade the Royal Thai Army, the communist Pathet Lao, the Royal Laotian Army, local police, and American spooks. "I felt a little uncomfortable for a moment and shifted the ten grand in my belly pouch nervously like some sitting duck," he wrote later.

A Laotian fisherman hid the American under his nets and took him across the river to Vientiane, and he made his way to the central market, where his partner was chewing betel nuts in her stall. She excitedly closed up shop and took him to inspect his crop. Dawson nearly fell over when he saw mamasan's sons turning a small mountain of perfectly dried, golden ganja with pitchforks. Next he went to a sawmill, had them cut thin wood panels, and build crates that he packed with the "Golden Voice." The smuggler fiberglassed the inside and padded the corners of his boxes with cotton. When they were ready for shipping, he pressed eleven tiny dots in the steel bands that held them together and shipped seventeen boxes from the Vientiane APO to Honolulu.

A few weeks later, Dawson and a nervous colleague picked up the boxes from a Honolulu post office, loaded them into a van, and drove to the North Shore, where he buried them in a grove of ironwood trees near his house at Kawela Bay. Over the next month, he dug up the crates as he needed them.

One afternoon when Terry Dawson returned to Kawela Bay for more pot, it looked like the forest had been bombed: not only had the trees been clear-cut, the land had been bulldozed to make way for the new Turtle Bay Hilton's golf course. Ralph Baxter's organized crime associates quickly "hired" the bulldozer crew for a few thousand dollars and spent the next three days fruitlessly churning the dirt and rubble in search of the boxes. Just as hope was beginning to fade, "the crates erupted from beneath the huge pile of debris." There was only one problem: most of the boxes were broken open and sand was now mixed into the ground pot. Dawson and his team spent the next few days living on Kit Kats and Dr. Pepper, trying to recover as much pot as they could. "We clawed at the golden footprints worth thousands apiece until the madness overwhelmed us," he wrote, "leaving a fortune flickering on the sands of time. I was physically ill, my insides tortured by the ulcer I'd quickly developed."

Finally, Dawson took the pot to his Kawela Bay house and used everything from fans to sifters to hairdryers in an effort to remove the sand. After a few days, the walls were covered with gold dust, and nothing could remove the finer particles, "the end result being years of girls getting their tits burned from red hot sand embers dropping from lit joints." The sand load proved to be this smuggler's breaking point. However, quitting was not so simple because he was now in bed with organized crime. "The syndicate was most displeased to hear of my retirement plans, and none of my macho friends wanted me to cut off the logistics of their profit or dementia." Dawson had no trouble finding a willing successor, but not all of his suitors were up to the task.[4]

Although Buddy Boy Kaohi was a well-known, larger-than-life character, his scams were small and haphazard; some even said that his motto was "Chance 'em, brah." When the Hawaiian heard that world champion surfer Jeff Hakman had recently gone to Lebanon to do a hash scam, he asked Hakman if he was interested in going to Thailand. Kaohi told him that there was a military base near Pattaya Beach where they could send the pot via APO. A week later, the pair arrived in Bangkok with no plan, no contacts, and no source. Buddy Boy managed to buy a couple hundred kilos of mediocre pot from a young Thai he met in a bar and then hustled an American bank manager (whom he also met in a bar) into shipping his "stereo equipment" APO to the North Shore of Oahu. Not content to fill six speakers with pot, Buddy Boy got greedy and also filled cardboard boxes. A few weeks later, when Hakman picked up the pot at the Haleiwa post office, the police were waiting. True to form, Buddy Boy was able to evade the authorities, return to Thailand, and make up the difference with a small load welded inside a scuba tank.[5]

Given his familiarity with Asia, Mike Ferguson was a much more likely successor for Terry Dawson. Ferguson had lived in Japan while his father was training pilots for Japan Airlines. The young American had recently traveled to Udorn, Thailand, where some of his dad's friends were flying for Air America. After the United States constructed a massive Air Force base there, the red dirt village was transformed into a Wild West boomtown. With Hanoi only 700 kilometers away, an endless stream of planes, everything from McDonnell F-4 Phantoms to Fairchild C-123 Providers, took off 24 hours a day. Just outside the gates of the base were R&R tents with rock and roll bands playing. Although there were kegs of beer, given all the puddles of puke on the ground and the scent of pot in the air, it seemed as if the soldiers were more interested in Thai sticks and heroin. "God, they were just young kids, it was really sad to see," recalled Ferguson.[6]

The Hawaiian met the musicians from one of the bands, and they introduced him to a cab driver who could get a load. With a Thai dictionary and sign language, he told the cab driver that he was a tropical agriculture graduate student interested in seeing a ganja farm. In one village near Udorn, his driver put out the call and everyone scattered. Within minutes, villagers returned with bags and bags of Thai sticks. "It was a cottage industry. They all did it, and it cost about three dollars a kilo!"

Ferguson put the load in custom-built boxes, labeled them scientific equipment, and shipped them back to Hawaii air freight. The Honolulu baggage handler he bribed to get the pot through customs stole it instead. Although Ferguson thought he was playing "Moscow Rules," surfer scammer Craig Williams heard through the grapevine that Ferguson had just put together another load, and contacted him. Ferguson knew of Williams because he'd made a name for himself by successfully sailing the first load of Papa Grande's *colitas* to Oahu. At the time, the seedless Mexican buds, made famous by the Eagles' hit song "Hotel California" (1974), were so much stronger than any other pot in Hawaii that the *Honolulu Advertiser* warned that a new "superpot" had invaded the islands.[7]

Ferguson and Williams traveled to Udorn and checked into a hotel frequented by Air America pilots, dressed for the part: safari suits, Rolex watches, ID wrist bracelets, flight cases, and Montagnard elephant-hair bracelets. They went to the same village, handpicked the best 50 kilos, and

Craig Williams tests the product in northern Thailand. Photo: Michael S. Ferguson

Thai villagers produce bags of Thai sticks. Photo: Michael S. Ferguson

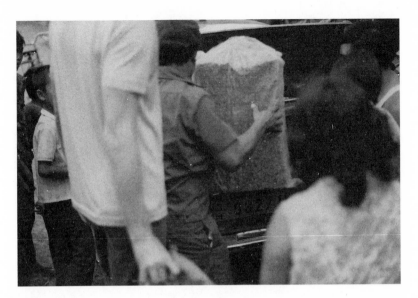

Ready for the road: Mike Ferguson. Photo: Michael S. Ferguson

packed them into boxes that they put into their first-class train car and unloaded at Bangkok's main train station, Hua Lamphong. Back in their hotel room, they packed the pot into small heat-sealed bags they wiped down with gasoline.

Finally, the pot went into three large aluminum Halliburton suitcases, and Mike Ferguson bought a first-class Pan Am ticket to San Francisco, with a stop in Hong Kong. He checked the bags at Bangkok's Don Muang Airport, and when the flight stopped in Hong Kong, he got off the plane and the suitcases continued to San Francisco. It was a very simple scam, and there were only three people involved; a financer, a pitcher, and a catcher. "It was the highest quality, just the best shit," said Williams. Ferguson and Williams continued their small but lucrative closed-cell "bro" scams. "This was down home, it was small. Five grand for stash, five grand for expenses, and it would all be over in two weeks. We used to be able to wholesale Thai sticks for two thousand a pound," said Williams. "We were just running wild. You're young, stupid, take risks, just say, 'Fuck it, we're lucky.'" Bangkok was wide open as long as you could hand off a little money here and there. "Later it got to be big money to big guys—they'd give you the big umbrella."[8]

Craig Williams with Thai sticks in Bangkok. Photo: Michael S. Ferguson

Thai sticks. Photo: Michael S. Ferguson

In some ways, smugglers had an advantage over legitimate businessmen in Thailand due to the nation's history. "Who smuggled commodities in colonial Southeast Asia?" asked Eric Taliacozzo in his book, *Secret Trades, Porous Borders*. "It would not be an exaggeration to answer, 'Just about everyone.'" Taliacozzo aptly described the illicit commerce as "undertrading." "No items in these waters were designated as contraband simply on ontological grounds. Rather, particular historical moments dictated to regional colonial governments whether or not it was in their self-interest to designate products as officially illegal." The only time smuggling raised Thai eyebrows was when it wasn't profitable.

Thailand has been home to smugglers and adventurous businessmen since King Rama I founded his dynasty in 1782. But despite the long tradition of free trade with the West, doing business in the kingdom is not as simple as it appears. Many Western businessmen were baffled by Thailand's Buddhist sensibility that seemed to value mental equilibrium and social grace as much as profit. "Some Westerners," King Bhumibol Adulyadej Rama IX explained to a *National Geographic* reporter, "may consider this sentiment to be a weakness, for it seems to lack, they call the spirit of 'push,' or of competition. They, of course, overlook the fact that the Thai spirit of *metta* is always based on a well-reasoned judgment, and is constantly reviewed against the background of changing circumstances." Joseph Balestier, one of the first U.S. envoys to Siam offended his Thai hosts during his trip to the kingdom in the mid-1800s. When Thai diplomats politely inquired about the U.S. President's health, the American ignored the question and skipped to matters of business. After making him wait for a few days, according to *The History of the Reign of King Rama III*, Thai Deputy Praklang informed the irate American that because he arrived in Bangkok alone, without any ceremony, he had violated royal customs and would not receive an audience with the king.[9]

What made the criminalization of the Asian pot trade particularly difficult was the fact that marijuana was considered by Southeast Asians little more than a medicinal or cooking herb and there was little or no stigma attached to it. Even more daunting to the American drug suppression efforts was the Thai culture of corruption. "What is called 'corruption' in Thailand dates back hundreds of years to when the ancient Thai kings would dispatch individuals to serve as government officials in their provinces," one retired DEA agent explained. "The meager salaries forced the Thai civil servants to keep their hands out just to survive. It evolved to where those who could pay the most had the greatest influence, and civil servants expected to be bribed."[10]

Well into the nineteenth century, there were thousands of state-licensed opium dens all over Siam and French Indochina. With so much opium so readily available, Asian governments wondered why Americans were so concerned about an old man's herb. Up until the 1970s, marijuana possession was only a misdemeanor in Thailand, and one U.S. government report noted that Thai police "have little interest" in marijuana suppression. "Almost every corner, every house, they have it in the yard growing. The older people, they will like it. The working heavy guy, he will like it," said a Thai broker. "They smoke in *bhang* [bamboo water pipe]. When they cooking something, they will cut one stem, something like that. So just add it in and you don't have to use MSG or any kind of flavor."[11]

Marijuana, also known as "*dinky di*," "*Ma Thi*," "the ghost that lives in dark corners," and "Chinese aspirin," has been grown in Thailand, Laos, Cambodia, and Vietnam for centuries and is used as an analgesic to treat migraine headaches, cholera, malaria, dysentery, asthma, indigestion, parasites, and dizziness, and as an aid for women after childbirth. "But they use for medicine also, when you really feel fever. So if you have nothing there, you can get like one branch, and ground it up," said one Thai grower. "And you can put it in the hot water, like two spoon. Cool it down right there and then you can take care of it later when you go to the hospital. It's very good." Thai farmers were even known to mix marijuana into their pigs' feed to increase the animals' appetites.

It is unclear when and by whom marijuana was introduced to Southeast Asia. Some speculate that Arabs brought it in the thirteenth or fourteenth century; others claim that it was the Spanish or the Portuguese in the sixteenth century. Linguistics provides the most compelling evidence that hemp was introduced by Indians, because the vernacular names for marijuana are derivatives of the Sanskrit word *ganja*; the Thais and Cambodians call it *kancha* or *kanhcha*, the Laotians call it *kan xa*, and the Vietnamese call it *can xa* or *gai ando*.[12] According to one anthropologist, Thais living in the northeast had three classifications for marijuana: Thai, Indian, and Chinese. Although they used the Sanskrit word, *ganja*, to describe the marijuana plant, they considered the Chinese ganja grown by the hill tribes along the Mekong River to be the most potent. Although it is impossible to know who brought this tradition of marijuana growing to Thailand and Laos, an educated guess suggests that China is as likely a source as India.

Not all marijuana in Southeast Asia was as potent as the Thai or Laotian variety; the difference between Thai sticks and most Vietnamese and Cambodian pot was like the difference between homemade wine and single malt scotch. The 1970 Stanton Report on drug abuse in Vietnam noted that unlike Vietnamese pot, Thai pot had a "very high THC content." The northeast corner of Thailand is populated by tribes that came from Nanchao (Yunan Province of southern China) who had been forced to pay tribute all the way back to the time of Kublai Khan in the thirteenth century. They fled the region and followed the Mekong River down to their present location in northeast Thailand and Laos.[13] These farmers took the same care with their marijuana plants that French vintners take with their grapevines. Among the hill tribes, some say the Yao, originally from Laos, are the best marijuana growers. "They know how to grow so nice, I mean how to take care of the flower, how to take out the male plant," said one Thai pot broker from the northeast. "They plant at nearly the end of the rainy season. If grow full cycle about six months, grow about two and half meter high. When the flower is heavy [indicating the size of his forearm], the flower grow yellow, then they check."[14] Leaf Fielding described a visit to a Udon village in 1971:

> The whole village was involved in the grass business. Talking pidgin and using fingers, we negotiated with the men while mothers and children sat in groups in the dirt, making up Buddha sticks. A stick held a dozen or more heads of grass, bound with fine hempen fibre around an eight-inch sliver of bamboo. Each stick weighed around four grams. Twenty of them made a brick. The bricks were being put together by the old people. A brick cost seventy-five US cents.[15]

By the early 1970s, the foreign demand for ganja had produced a boom in Isan, the poorest region of Thailand. Although it is in Nakhon Phanom Province, Thailand, the region's economic and social ties are closer to Laos. North of Udorn on the banks of the Mekong, Isan is a plateau the size of New England that floods during monsoon season and is arid and dusty in the dry season. Although rice fields are hard to irrigate and do not yield much, marijuana thrives thanks to the Mekong River, whose tributaries

Thai marijuana farm. Photo: Michael S. Ferguson

Mature Thai marijuana plants. Photo: Michael S. Ferguson

replenish the region with rich, silty soil. "This area [Nakhon Phanom] everyone have water, but the climate and the soil somehow make this area very good. The sun very good, very nice, and the night time very cold," said one Thai who began growing there in 1966. "If you grow same plant, same seed another place, have different taste."[16]

Ritter remembered the day he drove to his first pot farm in Isan. They turned down a dirt road a few kilometers past the charred remains of a frontier police post that the Pathet Lao had torched a week earlier. Even though the communists and the Thai government were still fighting over it, a poor farmer and his young wife had hacked out a plot in the same forest. At first, Ritter didn't realize that he was amid pot plants because they towered so far over his head and looked like Christmas trees. About the size of a suburban back yard, this garden sat next to a trickling stream that the farmer used to water his plants each day as he fertilized them with chicken manure and carefully examined them for bugs and male pollen pods. Male plants were immediately ripped from the ground because the female plants, if pollinated, produced seeds. Once harvested, the plants were hung upside down in the shade. Traditionally banana leaves were wrapped around the buds; when they turned brown, it meant the pot was perfectly dried. With a bit of luck, after a few successful seasons of growing, destitute farmers could earn enough to buy their own farms.[17]

Outside of a few riverfront trading posts, there were very few settlements in the northeast frontier until the United States built roads and infrastructure to support their military campaigns in Southeast Asia. Completed in 1960, the Mittraphap Friendship Highway, Thailand's first asphalt and concrete highway, made it possible to drive from Bangkok all the way to the Laotian border.

After the United States built five major military bases in Thailand and stationed tens of thousands of U.S. soldiers there, the marijuana industry exploded and cheap, powerful pot was as readily available as beer. One of the first things the Vietnamese, and later the Thais, noticed about the American soldiers was their "affinity not only for chewing gum but also for a weed that grew wild," wrote *The New York Times*. "With an eighty-cent bottle of gin purchased at the PX," a Vietnam veteran remembers, "you could trade for a pack of twenty Thai sticks." Although some claim Thai sticks were produced to cater to GIs, a stroll through any market in Thailand demonstrates that everything from flowers to frogs is tied to a stick.[18]

"They tie together. Put the stick. Make it nice. Sell for GI easy. One, two, or five for one dollar," recalled one Thai smuggler who got his start selling pot to U.S. soldiers. "Whatever place GI go, it started whenever they need. Some in Udorn, some in NKP [Nakhon Phanom], in Korat also," recalled another Thai broker. "Each person only grow just about a hundred plants so they can take care very good. So a lot of people here they will have it to sell and we know some area here they grow very good." At first the sticks were very small, about the size of a cigarette. "They would just wrap some newspaper around it, or any other paper, like a cigarette," a Thai grower speculated about the origins of the Thai stick. "When they like to smoke it, it is more easy for them. They can roll it in paper and just pull the stick out."[19]

Adrian Cronauer, the military disc jockey of *Good Morning, Vietnam* fame, joked on the air that there was no GI marijuana problem in Vietnam: "NO, it's not a problem. Everybody HAS it."[20] President Nixon's aide Emil Bud Krogh Jr. was sent to Vietnam to get a firsthand look at the drug problem. When he arrived at the first firebase on his tour, he saw four soldiers smoking a joint and approached them. "I'm here from the White House, and I've been asked to find out about the scope of the drug problem," Krogh announced. "Well, I'm from Mars," one soldier replied, and proceeded to tell him where he could find any drug he wanted. The aide concluded that "we weren't dealing with a problem. We were dealing with a condition. This was a fact in Vietnam."[21]

Even as early as 1966, one U.S. military survey found 29 "fixed outlets" to purchase marijuana in Saigon alone. Just blocks from Tan Son Nhut Air Force base sat Mom's Magic Shop. Mom, the wife of a South Vietnamese sergeant, sold marijuana, LSD, and girls. "We bought a bag of her special grass—pre-rolled canh sa—and sat down on the stone wall outside. We smoked, talked, and sipped warm Schlitz, which Mom also sold." U.S. Customs busted one Green Beret in 1967 for sending $12,000 worth of marijuana per week from Thailand to New Jersey. That same year, MPs raided the beachside bars in Vung Tau, arrested 25 soldiers, and confiscated 20 pounds of pot.[22]

As the ranks of the U.S. military swelled with counterculture draftees, marijuana use became rampant. Larry Heinemann described one soldier's introduction to pot in his novel *Close Quarters*. A new arrival is offered his first joint, and when he asks what it is, his comrade offers this soliloquy: "This here is one of the exotic de-lights of the East. Make a short man see over fences, a tall man see into the clouds, fat dudes crawl under screen doors. It'll slick up a wet dream, screw up a bad dream, fuck up a dufus. Cures heartburn, jungle rot, the Gee-fucken-Eyes, all them things. An' there ain't no muss, no fuss, no puke to clean up after. Smoke is m' little buddy."[23]

The U.S. military could no longer ignore marijuana after their 1969 study, "Marijuana Use in Vietnam," concluded that 35 percent of U.S. troops were regular pot smokers. Draftees were not the only ones indulging in the "exotic delight." An air force colonel who commanded a squadron at Tan Son Nhut was sentenced to three years of hard labor and given a $15,000 fine for sharing pot with the men he commanded. North Vietnam's Liberation Radio ridiculed drug-using American servicemen as "shabby, depraved playboys" who were "the embodiment of hopelessness, of a decadent fighting spirit." The army apprehended only 47 people for drug use or possession in 1965; by 1970, that number had climbed to 11,000. The air force set up special marijuana detection teams at the airports, including a German shepherd named Tuck who, on the command of "Mary Jane," sniffed bags for pot.[24]

The U.S. military's war on pot provided a preview of the kind of pyrrhic victories the U.S. government would rack up in the war on drugs. Just as the crackdown on pot began to show signs of success, soldiers began smoking heroin instead. Unlike pot, heroin is odorless and compact, and because it was so pure, soldiers did not need to inject it; they could pack a hit into the end of a cigarette and smoke undetected. According to one veteran, many U.S. soldiers thought it was "just another joint of marijuana." Prior to 1970, there were small amounts of red and purple No. 3 smoking heroin, but that year Vietnam and Thailand were awash with 90–98 percent pure No. 4 white heroin from the Golden Triangle of northern Thailand, eastern Burma, and western Laos. Although the poppy growers were simple hill tribesmen who had used opium and its derivatives for centuries, the remnants of Chiang Kai-shek's Chinese Irregular Forces (CIF), remnants of the Kuomintang (KMT) army, controlled the trade. Many of America's allies, the anticommunist Montagnard tribe, funded their guerrilla war effort by growing opium. Laotian Chief of Staff General Ouane Rattikone was forced to retire after he told newsmen that the opium trade was a good thing because it provided the hill tribes with a livelihood, and that prevented them from becoming communist.[25]

By 1970, it was becoming increasingly clear to American drug enforcement agents that the efforts against communism and drug trafficking did not always share the same agenda. American law enforcement agencies could not challenge the CIA's covert operations arm, some of whose most important allies were involved in the drug trade.[26] While the military reported only 309 people apprehended for heroin use in 1969, by 1970 that number had jumped to 854. After heading two army psychiatric teams in Vietnam, Dr. Joel Kaplan testified before a Senate subcommittee that when the military began to crack down on marijuana, soldiers simply shifted drugs: "Some men say they turned to heroin because the heat was on marijuana, and many would stick to marijuana if it wasn't for its detectability." Typical heroin users in Vietnam were nothing like the stereotypical users in the United States; many came from small towns and middle-class backgrounds. The heroin epidemic forced the military to take a more realistic view of pot. "If it would get them to give up the hard stuff," one army officer told *Newsweek*, "I would buy all the marijuana and hashish in the Delta as a present."[27]

The Nixon administration was humiliated into action by Congressmen Morgan Murphy and Robert H. Steele's 1971 world heroin report, which concluded that 10 to 15 percent of U.S. soldiers in Vietnam were addicted to the drug. After being offered it by children on the streets of Saigon, Steele described his trip to Vietnam as "a sobering and disheartening experience." The congressmen concluded that if the military could not get heroin abuse under control, the United States would have to withdraw from Vietnam. Even worse, huge shipments were arriving stateside via the APO. Even the command pilot for U.S. Ambassador Ellsworth Bunker was busted at Tan Son Nhut Air Base with $8 million worth of the drug in his plane.[28] By 1972, heroin use was so widespread in Bangkok that five American high school students attending the International School overdosed and died in a five-month period. When American diplomats attempted to pressure the Thai government, they were quickly reminded that drug abuse was not a Thai problem. To the Thais , the drug trade was governed by the basic economic law of supply and demand and if there was a market, there was bound to be a trade, either legal or illegal. To appease the Americans, the Thai government set up a new Narcotics

Suppression Committee in 1972 to focus on drug interdiction and to help the influx of DEA agents arriving in Thailand. Although there was a superficial shift in Thai policy, the market forces were too powerful.[29]

President Nixon's crusade against pot took a backseat as U.S. law enforcement focused on heroin, and it lost more momentum after even his hand-picked commission on marijuana concluded that it was basically harmless. When the National Commission on Marihuana and Drug Abuse, a.k.a. the Shafer Commission, finally published their report, "Marihuana: A Signal of Misunderstanding," in 1972, the President was horrified. The commission described marijuana smokers as "essentially indistinguishable from their non marihuana using peers by any fundamental criterion other than their marihuana use." They stated unequivocally that the fears about marijuana were "unfounded" and "exaggerated," and concluded that it "is unlikely that marihuana will affect the future strength, stability, or vitality of our social and political institutions." Even conservative commentators like William F. Buckley were now calling American marijuana laws "excruciatingly anachronistic."[30]

The Nixon administration's attempt to draw the line in their war on drugs at marijuana failed on a number of levels. First, it did not reduce the pot supply in the United States and created a domestic cannabis industry that had not previously existed. More important, it diverted attention away from the real drug scourge—heroin. American law enforcement agents made a practical triage decision and turned a blind eye to marijuana. "In DEA it was referred to as kiddy dope. For a long time we weren't allowed to work on it; you couldn't work on marijuana," said retired agent Jim Conklin. With both U.S. and Thai law enforcement so focused on heroin, Thai pot growers, brokers, and traders made the most of this window of opportunity.[31]

5

PATTAYA BEACH
GROUND ZERO

Anyone who has worked in Southeast Asia knows the importance of the "fixer." This key middleman stands between foreigners and whatever it is that they want. Not only does a fixer need great communication skills, he also must be capable of making fast decisions and winning trust in incredibly short periods of time. One of the first and most successful fixers in Thailand was a Vietnamese refugee from Udorn named Lek, who learned English after making friends with American soldiers at his sister's tailor shop. The soldiers took him to the Udorn base, where he drank his first beer and watched Thai girls dancing with GIs. Despite his family's hatred of Americans, he liked them.

One day Lek's brother asked him to buy diesel fuel on the base so they could resell it on the black market. When Lek saw a GI towing drums of fuel with a tractor, he offered him cash and speed pills in exchange for fuel. The soldier asked for the keys to the brother's truck and within minutes, the truck bed was overflowing with 50-gallon drums. In the following weeks, the sixteen-year-old made so much money that he was able to buy his own truck, and soon he was delivering steel and cement all over the country. "If we went to the northeast of Thailand, we might send oil, or household goods," he said. "On the return trip to Bangkok, we'd bring logs to the mills."[1]

Like any true venture capitalist, Lek wanted to earn even more money and considered selling opium, until a friend told him that Westerners were sailing into Pattaya, on the southeastern coast, on private yachts looking to buy ganja. "Back then, there was almost no market for ganja. Once in a while you could sell some," said Lek. "That was about the time the first Americans showed up looking for ganja." He decided to test the market and hid a few kilos of top-quality sticks inside a spare tire, then drove down to Pattaya. After he sold out in hours, he planned a trip to Isan to buy it directly from the farmers.

Typically, the pot growers in Thailand were independently contracted by traders who put up the capital for the seeds, fertilizer, and other growing expenses. The traders acted as the middlemen between the farmers and the buyers and were also responsible for packaging the product and transporting it to the coast. Over time, *kamnans*, the regional leaders who controlled multiple villages and large swaths of the northeast, got involved. They hired villagers to grow pot and carry it over the Phu Phan Mountains to avoid police highway checkpoints. The smugglers worked from 8 p.m. to 3 a.m., and each man was paid a few thousand baht for every 20 kilos successfully delivered. Often, men had to be short-roped to motorcycles and towed up steep mountainous sections to the caves where the marijuana was hidden. The police didn't dare venture into those communist (Thai Patriotic Front) strongholds at night.[2]

Back in Bali, Thai sticks were becoming increasingly common, and Mike Ritter wanted to enter the trade. After the surfing season ended, Ritter and an experienced Hippie Trail smuggler flew to Bangkok. After a few days in the city, Ritter hired a taxi that took a left at the end of Sukhumvit Road and headed southeast to the coast. Bangkok's noise and congestion was replaced by rice paddies, canals, and water lilies with pink and mauve flowers. High-speed, long-tailed boats roared by, and at the water's edge, giant scoop nets hung on poles from cantilevered towers. Ritter was amazed by the contrast between the capital and Pattaya, where road crews still stood on elephants' backs to trim tree branches.

The quiet fishing town was forever transformed during the late 1960s when it became an R&R destination for American soldiers. The girlie bars catering to the military were almost all located at the south end, where the water was deep and fishing boats came in to unload their catch. The more upscale hotels were located at the north end of the beach, and the lavish, Las Vegas–style resort built by deposed Thai Prime Minister Thanom Kittikachorn was farther south, on a private beach. The money behind it was rumored to have come from opium and vice. The constant tingle of fear that Ritter felt in Bali, knowing that each day he might paddle out into big surf, didn't exist in Pattaya. The Gulf of Thailand is shallow and narrow, and nowhere is it exposed to the open ocean swells. However, it wasn't the sea that lured surfers to the GI beach resort, it was the black market and the town's reputation as a pirate's free port. In many ways, Pattaya felt like Las Vegas before corporate ownership.[3]

Unlike the soldiers on R&R, who ate at Texas T Bones and flocked to sleazy bars like the Sandbox and the Fantasy Club, the scammers preferred to eat noodles and drink beer at the outdoor food stalls. The Thais, always quick to catch on to an opportunity to make a dollar, took note of the trend and soon provided more outdoor tables, choices of food, and bar girls. Most nights you could find a stocky, square-jawed American sitting with the big, smiling Hawaiian, Buddy Boy Kaohi, at one of South Pattaya's outdoor tables, drinking beer. Dick Petit had supposedly been sent over by a Laguna Beach smuggler as his front man and was paid a monthly stipend; Buddy Boy was working as his helper. Due to his language skills and local knowledge, Petit had an edge over the other expat scammers and became an important figure in the early years of the Thai ganja trade. Although he never made it big, the Thai sources he cultivated went on to dominate the high-end export trade. "In a way, Dick was instrumental in the whole process. He had a knack for working his way into the locals to find out what was going on behind the scenes. He was also instrumental in locating sources for weed," said Mike Ritter.[4]

The American expats in Pattaya were an unlikely mix of hippies and Vietnam veterans who shared little more than the fact that the Vietnam War was the defining event of their lives. For scammers, the draft had turned many into fugitives, and for career soldiers, Southeast Asia felt a lot more like home than America. Once word got out that it was easy to score Thai sticks in Pattaya, a Thailand–Bali smuggling axis began to develop, and no group was better represented than the surfer scammers. By the time they arrived in Thailand, most had already experienced some success as smugglers, and by the early 1970s, it was like Sutter's Mill during the Gold Rush because it was possible to make a fortune in one load. "All you had to do to get rich was bring a load of sticks back to the States," said Mike Ritter. "It wasn't merely the wrapping, the high, or the aroma; more than anything, Thai sticks were yet another mysterious and exotic import from the East." Thai marijuana smugglers were remarkably carefree, given how close they were to the fighting and horror of the wars in Cambodia, Vietnam, and Laos. From Pattaya, the closest border with Cambodia (Arranyapratet) was only 200 kilometers away. You could cross to Poipet, Cambodia, and if you were brave enough, take Cambodia's Highway 5 all the way to Phnom Penh. Most smugglers never went past the border station because they had heard horror stories about the Cambodian communist rampages in the countryside.

The Crow's Nest was a house on the north end of Pattaya with a third-story water tank that doubled as an observation post. While some scammers called it home, others dropped by to catch up on the news, get a stash, or just see who was in town. Mike Ritter remembered Buddy Boy starting each day at the Crow's Nest by chopping up Thai sticks on a butcher's block with a cleaver. "Buddy Boy would roll up half a dozen to ten joints—his 'ammunition' for the day. He would place one behind each ear, a couple under his hat, a couple in his shirt pocket, and the remainder here or there."

Mike Ritter rented a small hollow-brick house down the street for $100 a month where he cooked down several bags of Thai sticks to make oil in 50-gallon drums. Although the oil was fragrant like the fresh sticks, the color was green, not black or gold like the Afghani hash oil. After the 6 liters that made it to California inside of false-bottomed suitcases fetched only $36,000, Ritter lost all interest in labor-intensive hash oil and focused his efforts on fresh marijuana.

Anything that could be filled with marijuana—surfboards, windsurfers, small boats, Hobie Cats, scuba tanks, coolers—scammers packed with Thai sticks and shipped to Australia, Tahiti, Hawaii, New Zealand, and soon, the West Coast of the United States. "There was a whole group of people doing surfboards out of Pattaya and doing fiberglass boats out of Pattaya," said Tim Nicholson*, a Vietnam vet who returned to Thailand after the war and opened a pizza restaurant. "They were the people doing Afghanistan hash before, and they migrated here. They were sending sailboats to Australia, sailboats to the U.S., these types of things."[5]

Unlike the vast majority of the smugglers, who were surfers from California, Hawaii, and Australia, Nicholson was a former college football player who'd grown up on a dairy farm in the Midwest. Drafted in 1966, he served with U.S. intelligence in Thailand for six years and briefly returned to his Midwest farm town after the war, but quickly grew tired of "lying, hiding, not quite fitting in, and people not understanding." He knew that he could not stay and compared his status as a Vietnam veteran in the United States during the 1970s to that of "a leper or a dog. You were supposed to act like you did six years before, and I wasn't the same person. I didn't fit in, I couldn't live in America. I was close to going to a clock tower with a rifle." Nicholson casually met Mike Ritter and many of the first-generation Thai scammers because they were customers in his restaurant. One day someone asked him if he could put together a load of Thai sticks. "I poked around a bit with some of my sources and found that some of the intelligence sources we used were also sources for marijuana. I had the language skills; my part of it was providing loads."

Pattaya played such a central role in the early years of the trade because it was where the small sailboats came to buy pot. Expat American, Kiwi, Australian, and South African sailors used trimarans and ferrocement sailboats to move small loads of Thai sticks to Bali, Australia, and elsewhere. A Vietnam veteran who owned a yacht repair business in Thailand described the two kinds of yachtsmen he typically encountered during the 1970s. "Some—retired people, typically—were sailing around the world for pleasure," he told reporter David Kattenburg. "Then there were the 'scammers'—people smuggling pot. Most yachts heading south to Singapore and then up the Gulf of Thailand to Pattaya belonged to this second group."[6]

Tall, with closely cropped brown hair, early sailor/smuggler Robert Lietzman was anything but a hippie. Not only did he prefer bourbon to pot, one smuggler said that the American, who favored polyester pants with built-in belts, looked "like a country-western singer on vacation." Lietzman used his 16-meter trimaran to ferry pot from Pattaya to Australia and like many at the time, thought it was easy: "You buy it, you hide it, you ship it, and you sell it. Do all that carefully with a little common sense, and you're home and dry." More than anything else, Lietzman liked the freedom that smuggling provided. He believed that the sea was "one of the only places left in the world where you can call yourself a free man and mean it."[7]

One of the few female boat captains in Southeast Asia, Sally Waugh*, also saw pot smuggling as a means to a lifestyle end. The adventurous, 5' 10" brunette graduated cum laude from the University of Pennsylvania and spent three years in Thailand with the Peace Corps. She was sailing her custom-built 39' ferrocement sloop through Asia before she returned to the United States. Waugh had the advantage that she did not look like a hippie, and was a woman captain—virtually unheard of in those waters. For her, small-time smuggling was simple: she didn't want a percentage, just enough money up front "so that I wasn't broke and I could fix a few things on my boat, that's all I wanted." Like Robert Lietzman, she believed that she fell into it "because it was so easy."[8] When she and her two-man crew sailed to Bali, they spent a few weeks hanging around with surfer scammers. Initially, Sally and her crew had no idea they were smugglers. Although she enjoyed spending time with the scammers at the beach, she was struck by their hedonistic lives: "I don't think I met any of those men who had Western women; they were all with Thai women and sort of living on the edge kind of thing. It seemed like the ideal life, but there was absolutely no depth to it."[9]

Occasionally Robert Lietzman teamed with Brian Daniels, a tall, taciturn American with thinning fair hair who reminded Mike Ritter of the actor David Carradine. Raised in Long Beach, California, where his father was the West Coast Director of the Shipbuilders AFL-CIO, Daniels left for the Hippie Trail in 1969 after a divorce and a few uninspiring semesters at Long Beach Community College. He and his brother John got their start in Afghanistan, packing hash in Vauxhall vans that they drove to Europe. "Brian was always a drug smuggler from day one," said Tim Nicholson. "Very smart, talented, could do anything—anything he decided to do, he could do. He could go to sea, navigate; he could do all these things, very detailed." After Daniels married a Thai woman, he avoided the other expats and rented a place in South Pattaya, across the street from the bay. On a vacant lot he had a team of Thais building small plywood sailing catamarans that he planned to fill with pot and ship to the United States. The police found out about the operation and raided the factory, and although Brian Daniels managed to escape, his wife was arrested. Mike Ritter let Daniels hide out for a few days at the Crow's Nest and sent a Thai girl with food and information to see his wife in jail. In addition to the police, his unpaid partner, Lietzman, was also looking for him.[10]

When James "Abdul" Monroe* traveled to Pattaya for the first time, he wound up at the Crow's Nest, where he met Lek and scored Thai sticks. "You'd get these little bricks of twenty sticks, that were about this long [10 or 15 centimeters], on a piece of bamboo, like on a bamboo toothpick. It was all wrapped on there with bamboo string." Abdul bought the biggest Igloo coolers he could find, tore the foam insulation out of them, and replaced the foam with Thai sticks. "Twenty sticks, little bricks like that, really nicely packaged. We'd get those things and smash them down, and in one of those 'Sea Chests,' I could put in, like, six thousand sticks," he said, "it was just Thai sticks covered with plastic." He carefully glued the cooler back together, covered it with stickers, filled it with fishing gear, and took it to New Zealand or Tahiti, where it sold for $50,000.

After he left the States in 1970, Abdul didn't see his parents again until 1973, when his whole family met him in Australia. "Even then, they expected me to come begging to them for help with money or to take me back to the States or something," said Abdul. "They thought they'd see me and my teeth would have all fallen out, you know, from living in India and all." His father could not conceal his surprise when Abdul drove up in a brand-new Toyota Land Cruiser with a cabover camper and surfboards on the roof. "They expected me to be broke. My dad, the first thing, he goes, 'Hey, ding-a-ling, what are you doing for money? How do you get money?' 'I smuggled some hash out of Nepal while I was living there. I made about a hundred thousand bucks.'" When Abdul unscrewed a panel on the truck and pulled out $30,000 cash, his dad just shook his head.[11]

The first pot connections in Pattaya were cab drivers and hotel employees; Lek was probably the first to deal directly with the growers in Isan. After his first successful scam, the bold young Vietnamese-Thai never looked back. Ritter was taken aback when Lek, whom he had never met, called and said, "Hi, I'm Lek and I'm the guy for weed." "The first thing I noticed about Lek was his sparkling, mirthful eyes, almost challenging you to engage in some mischief," said Ritter. "He was skinny as a rail, like Ho Chi Minh, with soft white skin and a forgiving heart." After the American first met him, he felt that he had somehow graduated. "He and I were the same age and, as wildly different as our backgrounds were, I thought we understood each other as equals. Finally I had a weed connection I could really work with. I was thrilled."

Lek teamed with Jo, a street-smart Vietnamese-Laotian from Nong Khai. Although they knew each other growing up, the pair did not socialize because Jo was a street urchin and Lek was the son of merchants who owned a rice mill and a tailor shop. After his father died in a car accident, six-year-old Jo moved in with his opium-smoking grandfather and began selling ice cream to help support his family. "I carry big ice cream, make only one baht, fifty satang, fucking hurt shoulder!" His first foray into the underground economy was working as a ticket scalper; he would buy movie tickets in advance and then return at showtime after the box office had sold out.

Jo liked the free-spending American soldiers in Udorn but detested the war that had killed and displaced so many of his family members. "I feel terrible, this not right. Why they have to come and kill a lot of people?" he asked. "I have family there and innocent people there, what they do? What's going on, why they fucking bring airplane F-4?" To the young refugee, communism and capitalism were two sides of the same coin—both produced inequality and corruption once they obtained power: "So either side, just turn out the same thing. When the communists have a lot of power, so they try to get for themselves. So it's the same thing, nothing different—that's yin and yang; left and right. That's it." His favorite Americans were the Phantom F-4 pilots who faced MIGs and SAM missiles each day. "So you know when they take off, it carry full with bomb, and they coming back okay, light and easy. Happy and party all night, get all the girl, fucking," said Jo. "Tomorrow going again, they said, 'Fuck to hell tomorrow.' All the GIs, they say, 'Get killed, they never coming back, so do it tonight! So fucking getting whatever you can, have fun!'"

When Jo was eleven, he moved from Udorn to Nong Khai on the Laotian border, where he smoked his first ganja. In Isan, as in much of Thailand, marijuana plants were as common in family gardens as chili peppers; one of many medicinal herbs that had been used for centuries. "I smoke, farmer smoke, everyone smoke, just like tobacco for them. Because you working hard, they enjoy with it. I like it, because make you calm, not really harm and thinking good thing," said Jo. "Better than drinking. A lot of trouble start from drinking, not from smoking."

When Jo noticed how much the GIs liked to smoke pot, he began to sell it because it was such easy money. However, the young Thai's steadiest source of income was black-market cigarettes that he bought in Laos for eight baht and resold in Thailand for ten. Jo took a taxi boat across the river, hid the cigarettes under his shirt, and when he reached the Thai customs checkpoint, "We just run, fast you can, sometimes they chasing, if they catch it, they can have for free," he said. "But, fuck, in this cigarette business, it's a lot of fun, and a lot of problem because there is always guy wants to beat you up, get your cigarette." Soon Jo was making a great deal of money for a child and realized that his wealth bought freedom; now he went to movies and bought whatever he wanted to eat.

However, unbeknownst to him, there was a gung ho cop who had his eye on the young cigarette smuggler. When Surin, a burly Hindu officer fresh out of the police academy, first arrived in the frontier town, he cut quite a dashing profile on his BMW motorcycle. Although he organized police posses to catch Jo and his friends selling cigarettes, they were always too fast and ran away. Early one morning, Surin showed up at Jo's house, posing as a buyer looking to score a big quantity of cigarettes. The minute he saw Surin's belt, Jo knew that he was a cop and tried to run but could not get away. The policeman hauled the young smuggler down to the police station and asked who his parents were. Jo said that he had no parents and sold cigarettes to survive. When a friend came to the station and asked if he should get his grandfather, Jo told him, "Just let me deal with it myself." As day turned to night, the policeman's respect grew for the boy who refused to buckle under pressure. When Surin told him that he was free to leave after he paid a 10-baht fine, he said that he had no money. When the policeman told him that he would have to spend the night in jail if he could not pay the fine, Jo fished out a 10-baht from under his belt and handed it over. Although he didn't realize it at the time, the respect Jo earned that day would serve him for many years: Surin would become as much a guardian angel as a coconspirator.

Over time, Jo sold fewer cigarettes and more marijuana. "So whatever place GI go, it started whenever they need. So a lot of people here they will have it to sell and we know some area here they grow very good." To him, the pot business was like a passing train: "If you not get on the train, you going to miss it. That's it. And another thing that I see is the challenge, it's not easy." One day Jo heard from a mutual friend that Lek was selling pot to the Americans sailing into Pattaya on private yachts and wanted to buy it directly from the farmers in Isan. Jo put together a load to take down to the coast. After a few successful small loads, Lek and Jo were growing into a formidable team.[12]

By 1974, more and more surfer scammers were gravitating to Bali because of its surf and proximity to Thailand. One more veteran surfer scammer who migrated from Bali to Pattaya Beach in search of Thai sticks was yet another blond-haired Adonis named John Parten. An excellent surfer, Parten dated "Miss Teen USA" in high school and worked at the prestigious Harbour Surfboard shop in Seal Beach. During the 1960s and 1970s, surf shops were nothing like today's climate-controlled corporate chain stores. Most only sold surfboards, wax, resin, foam, and fiberglass and were as much cultural hubs as places of commerce. While some were square and straight and did not tolerate pot smoking, others provided convenient fronts for all forms of illicit commerce.

Seal Beach was the hometown of *Endless Summer* star Robert August, and as a result, a constant parade of international surfers passed through the town. One summer, Tony Vandenhoovel, one of South Africa's top surfers, showed up and enticed Parten with tales of minute-long rides at South Africa's legendary right point Jeffreys Bay. Two other surfers came back from Europe and described France's perfect waves; beautiful, surfer-loving women; and abundant hash. It was in the surf shop that Parten decided he would travel the world after high school. "I had my own program, and that was to go surfing." The extremely organized and goal-oriented teen saved his money and in the summer of 1969, flew on Icelandic Airlines to Frankfurt, Germany, with a surfboard and two foam surfboard blanks. He bought a VW van at a German police impound yard and drove it to Biarritz, France. The beautiful Basque town was already a major crossroads for traveling international surfers and a Hippie Trail hub teeming with hash. "Of course, everyone smoked," explained one French surfer. "Also, no big companies sponsored surfing at the time, so if you wanted to travel and surf, you needed a lot of money, and dealing drugs was one way to get it." While surfing the Côte des Basques, Parten ran into some old friends from Southern California who told him about the good surf and hash in Morocco. His friends had just purchased a fully outfitted, four-wheel drive Land Rover with a fake gas tank they planned to fill with hash. A few days later they drove to Cadiz, Spain, and put the Land Rover on a ferry to Morocco. John Parten decided to do a copycat scam and put his VW van on the same ferry a few days later.[13]

The first time he met the connection to buy his Moroccan hash, Parten was nervous because of all the stories he'd heard about people being sold henna dye (it looked like hash) or simply robbed. He quickly realized that by being polite and respectful of the local traditions, he could establish a lasting relationship. The American earned the Moroccan dealer's respect when he quietly pulled a weight from his pocket and tested his scale. "You had to treat them like you were going to come back twenty times." The surfer packed 8 kilos of hash under the plate that covered the van's clutch cable and wedged another 6 kilos into the spare tire. "I remember trying to get that damn tire back on the rim, full of hash. What you had to do was, you had to get the hash between the tube and the tire, so if they let the air out, it wouldn't smell," said Parten. "A scam's a unique thing because there's no manual for it."

John Parten drove off to the ferry in Cadiz, and while he was waiting in the customs line, he saw his friends' Land Rover sitting on jacks without an engine. "They're busted, and we're just choking. I mean, here we are, we had the spare tire mounted on the car. We drove right by there and we went through, but, man, our hearts were just pounding out of our chests." Parten breezed across the border. He built two hash-filled surfboards and shipped them to New York. Word traveled fast that the young surfer was a skilled craftsman with good connections, and he was soon involved in three other scams. "My expertise became dealing in the foreign countries, buying the pot. I never really had anything to do, in fifteen years, with selling the pot. I was the broker overseas. It started out in Morocco."

Soon, John Parten had more than enough money to continue his pilgrimage to Jeffreys Bay, South Africa. He put his van on a ship that traveled from Portugal to the Cape Verde Islands and then took another ship to Angola, where he began the long drive south. After the van's engine blew, Parten got a ride from a white hunter in a Land Rover filled with guns and camping supplies. When he crossed the border into South Africa, he felt like he was in Texas. Very few of the conservative white South Africans were willing to pick up the hippie with long blond hair. Finally, a road grader picked him up and he rode into the town of Jeffreys Bay on it. When the heavy equipment operator dropped him off in front of the Andorra Store, he ran into his South African friend Tony Vandenhoovel, who offered him a place to stay. "I see [Vandenhoovel] rolling this—they called it 'Dacha' or 'Durban Poison,' 'DP,' down there," said Parten. "They were buds, beautiful pot, and they came wrapped in these little newspaper things. They were about six inches long." Although some South Africans smoked joints mixed with tobacco, most smoked out of a conical clay pipe called a chillum. "And then you had a little rag you put over the bottom of the chillum so you didn't suck anything through," said Parten. "At the base [inside] of the chillum, there was this little seed or stone or something so you wouldn't suck the ash through."[14]

Like Maui's Honolua Bay, Jeffreys Bay was not just another surf spot; it was one of the finest right points in the world. "It was probably the best surf spot I've ever been in my life. Yes, there were three points in a row, and it was just a fantastic place. Those were amazing years." A Who's Who of the surfing elite passed through the small rural town. Even Bunker Spreckels, Clark Gable's stepson and the heir to the Spreckels sugar fortune, came for a visit. After he inherited somewhere in the neighborhood of $20 million at age 21, Spreckels redefined the surfing safari. His South African entourage included two Mercedes sedans, a personal photographer, his model girlfriend, a bodyguard, firearms of all calibers, and an unrivaled fleet of surfboards that he put through the paces at Jeffreys.

The conservative South African fishing village had never seen anything like this traveling circus of pot-smoking hippie surfers. The Afrikaners viewed marijuana as a black man's drug. One South African criminality textbook from the 1960s argued: "In extreme cases marijuana can so destroy a man's character that he mixes freely with persons of another race." Unlike the Afrikaners, who considered the black Africans inferior and called them "boy," most hippie surfers called them "brother" and treated them as equals. Although many of the Africans called white South Africans "master," some called the surfers "Children of God from the Sea."[15]

The Australians who worked at nearby oil refineries were among the first to smuggle South African pot. They were paid well for their six-week shifts and always arrived at Jeffreys with cases of beer and bundles of Durban Poison. The pot was grown by the Zulus around Durban, but sold by the Indians. "Everybody used to go to this Indian named Tex, in Durban. Somehow we heard about this valley, Ungane Valley," said Parten. The same marijuana that cost twenty cents in Durban resold for one dollar at Jeffreys. The American and a frenetic, fast-talking Aussie named Phil Hasting traveled to the river valley to buy it directly from the Zulus who grew it. They were taken to a thatched hut with polished mud floors, where their connection's two bare-breasted wives greeted them. "They had bracelets from their knees to their ankles, their wrists to their elbows, and beads hanging over the front of their chest," said Parten. Although the Africans were more interested in drinking homemade beer than smoking pot, they always found two white guys smoking pot "hilarious."

One afternoon, John Parten was fixing his surfboard with a Bondo-like adhesive substance called Pratley's Putty when the board fell to the ground and shells got stuck in it. A light bulb went on in Parten's mind. "We're all stoned, we were smoking a lot of really good pot then out of chillums, so we're looking at this and thinking, 'Okay, here's what we're going to do.'" With a metal cylinder tube and a car jack, he could reduce 2 kilos of Durban Poison into a 15-centimeter cube. He covered it with Pratley's, pushed decorative seashells into the putty, covered the bottom with felt, and mailed the "paperweights" all over the world. His Aussie friend was much more ambitious and audacious and running scams of all sorts, including incredibly bad hollow surfboards. "It was so obvious!" exclaimed Parten. "I remember holding it up on a bright sunny day after we made it, and you could just see these circles up in it! But he didn't care, Aussie Phil was so bold—he body packed, took surfboards, loaded suitcases up—he had nerve to spare!"

For his last Durban Poison scam, John Parten traveled to another underground surf Mecca, New Zealand's Mahia Peninsula, with two pot-filled boards. Although New Zealand had world-class waves, there was almost no pot, and it was worth more than gold. Parten's pot sold out quickly, so he returned to California, bought a large load of Mexican, hid it inside a pop-up car camper, and shipped it from Long Beach to Auckland. Soon the American had a regular pot run starting in Wellington and going all the way up the east coast of the North Island, selling the pot to surfers. Business was booming until the day the Bali surfer scammers showed up at the famous left point at Raglan with Thai sticks. "It was going pretty good, I'd probably sold about half of it, and then the boys showed up from Thailand with their Igloos—Ray Lee, Abdul, Bob Jones, and those guys—and that just ruined my market," said Parten. Always a shrewd businessman, he bought some of the Thai and expanded his inventory.[16]

Just as winter was approaching, John Parten collected his cash, flew to Bali, and spent the summer of 1974 surfing perfect waves with Abdul and the other scammers. "It was a great spot. At that point, you could buy Thai sticks down there; it was kind of a surfer hippie paradise." "The word was out about Bali. The village of Kuta was teeming with both major and bit players on the international surf scene. While there were some pro surfers, like Jeff [Hakman], working out between contests, by far the greater were traveling soul surfers, those people of mysterious means who seemed (and still do) to bob up on Maui or Mauritius, Hossengor or Hanalei Bay, Kuta or Cactus, wherever there is a chance of a surf and the certainty of a constant supply of recreational drugs," wrote journalist Phil Jarrat. "That's actually where the real hippies were, the ones that didn't surf—all the people from Goa would come down. Bali was now 'the rising star' for scammers transitioning to Thai marijuana," said Parten. When world champion surfer Nat Young visited Bali for the first time, "a tall, blonde-haired man with piercing blue eyes and a huge bundle of Thai sticks under his arm approached him on the beach, flashed a big smile, handed him two Thai sticks and kept walking." The Pied Piper of pot was none other than Big Eddie, a Hippie Trail standard-bearer who had migrated from Padama, Afghanistan, to Goa, India, to Kuta Beach, Bali.[17]

The Indonesian government had taken notice of all the hippie activity and declared Bali a transit point for "international drug traffickers." They were baffled by the fact that well-heeled Americans with no visible means of support chose to live there. "In Bali there was a whole group of us who were hanging out, and almost everybody was exclusively in the drug business," said Abdul. "We just started hanging out there, and then they got a bit like, 'What the hell's going on with these guys? They live in America and they want to be here. Something must be wrong.'"[18]

John Parten learned from Abdul and the others about the various Thai scams, like scuba tanks and coolers filled with pot; "then I believe they upgraded to jet skis or something like that. That was the progression down there." After the surfing season ended, Parten flew to Pattaya Beach and looked up American smuggler Dick Petit, who was doing a rubber sandal scam with Buddy Boy. The pair were cutting open platform rubber thong sandals, filling the soles with pot, and gluing them back together. Petit introduced the Californian to his Thai connection, Dom, whose Buddhist equanimity and sense of fair play impressed him immediately.

"Dom, my Thai connect, was great to all his family and his brothers and everybody involved," said Parten. "He was a model of fairness, there was no criminal element."

Given Parten's skill with fiberglass, Petit hired him to cut open two windsurfers and fill them with Thai sticks.[19] Runners took the windsurfers to Bali, where the pot was removed, placed in watertight drums, and loaded onto Sally Waugh's sailboat, which would take them to Darwin, Australia. Not only was Australia geographically close to Bali—roughly 950 nautical miles, less than half the distance from Thailand—Darwin was closer than Sydney. It was impossible for Australian Customs' two patrol boats to cover the thousands of kilometers of uninhabited territory that stretched from Broome in the northwest, to Darwin in the Northern Territory, to Port Douglas in northern Queensland. What made Australia most attractive to smugglers was that the police and customs agents had very little experience with drugs; in 1967–68, Australian Customs seized only one kilogram of marijuana, and as late as 1969, the number was up to only 25 kilos. There was little or no pot culture until American soldiers began to arrive in Sydney for R&R during the Vietnam War.[20]

John Parten flew to Darwin to meet Sally Waugh and drive the load to Sydney. When he arrived, the place looked like it had been bombed; a year earlier, Cyclone Tracy's 200 kph winds had just destroyed much of the city and left 43,000 people homeless. The smuggler bought a Volkswagen van and made a false compartment behind the engine to hide the pot. Sally sailed down the Timor Sea, across the Beagle Gulf, and into Darwin Harbor with the weighted barrels dragging under the keel. After the offload, the sticks were hidden in the van and Parten set out on the Stuart Highway and began the 3,000-kilometer race to Sydney. Probably a greater threat than Australian law enforcement were the cyclonic rainstorms known as "the wet." Northern Australia has only two seasons, "the dry," which lasts from May to October, and "the wet," which comes around Christmastime and delivers half of the year's rain in two months (up to 1.5 meters). "I recall the storms were coming in and we were making it in the nick of time," said Parten. "It got so muddy that the mud would keep building up in the wheel wells and stop the wheels."[21]

The smuggler made it to Sydney and sold all of the Thai sticks. Although his customers were surfers, Parten described them as "mini-gangsters" whose motto was, "If somebody put you in a position where they could rip you off, then it was their duty to rip you off. I liked them and I got on good, but I just made sure that I never let anybody be in the position that they could rip me off," said Parten. As in Hawaii, by 1974 the Australian marijuana industry was much more criminal than its American counterpart and would soon get much worse. Marty Johnstone's Mr. Asia syndicate and crooked New South Wales detective Murray Riley's "Ocker Nostra" cornered the pot market and forced many marijuana dealers into the heroin trade instead. Soon Australia would be flooded with cheap pure heroin that would decimate a generation of surfers. "There was a line in the sand and it was crossed the day smack came into town, and we were sitting ducks. Surfers as a tribe were total test pilots, 'cause we were living the dream of freedom. We thought we were bulletproof and there was no way this shit could harm us. We were so wrong," wrote professional surfer Wayne "Rabbit" Bartholomew. "Twelve of my friends bit the dust. It was invasion of the body snatchers, man."[22]

John Parten collected his money and flew back to Thailand in time to help Dick Petit load a small sailboat. In Pattaya Beach he ran into Rocko, an old surfing friend he had last seen in South Africa, who was trying to put together a load for David Ortiz, an experienced California surfer scammer. Ortiz had been impressed by Thai pot ever since the day in 1969 when a friend serving in Vietnam mailed him a joint: "We went out and smoked that fucking joint. Holy fuck! The best shit I'd ever had! I'll tell you, it was like, hash is pretty good—well, this shit was electric." He thought it was Vietnamese weed, but when his friend returned home from the war with a duffel bag full of inferior Vietnamese pot, he realized that Thai pot was in a league of its own. The first time David Ortiz saw a Thai stick was in 1973; he was so impressed by the lime green buds that he bought the entire kilo for $4,000; back home in California, it sold out in days.[23]

6

THE GREAT CIRCLE ROUTE
AND THE SEA OF GRASS

By 1975, the scammers were seeking their fortunes in Thailand like miners in the Old West. "It was like a gold rush, and every fucking guy with a pick and a shovel and a bit of adventure in his blood said, 'I'm gonna go over there and try my luck!'" said Craig Williams. "We were disorganized crime. It was just a bunch of idiot surfers running around like Laurel and Hardy on the high seas." "It was a very loose hierarchy," said Tim Nicholson*. "Michael [Ritter] was way up above me because he was actually able to purchase the load, he arranged the boats, he arranged the offload, and he supervised the sales."

The Ortiz brothers, David and Mike, were anomalies among the blond, blue-eyed surfer scammers because they were lower middle class and Hispanic. Descendents of a Spanish land grant family that moved to New Mexico in the 1600s, their parents migrated to Southern California after World War II to get jobs in the aerospace industry. The Ortiz family first lived in the Mexican part of Torrance, and it was rough; David regularly got robbed during his paper route. When they moved to middle-class Orange County, not only were there no blacks, they were almost the only

Mexican Americans. After David started surfing regularly at the age of fifteen, it was all he wanted to do. "In my senior year I missed fifty-two days and I surfed every day that I missed."[1]

Initially Ortiz believed that marijuana was the same as heroin, but when he tried it, he liked it. "I'd get my friends and I'd go, 'Okay, let's get five of us and all go in and buy a lid.' Then you think, 'Let's buy a few of them, we'll sell enough joints or whatever it is and get our money back.'" Soon the teenager was driving down to Laguna Beach and buying pot by the kilo. When he graduated from high school in 1969, the war in Vietnam was in full swing, but thanks to a low lottery number, he never even had to take his physical. By 1970, he was buying 5 kilos at a time and selling lids out of his bedroom window. When his father found a bag with $5,000 cash inside, he kicked him out of the house. "What the hell are you doing?" he asked. "All you do is go surfing, and now you're selling that shit? I want you out of here. I don't want your brother turning out like you."

Ortiz moved to Idyllwild in the California high desert and lived with a Mexican American friend. They drove pot across the border in a Plymouth station wagon with a false compartment and were moving 500 kilos a week. They had already smuggled three tons by the time Ortiz got busted at the immigration checkpoint in San Clemente. He was sentenced to two years in prison. One afternoon in the yard, a short-haired older convict asked him what he was in for, and Ortiz replied drug smuggling. "So am I. Let me show you around," he said. "I got 10 acres in Tahoe, I still got 50 grand. I was smuggling with airplanes. Fuck these guys. I'll introduce you around. Don't you worry about nothing." By the time Ortiz left prison, he had received a graduate education in smuggling.

One of the Mexicans he met in prison was heavily connected with the Mexican Mafia in Tijuana. After Ortiz was released, he drove south of the border, met with the Mexican gangsters, and struck a deal. They bribed a crooked U.S. border guard and brought 300 kilos across the border at a time. Ortiz worked his Mexican connection for a few years, but after his best friend was killed in a plane crash during a scam in Baja, he never went to Mexico again. Ortiz began sending runners to Nepal to bring back hash oil in false-bottomed suitcases. The smuggler quickly made $50,000 and moved to Santa Barbara, where he spent most of his time surfing the pristine waves of the Hollister Ranch.[2]

One day he ran into an Orange County surfer smuggler named Rocko*, who said that he could put together a Thai load if Ortiz could provide a boat and crew. The smuggler jumped at the opportunity to get into the Thai trade. "I'm going to go over there and I'm going to stay until I get the job done. This is too good of an opportunity," he told his brother. "I've seen what those guys did at the beach with Volkswagen vans. I'm getting in the fuckin' door right now. I ain't coming back till I do it." Ortiz and his partner, John Stansberry, another surfer from California, bought a brand new Cheoy Lee schooner in Hong Kong and flew to Thailand ahead of the boat to discuss the logistics with Rocko's source, John Parten, and his trusted Thai fixer, Dom. Although Stansberry knew nothing about Thailand, he insisted that they load near Pattaya. Parten wanted to go farther down the coast toward Chonburi because Pattaya was hot, but Stansberry was totally inflexible and refused to listen. Parten and Dom ignored their instincts, radioed the boat, and instructed it to come into a nearby cove to pick up their load.

They watched from the bushes as their pot-filled truck drove onto the beach. Just as Stansberry's boat came into the cove, so did a second fishing trawler, and a second truck pulled onto the beach and began to flash signal lights. "Oh fuck. There's another scam going on. Right here, right now," Parten said to Dom and called off the mission. Even though the other boat was smuggling TVs, Parten didn't like the commotion. As they were driving the pot back to their safe house, they came over a hill and saw a police roadblock. Although the load was covered by cassavas, because they were heading away from the market, the police were suspicious and searched the truck. When they found the pot, Dom began negotiating furiously; money changed hands, and although the police kept some of the pot, the smugglers managed to get most of it back.[3]

"I do remember Stansberry was shaking like a leaf that night, and he didn't want anything to do with it after that," said Parten, who returned to their original spot the next night and loaded the pot onto the trawler without incident. The Cheoy Lee sailed the Great Circle Route back to California, where Ortiz and his brother were waiting to offload. David Ortiz liked to use sailboats so that he didn't have to worry about the Department of Fish and Game boarding them because of fishing rods. They used O'Day sailboats to bring the pot in because they were the largest trailerable boats on the market. "It sailed for shit, it was like a fucking motor home. Twenty-five foot and it fits on a trailer, but you could put a ton in it of Thai weed and leave the hatch open. You couldn't even see it." The Ortiz brothers sailed to Santa Rosa Island, anchored in Beecher's Bay, and that night their mother ship arrived and transferred the pot. The next morning, one boat sailed to Santa Barbara Harbor and the other went to Oxnard Harbor, where waiting trucks pulled the boats out of the water and drove away to safe houses.[4]

John Parten flew to California to collect his money from the boats he had loaded in Thailand. He was quickly learning that possession was nine tenths of ownership in the marijuana trade. With the pot now successfully offloaded in California, his partners were trying to renegotiate the deal. "Same old scenario from South Africa, 'We did everything, we had the money, we sailed it,'" said Parten. "They didn't realize that once again, to do a scam, you have to have the product." Because the Thai police had confiscated part of the Ortiz load, there was less weight than anticipated, and Ortiz refused to pay the original price they had agreed to. The other sailboat Parten had loaded broke a backstay on the voyage home, so the crew had to bury their load on an island and sail into Singapore for repairs. Although successful, their trip took four months, and they too wanted to renegotiate.[5]

By the mid-1970s, the hippie era was ending, and with every deal there was outstanding money, misunderstanding, and a growing sense of distrust. The in-country guys like Parten and Ritter were often on the short end of the stick because they lost control of the product once it was on the boat. After their boats were loaded, many buyers quickly forgot that without the weed, there was no scam. Americans with little overseas experience didn't believe the Thais had to be paid just like the sailors, offloaders, and facilitators on the American side. Few were capable of doing it all: loading in Thailand, sailing across the Pacific, and then selling the pot in the United States. You had to rely on other people, and once the trust of the hippie era broke down, the Thai marijuana trade became a tough game.

Despite the setbacks in California, John Parten was fast establishing a reputation in Thailand as someone who could put together high-quality, well-packaged loads. This was especially important with Thai pot due to both the heat and the long sea voyage home. Many times smugglers successfully offloaded in California, only to open their packages and find "long white strings of mold, your beautiful Thai sticks now looked and smelled like Limburger cheese." Because mold was such a problem with Thai pot, Parten carefully hand-packed each box himself. "There was nothing worse than going to all this trouble and getting back and having the ammonia smell. I mean, right away, you were history. I prided myself on the fact that I checked every bit of pot I packed. I touched every ounce of pot that I ever smuggled," said Parten. He devised his own packing system and used a vacuum cleaner to suck the air out of the bags. "So basically, you had your cardboard box, two plastic vacuum bags over it, and then the tarpaulin bag, and then you would bind it up with a metal band." Parten was proving to be such a reliable customer that his Thai connection, Dom, took him to northeast Thailand to meet the farmers and sources in Nakhon Phanom. "I negotiated with these guys that I would pay them double, but I wanted larger sticks. So I got these beautiful big sticks,"[6] Parten recalled.

Like Dom, Lek was emerging as one of the main brokers putting together loads for Westerners. However, that was the only similarity; Dom was relatively straitlaced, while Lek and his sidekick Jo had become full-on pot-smoking hippies. Lek would make the deals in Bangkok and Jo would work upcountry with their contract farmers in Nakhon Phanom, Phon Sawan, Si Song Kram, the Phu Phan Mountains, and the northern tributaries of the Mekong River. "We tell them, 'Anyone want to do it, okay do it, but it have to be the good,'" said Jo, "and we come back and buy it. But we check it and not good enough, we won't buy it." In the beginning they simply loaded the pot into stake-sided trucks and covered it with seasonal produce like bananas, cucumbers, or cassavas. Most important, Lek and Jo always had a pocket full of cash for unanticipated problems. "If we can, we pay. Every time you have to have cash in your hand, so traveling, any trouble, you have to get out of trouble, it doesn't matter. Sometimes we have to tell them, then we pay first, but you have to know the right way to talk too. If you don't have the right way, they will get you too."

Once when Lek and Jo were trying to deliver a load to Bangkok, they saw a police roadblock in the distance and managed to turn the truck around in time. They hid the pot in a nearby village, but when they returned a few hours later, the roadblock was still there. They ate dinner and went back a third time, but the lone policeman was still at his post. Lek wanted to wait, but Jo got impatient. "Sitting, nothing is happening, stay there, look like a chicken," said Jo. "He stay here all day and we stay here all day. What we going to do? Better we go tell him."

Lek and Jo drove the pot-filled pickup to the roadblock. Jo got out, *wai*ed very deferentially, and said, "I need you help something, I tell you the truth one thing, I want to carry some ganja out. I want to do it and I saw you only one guy here anyway, I have to do anyway. You agree or not? Better you help me, we both happy. I have not much money, it's my job, to take care." The policeman looked at Jo as if he were crazy and asked if he was serious. "Yes," said Jo and added matter-of-factly that he would do it with or without the policeman's help. The policeman said, "I know you came last night. I remember plate registration, car, everything." Jo replied, "Yes, I know you know. That's why I come to talk with you. So what do you think? I have no money, I have a gold chain, but I promise you so you can have it." Jo took off his gold chain, handed it to the policeman, and asked, "You happy?" The policeman took the chain, nodded yes, and the smugglers drove through the checkpoint. "Solve the problem, that's my motto," said Jo.[7]

Doing business in the Kingdom was not as simple as many thought; not only was the demand for weed greater than the supply, the Thais had centuries of experience outwitting predatory foreigners. Scammers who believed that their bribes bought submission were sadly mistaken. "These people always had a penchant for speaking and talking and bragging, 'I've got this guy in my pocket.' I've worked with the Thais my whole life here, and you never have anyone in your pocket. You endanger them! They're not in your pocket," said Tim Nicholson.

Procuring a load of high-quality Thai sticks was no small feat; by the time it reached Pattaya Beach, farmers, police, power brokers, politicians, and the military had been paid off in an endless series of negotiations and renegotiations. Many Westerners badly misread the Thai sensibility; behind the smiling *wai* were some of the toughest people on earth. For Lek, the biggest problems came when people were not flexible and rushed him. "I didn't like that the people, the *farang*, they want to finish it in time, but they don't understand the situation. . . . They didn't understand that it was very complex. That there were many different parts to it and every step you have to be very careful."[8]

American scammers prepare a load for shipping. Photo: Michael S. Ferguson

Among those who most misunderstood the Thai marijuana trade were American law enforcement agents, who failed to realize that Westerners were responsible for the demand. "It's not the Thais' fault. It's the market, the demand. They thought the Thais were pushing it." As Nicholson pointed out, the pot trade was nothing like the opium trade; there was no neat pyramid structure. "One consistent misconception on the part of law enforcement is this picture of the marijuana business as this perfect hierarchical structure of organized crime with Mr. Big at the top and the inner group and then the sublieutenants." The pot business in Thailand was never so orderly, and although powerful individuals were involved, no one person controlled it.[9]

Those who had been in the Thai game for a few years, like Abdul and Mike Ritter, were beginning to specialize: for Abdul it was cargo shipping, for Ritter it was taking loads out to smugglers on Thai fishing boats. Experienced scammers were now arriving before the harvest, placing their orders, and putting down deposits. Mike Ritter was loading more boats in Thailand every year. To him, smuggling pot was similar to surfing; when a surfer paddled out, there were any number of floating variables that posed risks. More often than not, things did not go as planned: a load could be short, the quality off, or a boat late. The main dynamic was not the interplay between smugglers and law enforcement; much more terrifying than the DEA, established in 1973, were pirates, Khmer Rouge patrol boats, and the Vietnamese Navy—the list of things to worry about was endless. "Usually you didn't worry about them and usually they weren't a problem," said Ritter, who believed that the most valuable talent a smuggler could have was the ability to improvise and deal with people from all walks of life.

The price of Thai sticks was attracting the attention of veteran smugglers like Mike Carter. The 6' 3" blonde looked like a cross between Gary Cooper and Ken Kesey and was one of the best in the business. A former abalone diver, he was a waterman of the highest order, and this knowledge and skill set made him a natural marijuana smuggler. "I was at home, totally at home in the water, on the water, under the water," he said. "You've got the open ocean, and you go out there, and you go, and there's no laws out there except the law of nature." When he went to sea, a big weight came off his shoulders. "It's more of a natural thing that you can see and have more tangible reality instead of just arbitrary laws."[10]

After a few years of abalone diving, Carter shifted to albacore fishing. Like sea gypsies, the albacore fleet is a close-knit community of tough, independent, resourceful, and extremely capable mariners. Unlike most other forms of commercial fishing, albacore are caught with rods using lines and feather jigs. The boats do not use nets or large winches, and although they are smaller (between 16 and 32 meters), they are extremely stout and capable of handling just about anything the Pacific can throw at them. Not only were these craft perfect for smuggling, the Pacific Ocean was already their home. Much of the fleet begins the season in Hawaii and follows the fish all over the South Pacific. "You don't know where you're going to end up. But you know the coast," he said. "You know what to expect. It's kind of a flexibility, a looseness that you just follow the fish."

Carter bought a fishing boat but fell behind on taxes; his boat was seized, and his wife left him. One of his old diving buddies offered him a way out of his financial dilemma. All he had to do was take a boat down to Mexico, pick up 400 kilos of pot, and bring it back to Oceanside. He ran down to Puerto Nuevo, a small lobster-fishing village between Tijuana and Ensenada. He anchored just outside the surf, took his Zodiac through the breakers, and found his friend waiting on the beach with the pot. The surf was big and consistent; when they launched the loaded Zodiac, the first wave capsized the boat and washed it back up the beach. As they were righting the boat, someone shone a light on them and his partner wanted to abort the mission, but Carter refused.

When he tried to punch through the surf a second time, another wave capsized the inflatable and washed it up the beach. Carter tried to get through a third time, and although the first wave did not flip his boat, it washed him off the stern. Although he never let go of the throttle, the prop was spinning between his legs. "I knew the propeller was down there, and I was in the water, right behind it, hanging onto the throttle," he said. "I just kept it on, kept it on, and I got over the next wave, and I got back on the boat, and I said a prayer. 'If there's a God up there, I want a miracle now. I'm asking for a miracle.'" The smuggler made it out to his boat, got the pot on board, and headed north; by the time he reached the Broderick Street landing in San Diego, the sun was up. He offloaded in broad daylight with total confidence. "There was nothing really unusual for me, because being an abalone diver, you do that sometimes," he said. "We weren't out of context or anything like that."

Unlike Ritter and Abdul, Mike Carter was a commercial fisherman, not a hippie. He liked smuggling because it offered a chance to advance socially and economically. "Instead of the old money, the old royalty, the old high social standards or status, this is a way that the common man had a chance to do something," he said. "I saw peons down in Mexico who had no way of rising in the social structure. Getting involved in marijuana, the peons driving a truck or beach loading were able to make money and do things."

Carter moved from Southern California to Central California and continued to run larger and larger loads of pot. After successfully delivering

The *Ancient Mariner*. Photo: Mike Carter

and offloading a dozen loads in a three-year period, he earned a reputation as an extremely competent and reliable smuggler. One day his partner asked if he would captain the *Ancient Mariner*, a 32-meter halibut schooner built in Seattle in 1913, on a voyage to Thailand to pick up one of the first multiton loads of Thai sticks. Just before the boat left Newport Beach, California, Carter's father, a career navy man, came down to the dock and went aboard. When his son told him what they planned to do, he shrugged and said, "So what?" Although his dad was conservative, he saw nothing wrong with smuggling pot.

The old fishing boat left Southern California in the summer of 1975 with Carter, his army buddy, Goat Bill, and a mechanic they called "the Professor" on board. From California to Hawaii, they were an albacore boat; once they passed Hawaii, they became a research vessel. They reached the Philippines via Guam, passed through the San Bernardino Strait down to the South China Sea, and waited in Singapore for word that the load was ready. The brother of the Thai captain transporting the weed flew to Singapore and would be traveling aboard the *Ancient Mariner* to their rendezvous location in the Gulf of Thailand.

One week later, the *Ancient Mariner* motored into the gulf and drifted near Ko Tao Island. Due to fears of piracy, the smuggler had a .45 strapped to his side and Molotov cocktails in the crow's nest. "If anything went down, somebody would try to get up there and smash the other boat. You know, we didn't know what to expect. It was our first trip over there." When Carter saw a big *sampan* in the distance, signals were exchanged with copper lanterns. They tied up alongside and the two captains shared a beer as the Thais began to transfer the load and thousands of gallons of diesel fuel. Seven and a half tons of Thai sticks were packed into cardboard-lined sheet metal boxes that were soldered shut. "That was real nice stuff, that lime green stuff," said Carter. "All still good. It was sticks. Sticks and sticky. And it was fresh, too."

Before leaving California, they had had two giant plastic fuel bladders built to supply the long trip home. After they finished loading over one hundred fifty-gallon barrels of fuel and started back to America, somewhere near the Philippines, U.S. Air Force jets began to buzz the *Ancient Mariner*. Although he was worried, Carter went on deck and waved at them. Other than that fleeting encounter, the voyage was routine until they neared Alaska and a massive storm caught them 110 kilometers from Adak Island in the Bering Sea: "The seas were big enough to smash into the *Ancient Mariner*'s crow's nest; some even broke over it. The wind was so strong it was just blowing froth, it was beautiful. Things get so bad that it becomes beautiful, especially in the ocean—huge, huge seas, biggest seas I've ever seen, I'd say 40-foot seas."

Carter steered the old fishing boat down the faces of the giant swells until water came over the stern and down the stairs into the engine room. He turned the boat around and began jogging up the faces of the swells. "You've seen *The Perfect Storm*, and I've seen the same waves. You're idling up these things, and you've got to idle straight into them. You can't take it sideways or you're going to roll over. You take it nose into it, you're all right." It took seven turns of the ship's big steering wheel, lock to lock, to turn around. "You had to turn it all the way over, rev it up, get the boat turned around, and—it was like constant physical work, just holding that thing. The storm did not subside."

At one point in the night, a wave broke over the *Ancient Mariner* and knocked out all the windows on one side. Although the wheelhouse was on an elevated storm deck, there was three feet of water in the companionway and every time the door opened, water rushed down into the engine room. A vent pipe from the fuel tank broke off and the tank began to take on salt water. Suddenly they lost all electrical power and everything went black. When the professor burst into the wheelhouse and told Carter that engine room was flooding, the captain replied, "I can't leave the wheel. I leave the wheel we're dead." They managed to get a DC generator going, but although the main engine was running, it was now shooting sparks.

The *Ancient Mariner* had left Newport Beach with cases of gin, vodka, and Scotch. "No one drank Scotch. There was only a case of Scotch left. So me and the Goat guy held the wheel, drinking Scotch all night long, and you [could] only hold the wheel for fifteen minutes at a time before you're totally physically exhausted, because you had to try to see the waves." Finally, after three days, the wind dropped to thirty knots and they knew the worst of it was over. "Once you go through a storm—you have to go through a storm more vicious to get scared. Anything under that is nothing. I mean, it was another baptism," said Carter. "After that, nothing else ever scared me in the ocean."

By the time the *Ancient Mariner* reached Alaska, they were nearly out of supplies and were warming cans on the engine's exhaust manifold. "We didn't know what it was. Could be peas, corn. The labels were washed off the cans," said Carter. "You didn't know what you were getting. So that's how we ate for two days, three days. No coffee." When the seas finally calmed, they built an oven out of a fuel drum and cooked a standing rib roast. "You could feel the food all the way down your gullet, so good," said Carter. "The soot from the stove came into the cabin, nobody was washing, and everyone was eating meat, it smelled like a dog kennel."

When the *Ancient Mariner* finally made contact with their offload team on the one working VHF radio, they were instructed to come to a predesignated spot near the Columbia River in Oregon. They were a kilometer offshore when his partner called and told him not to ask any questions, but to head back out to sea immediately and go to Plan B— Bear Harbor in Northern California. A few days later Carter anchored the *Ancient Mariner* as tight as possible, ran his Zodiac to shore, and saw his partners for the first time in eight months. They got all the pot off the mother ship and loaded it onto trucks, and as they were driving away, the financer of the operation turned to the smuggler and said, "Okay, go out and sink the boat now." "Fuck you!" said Carter. "Here's the keys, you fuckin' sink the boat! I ain't sinkin' that boat, I ain't sinkin' no boat that saved my life!" Instead he ran the *Ancient Mariner* to Crescent City, entered the harbor like any other commercial fisherman, and called his mom. She told him that his father was in the hospital with an aneurysm and probably wouldn't live much longer.

The smuggler drove straight down to the hospital in Newport Beach, and when he saw his father, he could no longer talk and was barely alive. "I told him, 'Hey, Dad, I did it! Guess what? I'm a millionaire now.' He smiled. It was great, you know? And we talked for a while—or I talked to him; he couldn't talk." Carter returned to the hospital later that afternoon. When his father saw him coming down the hall, "his eyes opened up, and, like, [sigh]—you know? I can just see that—'My son. I'm proud of him.'" Suddenly he slumped over and the doctors rushed in and tried to revive him, but he was dead. For the first time Carter noticed a map on the wall with thumbtacks in it; his father had charted the *Ancient Mariner*'s entire voyage.

After he paid his crew, Mike Carter kept collecting money and vacuum bagging it; the bags went into Igloo coolers that he deposited in "The Bank of the Igloo underground." "We just kept collecting the money and putting it in the ground, collecting money and putting it in Igloos. I had about a dozen holes back here." When he finally dug up the coolers and counted the money, the seven and a half tons aboard the *Ancient Mariner* had netted close to $20 million. "That trip—I believe that was the first boatload that went to Thailand, that came out of Thailand. I don't know how I can verify that, but I believe that was, and I believe that made a lot of guys millionaires on that trip. I mean, that opened a lot of people's eyes up to what was to come over there."[11]

There were few significant West Coast marijuana seizures well into the mid-1970s. However, by 1976, more and more Thai marijuana was landing on the Pacific Coast of the United States. Thanks to an informant, San Luis Obispo sheriffs were waiting for the *Dong Phat* when it pulled into a remote cove on the Hearst Ranch on Halloween. For almost two hours, the fishing boat loaded wooden boxes onto a skiff before heading back out to sea. When the skiff came to shore, the boxes were put inside a waiting rental truck that was intercepted by the sheriffs as it headed toward Highway One. After a 90-kilometer open-ocean chase, the Coast Guard cutter *Cape Hedges* caught the fishing boat. Law enforcement recovered over six tons of marijuana. Initially, the pot was valued at close to $1 million, but when police realized that "the illicit shipment was made up entirely of Thai-sticks," the value jumped to $40 million.[12]

After the *Ancient Mariner* voyage, Mike Carter captained a few more loads but mostly focused on offloading. He liked Northern California because it was so desolate and there were so many small coves. One night in the Mendocino Hotel he noticed old photos of lumber schooners loading logs in the tiny coves called "dog hole" harbors. Near sawmill towns like Usal, Needle Rock, and Bear Harbor, the schooners had rigged elaborate block and tackle systems called yarders to load redwood and Douglas fir logs. He figured if nineteenth-century ships could load giant timber with high lines that ran from the tops of the cliffs to offshore rocks, why couldn't technology be updated to offload much less cumbersome cargo, like bales of marijuana?[13]

7

THE GOLD RUSH

The successful voyages of boats like the *Ancient Mariner* drew the attention of a number of big-time smugglers who decided to pool their talents on a large Thai load. Unlike the commercial fishermen who had come to Thailand the previous year, this new group was a Who's Who of the scamming world. Ritter regretted not investing in Mike Carter's scam the year before, so when this consortium of high-profile Western smugglers approached him for assistance, he eagerly agreed to deliver 10 tons to their mother ship. They would use the same financial arrangement that had worked so well for the investors in the *Ancient Mariner*. Ritter and Tim Nicholson* were supposed to receive one quarter of the profit once the pot landed in the United States.

Brothers Bill and Chris Shaffer were in charge of the *Sol*, a 36-meter triple-masted schooner that would transport the pot across the Pacific. At the leading edge of the second wave of Thai smugglers, the Shaffers had grown up in Europe and were the antithesis of the surfer scammers. Bill Shaffer had previously smuggled cocaine and led a very high-profile life, dating celebrities and providing a preview of the conspicuous consumption of the 1980s. He handled the business, while the more down-to-earth brother, Chris, ran the boat with his wife and used dive work as his cover. "Everybody and his brother wanted in on the *Sol*, and they were all in Bangkok, staying in first-class hotels, dining at the best restaurants, and passing time sightseeing, golfing, and chasing the same bar girls as the DEA agents," recalled Ritter.[1]

Although a sturdy boat and crew capable of crossing the Pacific was a primary component of a successful smuggle, it had to be followed by a competent offload and a well-run sales effort. Many groups arrived in Thailand believing that getting a load packed and delivered offshore was just like Columbia's Guijara Peninsula, where pot-filled dump trucks lined up on the beach. Mike Ritter initially told Lek to get 10 tons of grade-A Thai sticks, but over the next few weeks, different scammers approached him and tried to add more and more weight. However, when Ritter informed them that the price was $50,000 per ton plus delivery costs, excuses followed promises, and he received only a fraction of the deposit. "I was told I would have the balance after delivery onto the *Sol*. They even asked if Lek would front the weed and accept his money after the load was sold in California."

As the delivery date drew close, Mike Ritter traveled to Singapore to meet the Shaffer brothers and their main investor. When he knocked on their hotel room door, Ritter heard shouting inside. They finally answered and told him dismissively to come back in a few hours. He returned a few hours later, their argument was still raging and they told him, even more dismissively, to go away. Ritter was stunned. He was the one supplying the load, and they were too busy arguing to meet him! Although his bad feelings about this scam were growing worse, he ignored them.[2] Ritter returned to the hotel the next day, and when he finally met Bill Shaffer, he disliked him on sight. A thin-haired blond with a weak chin and a pasty complexion, Shaffer was a persuasive talker with a mesmerizing voice and a pushy, know-it-all arrogance. Ritter was used to working with hippie surfers who, "despite youthful ambition and a natural competitiveness, still retained an underlying sense of fairness." Shaffer was always calculating how he could get the advantage, and Ritter knew nothing caused more strife in a scam. "To give full focus to your specific task, you needed to feel relaxed about the people you were working with," he said. "If you had concerns about their honesty, then obviously your focus was compromised."

Ritter and Bill Shaffer took a taxi from Singapore up the east coast of Malaysia to the port town of Mersing, where the *Sol* was anchored. During the ride, Shaffer doled out heaping spoonfuls of cocaine and showed Ritter photographs of himself with Hollywood starlets. Shaffer's coke-fueled monologue continued until they reached a small hotel, where his brother Chris was waiting. They sat down for dinner, and the brothers hailed the waiters with endless requests as if they were eating at a three-star Parisian restaurant. While the local lobster and imported wine were excellent, Ritter thought, the brothers' behavior drew too much attention. He preferred "to move quietly and leave no wake. I thought they were show-offs who liked to be known as the biggest spenders in town." The next day, when he went out to the *Sol*, he was impressed by the steel-hulled sailboat, but in the end, they only discussed the most superficial details: chart coordinates, radio frequencies, and code words. The most important aspect of any Thai scam—the contingency plan was left unaddressed.[3]

Ritter returned to Thailand and was surprised when Bill Shaffer showed up unannounced and left as quickly as he'd arrived. At the airport, Shaffer was stopped by Thai Customs after his belt buckle, which contained a knife and brass knuckles, set off the metal detector. "Did he really think he might need such a weapon?" asked Ritter. "A little diplomacy might have proved a lot more useful a defense." Because of the knife, customs did a complete search and found $50,000 cash. Rather than offer a fraction of the money as a bribe, a rattled Shaffer offered all of it to the Thai Customs agent. The Thais were anticipating a payoff, but never that much. "Those fools gave it all away."

In the end, the load turned out to be just under 10 tons of excellent weed that Lek had handpicked from dozens of farms between Udorn and Nakhon Phanom. All of it was carefully sealed in small plastic bags that were bundled inside large gunny sacks. Ritter successfully delivered the pot from upcountry to the coast, and now he and his Thai crew were waiting at the beach. The plan was to transfer the pot onto the small boats that would carry it out to the fishing trawlers loitering a few hundred meters out. Excited that after all the work, it was coming together according to plan, Ritter rechecked his navigation gear and made sure he hadn't forgotten anything. Just as he was about to leave, one of Lek's Thai workers arrived breathlessly to inform him that the police had captured the pot, and arrested part of the team.

Mike Ritter still wasn't convinced it was a lost cause. Several times Lek had been able to buy back loads from the police, so they decided to go to the station and try to make a deal with the commanding officer. "Bad choice," said Ritter. "He searched us and our car, busted us, and placed us in their lockup." Rural police stations in Thailand are built on posts raised one to three meters off the ground. The actual cell was a two-meter-square bamboo cage that sat on the floor. "It reminded me of the kind of cage you might see in an old Hollywood movie about capturing wild animals in Africa," Ritter said. "Anyone passing by could see you inside, like monkeys in the zoo." Next to the police station was a school and every time class let out, a gang of schoolboys came over to look and laugh at the *farang* in the cage. Worried that the *Sol* might be waiting offshore, Ritter asked Lek to contact his associates and let them know what had happened.

Two days later, the American was transferred to a provincial prison in Chumphon and placed in a large room with the other inmates. In the center was a cage that contained a grinning lunatic, said to be a psychopathic killer, shuffling around in ankle irons. Drug offenders, thieves, and murderers were all mixed together, and Ritter was the only foreigner. At night the American slept with other prisoners on bamboo mats squished together like sardines. Lek paid someone in the nearby town to bring Ritter food so he didn't have to eat the same rice gruel as the rest of the prisoners. After two weeks, the necessary bribes were paid and Ritter was released. In the weeks that followed, Lek spent a lot of money entertaining the police chief and his associates, but in the end, all the smugglers gained was a questionable friendship with a bent cop—their beautiful 10-ton load was lost.

When he returned to Bangkok, Mike Ritter learned that the *Sol* had broken a steering gear shortly after leaving Malaysia and returned to port without notifying anyone in Thailand. He wondered what they would have expected him to do if he had arrived at the rendezvous location and there was no mother ship. Lek did what he could to find more weed, but because it was late in the season, he was only able to come up with four tons. With almost no money, they accepted whatever was offered, and most of it was junk. Ritter scrounged another radio, loaded the four tons onto a Thai trawler, and set out to meet the *Sol*. Using only a compass and a taffrail log spinner, he steered east 100 kilometers offshore, then another 60 kilometers due south, and spotted the *Sol* on the horizon the next morning. After all the disappointment, this was a small reward. When he came alongside the large sailboat, Ritter noticed that Chris Shaffer's wife was at the helm, she handled the transfer masterfully. When the *Sol* reached the North Pacific a month later, she ran out of fuel and was adrift in the giant, freezing seas. Finally, a passing ship spotted them and pulled alongside; when they slung a fuel hose over to the rail, diesel fuel sprayed all over the deck, got into the hold, and saturated much of the weed. The Shaffers cherry-picked the best pot and secretly offloaded it.[4]

Before he left for California to collect his money for the pot, Mike Ritter's Thai girlfriend, Dang, begged him to get married. The nineteen-year-old beauty was not a bar girl; her mother was a respected writer and her father a well-known artist. Dang had just returned from studying in Paris when the American spotted her sipping daintily from a straw in a Bangkok café and was entranced. Ritter forced himself to overcome his shyness with women and approached her. They went out on a date that night, and although they fell in love in short order, Ritter did not want to commit to a woman until he had made his fortune. "I didn't think it would be fair to ask her to commit to me, when my commitments were still consumed by marijuana smuggling." To him, a smuggling conspiracy was like a marriage. "Your first obligation is to your partners. A team's well-being and even their lives depended on everyone making the right choices." The smuggler believed that women interfered with that bond because many did not like the competition for attention. "I had witnessed several smugglers take a tumble from the law because of women—either through their own carelessness or outright betrayal from their women," said Ritter. "I made up my mind to wait until I earned my fortune before I had a wife."

When the *Sol* reached California, Mike Ritter left Dang and flew there to sell Lek's inferior weed. It took much longer than he anticipated, and by the time it was all gone, his nerves were shot, friendships had been destroyed, and most of the investors were pissed off. The Shaffer brothers were off to a very inauspicious start. "Too much cocaine and too much fantasy, there was no real substance to them at all. They were just bad," said Tim Nicholson. "Every deal, there was outstanding money. Every deal had a problem. We lost control of the product once it got on the boat. Michael lost control of it once he offloaded it because he was at the mercy of the sellers."[5] Ritter left California with $250,000 and a great sense of disappointment. Not only did he still have to pay Lek and the rest of his Thai crew, it was impossible for him not to compare his meager earnings to the great successes of his peers. Abdul had already salted away millions. Ritter blamed Lek because he believed that he gave all the good weed to Abdul. "It would have been better had he just told me that he couldn't fill my request; then I would have looked elsewhere," said Ritter. "But with the typical Thai attitude of not wanting to disappoint, he led me on."

Lek found it difficult to say no to hard-driving Americans. "If they make their face sad, and then I will do it right away. All honest man too, all very good person, so that I never worried about the money," he said. While Ritter was in California struggling to sell the mediocre pot, he reevaluated his life. First and foremost on his mind was his girlfriend Dang. After this business disappointment, he decided to propose to her once he returned to Thailand. However, he never got the chance: to his absolute shock and horror, he learned that she was now living with Abdul. "I was devastated. The person who had stolen my chance for success in the marijuana business had now taken my woman." Heartbroken, Ritter couldn't focus on anything; after three mediocre loads and his nemesis stealing his girlfriend, his self-esteem was at an all-time low. He stopped working with Lek, quit making deals, and stuck to logistics. Although he considered retiring from the marijuana business, Ritter had no clear idea what to do next—he was thirty years old, with no significant training or experience in any field other than pot smuggling. Moreover, he had not shed his antiestablishment attitude, and a million dollars seemed within his grasp. "I wanted to make it in the marijuana business. Thailand sucked me back."

As Ritter grew older, he decided to set surfing aside until he quit the business altogether. Although he never lost his enthusiasm for the sport, and in fact, missed it greatly, he had become so totally focused on marijuana smuggling that surfing seemed like a luxurious distraction he could no longer afford: "Like a soldier locked in a life-and-death struggle during war, I was afraid to take my eye off the action and stumble into one of the many, ever changing, pitfalls that could easily spell disaster." Not only did the desire to succeed consume him, the loads were growing so fast and so many people were now involved that, illegal or not, smuggling was serious business with big responsibilities. Ritter withdrew to a smaller and smaller group of smuggler friends. "Eventually all that remained of my social contacts were just a few distorted souls like myself."[6]

James "Abdul" Monroe*, on the other hand, was so successful that he had stopped counting his money. "It was just there, like ten million dollars in cash money, just a room full of money," he recalled. "Once I started making millions, I didn't really change anything. Things became more available, but the money, it was just kind of tossed away somewhere, you know." His first big loads traveled to the United States via commercial shipping companies. Lek and Jo would collect the pot in northeast Thailand, bring it down to Bangkok, and pack it into tin boxes that were soldered shut and placed inside wooden crates. "The tin box would fit down inside, and then we'd just load like the last top foot of it with silk shirts, big crates, seven foot long, six foot high, five foot wide—big, big things," said Abdul. After several successful loads, he grew confident enough to fill an entire shipping container with Thai sticks. Ten-wheeled trucks full of pot pulled right into the driveway of his rented house near Ladprao in central Bangkok. Inside, Thai women sat in front of huge piles of weed, picking out buds, tying them onto sticks, and lightly pressing them into perfect one-kilo bricks. "By then, we weren't even trying to conceal it, we'd just fill the container up," he recalled.

When a container was full, a truck would tow it to the Thai Customs dock at Klong Toey. From behind the tinted windows of his Datsun B210, Abdul watched a corrupt Thai Customs officer put the official wire lock and stamp on the door of the container. "He'd twist the wire, like, seven times to the right," said Abdul, "then he'd do something to it, and then he'd do, like, three times back to the left, then he'd put on one of those little lead sealer things, crush it, and that would make the wire lock the door." The containers traveled by ship to Abdul's Mexican Mafia associates in Manzanillo, where they had contracted the Mexican army to transport it to warehouses on the border. The Mexicans knew how valuable Thai pot was and got 30 percent of the load. "They'd pay off the border guards and they'd bring it through in fuel trucks or whatever."[7]

The American marijuana smuggler got to a point in Thailand where he felt "untouchable." Abdul knew enough people and had enough money to buy his way out of almost any situation. He rented a house from the vice president of Bangkok's biggest bank. "He didn't know exactly what we were doing, but he knew it was probably something illegal." One day while they were playing golf, the banker turned to Abdul and told him that he would do anything for him, short of strapping heroin to his body and flying to the United States.

The smuggler was on a roll. Every time he sent a load, he would buy Buddha statues, have a monk bless them, and send them with the pot. Even his superstitious Thai associate Lek admitted, "Abdul have very good luck." When there were problems, Lek and Jo were able to smooth them out with well-placed bribes and the help of their old guardian angel, the respected Hindu-Thai police captain called Surin. When one truckload of pot was intercepted by the highway patrol, Jo walked straight into the police station, asked who was in charge, approached him with a respectful *wai*, and negotiated a deal on behalf of the "top boss in Bangkok." In the end, the police kept a small part of the load, but Jo left with the majority and even managed to recover the truck. "So nothing harm, everyone happy. So like I tell you not many people can do, you have to know the right way to talk too," Jo explained. "If you don't have the right way, they will get you too." If the problem was especially difficult or delicate, they brought in their fixer, Surin. Once in Pranburi the police captured one of Abdul's trucks carrying a ton and a half of pot. When the local police chief refused a bribe, Surin spoke to his boss and a deal was struck. The chief was allowed to refuse the bribe, but out of respect for his boss and Surin, the smugglers were allowed to take back their pot after they replaced it with the same amount of inferior marijuana. Jo and his guys stayed in jail for a few weeks, then were quietly released one by one.[8]

Abdul quickly learned that money presented its own set of problems, and found himself surrounded by what he described as "the best friends money could buy." Although he wanted to share his fortune and help his friends, no good deed went unpunished. Even with those he had made millionaires, the laws of greed and jealousy prevailed; the 1960s hippie scammer ethos had been replaced by a cocaine-fueled, "he who has the most wins" philosophy. "It just showed me so much bad stuff. I saw so many bad aspects of people that I probably never would have seen without all that greed and excessiveness," said Abdul. A small, but telling example was a meal in a restaurant: "Everybody would just sit there, you know, and expect me to pay because I had more." Honesty and personal honor mattered a great deal to the smuggler; for him there was no gray area. "You couldn't be just a little bad."[9]

Abdul witnessed the most naked greed when he paid couriers to move large amounts of cash from the United States to Thailand, to pay for the next year's load. Several couriers disappeared with hundreds of thousands of dollars, only to reappear a few days later with bad stories and no money. One of his couriers simply gave himself a $15,000 bonus and told Abdul, "Well, I didn't think you'd mind, I thought that would be fair; it was only 10 percent of the money." There was one person Abdul knew he could trust, and that was his old high school buddy, Jim Lawton*. The pair had lived together in Laguna Beach during the 1960s and sold pot, LSD, and hashish. Although Lawton still did the occasional offload, he mostly worked as a commercial fisherman.[10]

Jim Lawton got his start driving four-wheel-drive trucks with hidden compartments to mainland Mexico. After filling them with pot, he and his truck took a ferry to the Baja peninsula. When he drove off the boat in La Paz, Baja California Sur, there were no paved roads for 500 miles. His truck had reinforced suspension, heavy-duty shock absorbers, leaf springs, reinforced engine mounts, a winch, tow hooks, tow straps, shovels, sand anchors, and much more. To keep the smell down, he soaked a rag in Pine Sol and placed it next to the big dog that traveled in the camper, "like the dog barfed and I cleaned it up with Pine Sol." Lawton was very conscious of his image when working; he never looked like a hippie. "We'd . . . look like college prep, rather than cool beach guys. I had polyester clothes sometimes to wear. They were like outfits—like Zorro puts on a suit, Superman puts on a suit," he said. "We'd make sure we didn't have stains on our fingers from holding joints, and we carried it to short haircuts and always really played it up." The commercial fisherman approached smuggling very methodically and followed his own set of self-imposed rules. "Never have I ever crossed a border with so much as a joint, I never tried to do that. That would be really dumb. Rule number one: don't stick it under their nose. Rule number two was keep quiet, keep to yourself, and keep the load moving."[11]

When Abdul asked Jim Lawton if he was interested in carrying $300,000 to Bali, he jumped at the chance. After he successfully completed the mission, the old friends were reunited in Bangkok, where Abdul bought Lawton his "drug dealer's dog tag." The round-linked, 22-karat yellow gold necklace was a symbol during the 1970s. "That was a dead giveaway at one certain stage." After his first taste of Asia, Lawton wanted to do a scam of his own. Having sailed loads from Mexico, crewed on transpacific races, and delivered yachts, he now wanted to captain a load from Thailand. Although sailing a load to the United States sounded like a very lucrative adventure, the South China Sea was an especially dangerous place after the fall of South Vietnam and Cambodia in 1975. Pirates were at large with no law enforcement agents to hinder them.

It wasn't as if piracy was a new development; as Stefan Eklof points out in his book *Pirates in Paradise*, "In terms of geography, few other regions in the world seem as favorable for piratical activity as maritime Southeast Asia."[12] However, the mass exodus of Vietnamese, Cambodian, and Laotian "boat people" trying to escape by sea with only the valuables they could carry—mostly cash, gold, and jewelry—drew pirates the same way schools of scared pilchards attract sharks. According to the United Nations High Commission for Refugees, one third of the boat people died at sea, and of the boats that made it to safety, most were robbed, on the average, three times. One boat loaded with over 100 Vietnamese refugees was attacked by four different groups of pirates in eight days—even their engines were stolen. Mike Ritter remembered the first time one of his pot transport boats happened upon a boat full of refugees; as he was handing them water from the bow, the Thai fishermen he'd contracted to haul the pot were boarding and robbing the Vietnamese until he ordered them to stop.[13]

The lucky ones were only robbed. The pirates towed most unfortunate victims' boats to Koh Kra, an uninhabited island 280 kilometers south of Koh Samui, Thailand. There, the pirates would usually kill the men and then fight over who got to rape the women first. If word of freshly captured women got out, dozens of ships descended on Koh Kra. A human rights worker debriefed one Vietnamese woman who survived her ordeal on the island:

The pirates didn't bother to take them off to some hidden place, but went right ahead with their rape right there on the beach in front of everyone. The next days, from Mar. 24 to April 1, hundreds of pirates arrived from numerous boats and barbarous scenes took place each day: the hunting of women and torture of men. The women spread out, some hiding in the jungle, some climbing the mountain, but by now the pirates were well acquainted with the territory and kept up the search. Sometimes they set fire to the jungle to drive the women out as drunken crews would fight over booty.[14]

Although Jim Lawton had heard a few horror stories about storms and pirates, he wasn't worried. Given his sterling reputation as both a scammer and a mariner, Brotherhood of Eternal Love member David Hall offered to buy him a boat and provide a load. When Lawton and his two-man crew landed in Singapore in 1977, things got off to a bad start. Hall and his partner met the boat crew after they cleared customs and as soon as they got outside of the airport, he turned to them and asked, "Where's my ounce of coke?" When Lawton explained that he refused to violate his personal code by smuggling coke across an international border, they exploded with anger; their navigator got such a bad feeling about the scam that he caught the next flight back to the United States.[15]

Due to their limited budget, Jim Lawton had to settle for a cheap Taiwanese production ketch called the *Sea Tiger*. He had no idea how the boat sailed, but it was the right size and more important, one of the only boats in Singapore that he could afford. "I knew that it was going to be like a five-knot average boat, not much fuel capacity, a small diesel with a terrible prop, a small sail plan, and a kind of a round, roly-poly bottom." Although his backers were staying in an expensive hotel and spending money hand over fist, they refused to give their two-man crew enough cash to buy a radio, decent charts, or even a pair of binoculars. "We were under the gun and these guys were pushing us," Lawton recalled. "Vietnam and Cambodia never even got mentioned. It was like we were going to Catalina."

When Lawton set sail from Singapore, he was still confident that the voyage would be a milk run. As soon as the *Sea Tiger* reached the Singapore Straits, before he had even calibrated the boat's steering vanes, a giant storm hit. At first they tried to run with it on a broad reach, sailing far off the wind but not directly downwind, but finally they dropped the main sail and wallowed through the big squalls. When the storm subsided and the skies cleared, the horizon was filled with tiny, palm-covered islands. The sailboat had been blown into Vietnamese waters, and as they approached Phu Quoc Island, home to one of the largest POW camps during the Vietnam War, big patrol boats that looked like PT-109s came out of nowhere. When AK-47 rounds began buzzing over their heads like angry hornets, Lawton eased the main sheet and noticed that his partner was guzzling a bottle of Grand Marnier, the only liquor on board.

The Vietnamese boats pulled alongside and soldiers screamed, "Ho Chi Minh, Ho Chi Minh," piled onto the *Sea Tiger*, captured the two Americans, and put them aboard a patrol boat. After they reached shore, they were put inside a waiting helicopter. Lawton thought they would be pushed out mid-flight and was relieved when they began to descend and landed at an airport littered with discarded American military aircraft, trucks, typewriters, trailers, tanks, and jeeps. In Saigon, the prisoners were taken inside a French colonial building with high ceilings and thick plaster walls. In addition to the interrogator and interpreter, there was a table full of men in brown military uniforms and a couple of guys in civilian clothes. Everyone smoked cigarettes and drank tea.

After the Vietnamese found the American's Nikonos underwater camera, a Pentax 35 mm with telephoto lens, scuba tanks, and an inflatable boat, they were convinced the pair were spies and kept asking where the rest of the frogmen were. "I can understand totally," said Lawton. "Here's all of a sudden some guys that are wearing Hang-Ten shirts from America showing up. There was no explaining the irony of it to them. They must have just figured it was the most clever lie to have anything that crazy: 'Wait a minute, let me get this straight, you are a draft dodger and you are in Vietnam.'" There were no phone calls, letters, consulates, lawyers, charges, courtrooms, visits, or doctors. Nobody even knew that the two Americans were in a Vietnamese jail because the U.S. State Department had no embassy in Vietnam. In fact, Lawton and the handful of other Western marijuana smugglers captured by the Vietnamese were erroneously identified as POW-MIAs from the Vietnam War.

In the months following his disappearance, Jim Lawton's friends and family heard nothing and assumed that he had been lost at sea. "None of our support team did anything. They didn't even give us any expense money when we left Singapore," he said. "These guys just pushed us out in the cold and said, 'Go for it.' It was really a wake-up call." David Hall had waited with the weed near an island on the Cambodian border for a few days. When the *Sea Tiger* never arrived, he assumed that pirates got them. "If they're in jail, they'll call; if they don't call, they're dead." When Hall ran into Abdul in Bali, he casually informed him that his old friend had disappeared at sea. "'Man, you better fuckin' do something,'" Abdul replied. "'You should go do something. You're down here, spending money, vacationing in Bali when those guys are lost? Man, at least have somebody go to the embassy or report 'em missing,' [but] he [Hall] never did anything." Although Abdul could not go to the U.S. Embassy because he was a fugitive, he sent a friend to report Jim Lawton lost at sea.[16]

The Americans were transferred to a prison in the countryside that was surrounded by rolling hills and tea plantations. The monotony of day-to-day life was the hardest part of his imprisonment. On an average day, a gong went off, Radio Hanoi played the national anthem, and next came calisthenics, the commune report, and finally the political news. Sunday was the best day of the week because they broadcast a soccer game and classical music. Each day after lunch, Lawton was allowed out of his cell to dump his chamber pot and given a bucket of water to wash with. Although he wasn't a cigarette smoker when he arrived, the prisoner received six cigarettes a day that he smoked like joints. "You'd get dizzy and get a buzz. That was our way of getting high," he said. "That was the big thing, to have some cigarettes and hope." The spiders in his cell became friends; he would catch mosquitos mid-air, throw them into their webs, and watch the spiders grab them, "just like the Vietnamese grabbed us."

Lawton nearly had a nervous breakdown the day a smiling guard squatted outside his cell and began to whittle pieces of dried bamboo into long, sharp slivers: "I was just flipping out, I'm going, 'Fuck, this is it. These guys are getting ready to torture me and I'm going to have to fight for my life here. I'm not going to let them do this to me. I'm going to fight, it's time to fight now.' I'm trying to think of some kind of plan to keep from getting those bamboo things shoved underneath my toenails and fingernails and soaked in gasoline and lit on fire, like I seen in the movies and read in the books." When the guard finally handed the prisoner one of the sharpened pieces of bamboo, he was baffled. "I take this piece of bamboo and I'm going, what does he want me to do? Shove it in my eye or what? He takes one too and he pokes it in his teeth, between his teeth, like a toothpick. He's handing me toothpicks. I was almost ready to laugh and cry at the same time."

Jim Lawton compared his time in the Vietnamese jail to meditation: above all, he had to remain centered under the stress to survive. Memories of friends meant more to him than anything else. "I don't have gods, I don't have religions, I don't have anything. I have friends and memories, and that's the kind of stuff that kept me going through that whole thing." At times his imagination would run wild and he would get depressed that his father would outlive him. To keep his mind busy, Lawton designed a sailboat on cigarette papers and included every detail: the rigging, sail plans, measurements, lofting, frames, materials, and how many gallons of resin it would take to build the hull.

For a year and half, the Vietnamese made the Americans write their biographies over and over: "They would compare, like good detectives— they must have fingerprinted me ten times over the period, and they drew pictures of us and took photos of us and drew pictures of our ears like fingerprints. In that part of the world before they had the technology to do fingerprints, they drew pictures of ears to identify people." Finally, the smugglers decided to admit that they had been on their way to Thailand to pick up marijuana. "'Okay, I'll tell you the truth. We were on our way to go get this weed, but we are not spies,'" said Lawton. "'We are hippies—like American hippies, you get it? I'm a draft dodger. I'm antiwar activist from when I went to college. You've heard of Jane Fonda? She came to Hanoi.'" After a year, the Vietnamese guards began to loosen up; they realized the Americans posed no threat. "You could kind of tell that they felt guilty that they were having to hold us so long, when a lot of them understood that we were just boat guys doing this trip to Thailand," said Lawton. "The high government guys way off in Hanoi wouldn't cut us loose, I guess."

One day toward the end of 1978, a Vietnamese official told the Americans that they would be released. After a farewell party in a Hanoi hotel, they were driven to the airport and handed their passports and tickets for an Aeroflot flight to Bangkok. Two hours later, Jim Lawton was standing in the customs line at Don Muang Airport in threadbare clothes, with broken suitcases held together by string and only the 35 Singaporean cents that he found in the bottom of his suitcase to his name. When he was able to make a collect call to a friend in Santa Barbara, the friend told him Jim Lawton had been lost at sea. "No, no, no," Lawton replied. "I'm here. This is me, I'm here." Although the Americans spent eighteen months in a Vietnamese prison, they can be considered very fortunate compared to the young Westerners captured off the Cambodian coast by units of the Khmer Rouge's 3rd Division.

8

PIRATES AND PERILS

For pot smugglers like Mike Ritter, who regularly took loads out into the Gulf of Thailand, the greatest fear was being captured by the Khmer Rouge; it was certain death. "I'd look over there and I would just get cold shivers looking at it. My image of the country at that time was comparable to Tolkien's Mordor, a black hole where all regard for life and civilized behavior broke down. I choked at the thought of dying slowly in a Cambodian prison."

After their successful 1975 revolution, Cambodia's Chinese-backed Khmer Rouge attempted to take the nation back to premodernity. The nation's cities were emptied; all urbanities were labeled "New People" and forced to work as slave laborers in a series of agricultural gulags under the control of a mysterious leadership known only as "the Angkar." In the end, approximately two million Cambodians died in a four-year experiment that even East German communist ideologues condemned as "stone-age communism." While many were executed, most died from disease and starvation.[1]

Between the Cambodian port of Kompong Som and the Ream Naval Base, the Khmer Rouge had eight Chinese escort boats, a dozen fast torpedo boats, and a number of armed fishing boats aggressively patrolling their small stretch of coastline. The 15-meter sloop *Iwalani* was en route to Thailand to pick up a load of marijuana in late November 1978. They were within sight of Cambodia's offshore islands when her crew, Chris Delance and Michael Deeds spotted a Khmer Route patrol boat. They tacked abruptly and headed back out to sea in an attempt to avoid their worst nightmare—a Khmer Rouge patrol boat.[2]

The two Americans had grown up in the water and on the beaches of Long Beach, California, and had been friends since seventh grade. Deeds's father, Cameron "Scotty" Deeds, was a legendary tennis coach at Cal State Long Beach. Easygoing, artistic, and well liked by his friends and family, Mike Deeds moved to Maui after graduating from Woodrow Wilson High School in 1969. Although he worked in the construction trade, his true passion was music. The gifted guitar and ukulele player hoped to one day record an album and was growing tired of dead-end jobs. An expert sailor and skilled surfer, Chris Delance was the son of a Long Beach yacht broker who also moved to Maui after high school. Married with a young daughter, Delance was also feeling the pressures of adult life due to Maui's high cost of living and the limited employment opportunities.

When their friend Ron Jackson* proposed using his sailboat to do a Thai scam, Deeds and Delance both agreed. Jackson was a sailboat racer whose teak-decked Nicholson 45 was one of seven built by Camper & Nicholsons, the oldest leisure boat company in the world. The smuggler planned to use sailboat racing as his cover.[3] After he purchased *Yeoman 18* in England, Jackson raced in the Admiral's Cup Series, then sailed from Morocco to the East Coast of the United States, and from there shipped his boat overland to California. By the time Deeds and Delance sailed her to Singapore, the boat had been repainted and renamed *Iwalani*, after Hawaii's albatrosslike state bird. Jackson traveled to Bangkok to organize their load while Delance and Deeds lived aboard the sloop at the Royal Singapore Yacht Club. Although Jackson had set up a deal a year earlier, because he had arrived late, his source was out of pot. He turned to Mike Ritter and John Hagee* for a load, but even with their collective efforts, they could not locate decent pot that late in the season. Weeks turned to months, and Jackson grew frustrated; according to Hagee, one day "Jackson went ballistic" and demanded that they go to Pattaya to look for another source. There Jackson ran into Todd*, a first-generation scammer who had followed the Hippie Trail from Nepal to Thailand.

After Todd scored the load, Jackson contacted his crew and told Deeds and Delance to set sail for Thailand. The plan was to rendezvous with the Thai military vessel carrying their pot, then the three Americans would sail home to Maui. A Thai Navy boat with Ron Jackson and his pot onboard left Sattahip, but when they reached their rally point, the *Iwilani* was nowhere to be found. After three days and nights of waiting, they returned to Thailand with the pot still on board. "That was November 23, 1978," recalled Jackson. "I spent the last four days of November, all December, and the first week of January going up and down the Malaysian coast in case they'd been blown off or shipwrecked. The only thing we couldn't do was get into Cambodia. They just disappeared into the void."[4]

Deeds and Delance had tried to outrun the Khmer Rouge patrol boat, but when the boat began to fire warning shots, the Americans lowered their sails and awaited their fate. The Cambodian boat closed the distance quickly and didn't even bother to pull alongside; they smashed right into the *Iwalani*'s fiberglass bow. Deeds and Delance were swiftly overwhelmed by aggressive men with AK-47s who spilled onto their deck and wasted no time in subduing and blindfolding them. By the time the Cambodians had towed the *Iwalani* to port, other soldiers from the 3rd Division had heard over the radio that an American boat had been captured and were waiting at the dock. Many of these Cambodian sailors had fought against the U.S. Marines on Koh Tang Island during the *Mayaguez* affair and wondered if these were American spies.

After the Khmer Rouge captured the American merchant ship *U.S.S. Mayaguez* in 1975, U.S. Marines landed on the remote Cambodian island of Koh Tang and were met by heavy resistance from the battle-hardened Khmer Rouge 3rd Division. The Cambodian soldiers defending the island shot down three U.S. helicopters, and the fighting raged for three days. In the end, fifteen Americans and thirteen Khmer Rouge soldiers died. A week after the final battle, the Khmer Rouge soldiers noticed that each night someone was stealing their leftover rice; they suspected each other until they found "the Mike Force boot [print] of Americans." That night they set up an ambush and captured U.S. Marines Gary Hall and Danny Marshall. "They looked starved and [had] no spirit for fighting, they looked for life. We brought them to our base, no one spoke English or French," recalled Nek Long*. "We only knew that they missed the planes."

Nek Long heard over his radio that another patrol boat had captured an American sailboat with two men dressed like civilians aboard it. After the *Mayaguez* incident, the Cambodians were on the lookout for American intelligence agents and thought Deeds and Delance "might be spies who were ordered to take photographs for military actions because Americans were preparing for another navy fight. We understood that they were supported by other ships or something else, that the boat could travel on its own." When the sailboat came into port under tow, Nek Long saw two blindfolded white men. "Among the men I saw that time, there was one tall, big guy and another guy who was neither big nor tall."[5]

Sok Sann, one of the Khmer Rouge soldiers who shot down an American helicopter with an RPG, also noticed the strange boat. "We didn't have such a boat in Cambodia," he said. "The sail had already been pulled down when it was captured. We had never seen this boat before, it was very modern, it was made of neither metal nor wood." When San and his

Khmer Rouge soldiers in front of Angkor Wat. Photo: Documentation Center of Cambodia

curious comrades walked over to have a closer look, someone turned on floodlights and ordered the Americans to climb onto the pier. "Because they were blindfolded they couldn't see, so they held their arms and walked them," recalled Sann. The Khmer Rouge sailor thought the two white sailors had accidentally strayed into Cambodian waters and would be released after questioning in Phnom Penh. "In our mind, we had a lot of doubts, we didn't feel any hatred, as when we saw the Vietnamese," said Sann. "I didn't think the Americans were in such a bad situation as the Vietnamese. If the Vietnamese were captured, they would have been killed once they were brought onto shore."[6]

Deeds and Delance were loaded into a car that drove inland for a few hours before it turned down a hot, dusty road on the outskirts of Phnom Penh and stopped at the reinforced gates of Tuol Svay Pray High School. The Khmer Rouge had renamed the school "S-21" in 1976. Also known as Tuol Sleng Prison, this was the end of the road; of the approximately 20,000 people known to have entered, possibly a dozen survived. Unlike the majority of Cambodian prisoners, who were photographed and put in mass cells, ankle-cuffed to large steel poles, the Americans were photographed and taken to a house for "special" prisoners just outside the gates.

The head of S-21 was a former academic named Kang Keck Ieu, better known as Brother Duch. The torturers, guards, and prison staff numbered around 1,500 young men and women between the ages of 15 and 19, all from what their intellectual leaders considered "pure" or "clean" peasant backgrounds. Before they were selected to work at the prison, the future staffers were subjected to months of harsh military training at a camp outside Phnom Penh, where they were ordered to forget about their parents and to think only of the revolution. Their rations consisted of little more than banana stalks, papaya roots, and bugs. Even the slightest infractions were severely punished, and some trainees were even executed.[7]

The climate of fear and distrust at S-21 has few equals in twentieth-century history. One former S-21 cadre recalled the hardening process: "At that time, the Khmer Rouge taught us to hate our parents and not to call them 'Pok' and 'Me' [Mom and Dad] because our parents did not deserve

S-21 prisoner portrait. Photo: Documentation Center of Cambodia

to be 'Pok Me,' only Angkar [the nation] deserved to be children's parents [Pok Me]. We believed what they said, and step by step they slowly made us crazy."[8] Although these self-righteous teens served as the praetorian guards of Pol Pot's revolution, in truth, their lives were little more secure than those of the prisoners. According to S-21 records, 563 guards and other members of the prison staff were killed between 1976 and 1979. Disobeying orders at S-21 was a life or death decision. One guard was killed for burning a wasp's nest, another for shouting "The house is on fire" in his sleep. One of the most striking things about S-21 Prison was the all-pervasive culture of paranoia—every ally was also a potential enemy.[9]

The prison workers were divided into three main departments: interrogation, documentation, and security. In addition to being interrogated, many of the prisoners were photographed in some of the most haunting images of the century. The most feared unit at S-21 Prison were the "catchers," who were responsible for capturing people and bringing them to prison, and then for executing them after interrogation. By 1977, the Khmer Rouge leaders were ordering so many killings that every few weeks truckloads of bound and blindfolded prisoners were driven in trucks to Cheung Ek, 15 kilometers southwest of Phnom Penh. The "catchers" forced the prisoners to kneel at the edge of a pit and clubbed them in the back of the neck with an iron bar. The shallow mass graves they were buried in came to symbolize Cambodia's Killing Fields.[10]

The interrogators worked in three-man teams composed of a transcriber, an interrogator, and a torturer. Torture came in a variety of forms: beating with fists, feet, sticks, or electric wire; burning with cigarettes; electric shocks; being forced to eat feces; jabbing with needles; ripping out fingernails; suffocation with plastic bags; waterboarding; and being covered with angry centipedes and scorpions. Different teams specialized in "mild," "hot," or "chewing" interrogations. Many of the questions asked revolved around charges of sedition. Individuals were accused of being agents of "C" or "K," shorthand for the CIA and the KGB. Typically, the victim was asked a battery of questions that had no correct answer. A manual found at S-21 discouraged torture that ended with death, or what it called "a loss of mastery." The objective was "to do politics," to extract all the information possible before killing the prisoner. The goal of the torture was, according to Brother Duch, to loosen memories: "Beat until he tells everything, beat him to get at the deep things." Interrogators were carefully instructed how to write down prisoners' torture-induced personal histories. One interrogator's note to Duch recounts a typical session: "In the afternoon and evening of 21.7.77 I pressured him again, using electric cord and shit. On this occasion, he insulted the person who was beating him: 'You people who are beating me will kill me,' he said. He was given 2–3 spoonfuls of shit to eat, and after that he was able to answer questions about the contemptible Hing, Chau, Sac, Va, etc. That night I beat him with electric cord again." One Khmer Rouge lie detector was especially crude: a plastic bag went over the suspect's head, and if his or her carotid artery throbbed, the person was guilty. [11]

Tuol Sleng's terrifying head interrogator, Mam Nai, alias "Chan," probably questioned the Americans because he was one of the few members of the staff who could speak English. Exceptionally tall for a Cambodian, with thick lips, he had skin and eyes so light that many thought he was an albino. When journalist Nate Thayer saw him in a Khmer Rouge camp decades later, he described Chan as "the most-frightening" man he had ever seen. In a notebook that was left behind at S-21, Chan wrote, "Apply political pressure and then beat them until [the truth] emerges. Thinking only of torture is like walking on one leg—there must be political pressure [so that we can] walk on two legs."[12]

Throughout December 1978, Mike Deeds and Chris Delance were tortured and forced to write their confessions. Of limited historical worth, the Americans' confessions are more a testament to man's remarkable creativity under extreme duress. Both men wove facts from life with fiction to tell a more convincing story. Mike Deeds claimed to have been recruited by a CIA agent named Lazeby. After tactical training in Virginia and California and a sixteen-week course at the CIA's intelligence and operation school in Washington, D.C., he was given his certificate that declared him a CIA "operation officer." Before he left for Cambodia, the CIA sent him to Long Beach University to keep track of student organizations that opposed the U.S. government. He went on a mission to follow a Colombian drug dealer and revolutionary, and finally to Hawaii, where he infiltrated a radical environmental group. Deeds's stated objective was "to impede effectively the communist influence."[13]

Chris Delance wrote that the CIA recruited him in 1969 to infiltrate radical student organizations and "defend my country from within against communist insurgents." He claimed that he was trained by "Commander Branley" at the nonexistent U.S. Special Services School; his "CIA number," 570 80 5777, was strangely similar to a Social Security number. According to his confession, after Delance moved to Maui, the CIA instructed him to infiltrate a cult called "The Source" and the Hare Krishna Temple. After that, he was sent to Jamaica and Haiti to pose as a hippie yachter and to learn more about an arms- and drug-smuggling ring. Delance wrote that his mission in Cambodia was to make contact with Cambodian fishermen, turn them into spies, and sent them to photograph a Khmer Rouge military base. The American tried to flatter his captors by inflating their international political significance. "The government of Kampuchea is strong and functioning well. The economy is in good shape and the country is prospering. The only way to defeat Cambodia would be a full scale nuclear attack (out of the question)," the prisoner wrote. "This makes any form of bombing out of the question, and on the ground Kampuchea has already demonstrated her superiority to U.S. forces." Delance claimed that they had been taking photographs for an hour when they saw the Cambodian naval vessel and threw their camera overboard. After a series of warning shots, they were boarded by five or six soldiers who "immediately tied and blindfolded us."[14]

By the first week of January 1979, the Vietnamese army had taken Phnom Penh. The Khmer Rouge leaders and their Chinese advisors were running for the Thai border. Just two days before the Vietnamese army discovered S-21 Prison, Deeds and Delance were burned alive. "The Westerners, they came in pairs, and at that time Nuon Chea [a.k.a. Brother Number Two, second in command to Pol Pot] said that the long-nosed prisoners should be taken out and I was ordered by him to burn them to ashes and not to leave any remaining behind," Brother Duch told a UN war crimes tribunal in 2011. Ho Van Tay, a Vietnamese combat photographer, followed the smell of rotting corpses all the way to the gate of S-21 and first discovered the hastily abandoned prison.[15]

At roughly the same time, Ron Jackson called Mike Ritter and John Hagee in a state of panic and asked them to meet him by the old Oriental Hotel in Bangkok. An agitated Jackson had no idea what had happened to his friends and his boat. He told them that he would continue searching for them. When he returned a few weeks later, not only was he even more mentally and physically exhausted, he was out of ideas. When Mike Deeds left for Asia in 1978, he told his family that he was going to Molokai's Halawa Valley and would be out of contact for a few months. He had now been out of touch for more than six months, and neither Jackson nor anyone else who knew about the disappearance alerted his family. "Everybody was holding to the creed—Don't say anything," recalled Mike's brother Karl. It was not until the summer of 1979, at a ten-year high school reunion, that Karl Deeds learned that his brother had even been in Asia. He was talking to an old friend, and when the subject got around to Michael's disappearance, she realized that Karl didn't know the full story and got angry. "'I am tired of this bullshit!" she exclaimed. "Nobody has told you? Last thing we heard, they were in Singapore."

Karl Deeds continued to look for leads about his brother's disappearance, but a full year after his capture, still knew very little. Karl was working as a Navy corpsman at Clark Air Force Base in the Philippines and watching the ABC evening news on November 25, 1979. Jim Lorrie was among the first American newsmen to visit Vietnamese-occupied Cambodia and was reporting from S-21 Prison. "'Oh my God, this is horrible,'" Karl remembered thinking as he watched the report. Suddenly he heard his brother's name. "It was like a dagger." He knew, in that instant, that his brother was dead.[16]

Other claims have further confused the Deeds and Delance cases. Bill Bell, former chief of the U.S. Office of POW and MIA Affairs, wrote that Deeds and Delance were "initially captured by Vietnamese forces, sent to a prison in Vietnam near the border of Cambodia and eventually transferred by the Vietnamese to the Cambodian Khmer Rouge." Dean Temper*, a friend of Delance and acquaintance of Deeds, made an even more unlikely claim that he was aboard the *Iwilani* when it was captured. He said that he jumped into the water and survived the attack by clinging onto a cooler. "I was picked up and not unexpectedly," said Temper. "The entire incident from the time that we were approached, boarded, and the vessel was taken under tow took less than ten minutes; it was a hit and run. It did not happen in Cambodian waters." When told of Temper's story, Ron Jackson exploded with indignation: "WHAT! WHAT! WHAT! Dean Temper told you he was the third man on the boat! No, no, no, no, no! Fuck no, a million times no!"[17]

During the summer of 2012, 1,427 never before seen inmate photographs from S-21 Prison were anonymously donated to the Documentation Center of Cambodia in Phnom Penh; two were of Westerners. One was identified as French Embassy employee Andre Gaston Courtigne. The other photo is a torn image of a handsome, light-eyed Caucasian, wearing a collared shirt and staring straight ahead with open eyes and dilated pupils, his fear palpable. The man remained unidentified for more than two weeks, as neither the Documentation Center nor the U.S. Department of Defense's Joint POW/MIA Command could name him. DC Cam researchers even took the photograph to imprisoned S-21 commandant Brother Duch; he too was stumped. But it took the surfing fraternity's coconut wireless less than twelve hours to identify the man "as American sailor Christopher Edward DeLance [*sic*], who was seized by the Khmer Rouge while boating off the Cambodian coast in 1978," reported *The Phnom Penh Post* on September 3, 2012.[18]

Chris Delance at S-21 Prison. Photo: Documentation Center of Cambodia

Declaration of Michael Scott DEEDS

My name is Michael Scott DEEDS. I am American citizen. I was born on november 15th. 1949 at Long Beach, California.

My father's name is Cameron Scott DEEDS and my mother's name Katheen DEEDS. They have 4 son and I am the second son. My father is professor of physical education. He teaches tennis and leads and controls the other sports. My mother is a wifehouse. They Their home address is 592 Appian Way, Long Beach, California. My father is 58 years old and my mother 57 years old. My young brother names Robert and is 31 years old. And my two other young brothers are Karl and Timothy.

I was captured on november ~~24~~ 1978.

DATED ENTER PRISON TUOL SLENG
November 26th. 1978

Mike Deeds's S-21 Prison confession signature. Photo: Documentation Center of Cambodia

By the late 1970s, pirates posed enough of a threat that a handful of scammers had begun to arm themselves and fight back. When an aggressive Cambodian patrol boat approached a Baltic schooner with 9,000 kilos of Thai aboard, one of the crew members, a South African with recent combat experience, was ready. He had fashioned a homemade flamethrower, and once the Cambodian boat was in range, "'Bam, bam, kruuah!' Incinerated all of them! And sunk them!" recalled one smuggler.[19] Regardless of the risks, more and larger loads of Thai marijuana were finding their way to the West Coast of the United States because the rewards were so great. Jimmy Carter was now president, and marijuana legalization seemed to be in sight after Carter pointed to the Shafer Commission's recommendation that marijuana be legalized. This, coupled with the U.S. government's decision to continue spraying Mexican pot fields with the herbicide paraquat, pushed many smugglers to Thailand. Maritime marijuana seizures in American waters leaped from just over 200,000 pounds in 1975 to 3,000,000 pounds by 1978.[20]

Since Mike Ritter's disappointments with the *Sol* and his girlfriend Dang, he had gone back to logistics and teamed with a Thai smuggler/pirate named Sa, who had his own warehouse and pier near the city of Trat, on the eastern seaboard near the Cambodian border. Although Sa usually trafficked in fuel, cigarettes, and TVs, the Thai was open to hauling marijuana because it was so profitable. Ritter's job was especially precarious because Sa, like most other Thai smugglers, refused to use his good boats due to the possibility of loss. The American never knew if the boat he was about to board as the "warrior captain" was even seaworthy. "I carried my own radios and navigation gear with me. Usually I brought a compass, because you couldn't count on the Thai boat having one. If something broke, they never had spare parts."

Mike Ritter would arrive in the early evening at Sa's pier, go to the upstairs of the warehouse, and be out of sight by the time the load arrived. The American would hear the big ten-wheeled trucks long before he could see them through the cracks in the wooden walls. The pier planks banged loudly, as each truck carried a ton and a half, and when the drivers shut down the loud engines, the next sounds were of shouting Thais. The burlap bales flew from the trucks into the open mouth of the trawler's fish hold. Once the boat's diesel was fired up and belching black smoke, Ritter only had a moment to grab his gear and get onboard. They headed south into the Gulf of Thailand and as the lights of the shoreline receded, the sea breeze picked up. By dawn, land was almost out of sight. Some smugglers transferred their pot within sight of shore, but the American was not comfortable loading inside the horseshoe-shaped gulf and preferred to go well outside it.

Ritter's old friend from Bali, Vietnam veteran Bob Martin, contracted him in the summer of 1978 to provide a load and sent his partner, Bobby Clark, to coordinate the details. The son of a gypsy fortune teller, Clark had gotten his start by driving to Kansas, picking wild hemp (that did not get people high), and selling it in California to college students and hippies. Clark met Ritter at his house on Sukhumvit soi 43, and although he agreed to pay $50,000 per ton plus delivery charges, Ritter was shocked when Clark handed him only $15,000. "I took the 15 but wondered if he would send more money and, if not, what he was expecting for $15,000," he said, "More to the point, what was I thinking, signing up for a project that I couldn't pay for? I was so captivated by lure of adventure and fortune back then, I jumped for it." Lek agreed to front the rest of the load. "Lek was like me in that regard. He would say 'Yes, yes' because he wanted to please, but without being sure if he could perform. So on we went."

When Ritter finally saw the pot in a farmer's shed near Chumphon, he was devastated by how bad the small, dry buds looked. The Thais were getting greedy, and after 1978 it became increasingly difficult to get large quantities of high-quality, well-packaged product. Thai brokers were wrapping such bad pot onto sticks that consumers no longer wanted Thai sticks. The rush of scammers anticipating huge profits blew the cottage industry wide open. The shortage was exacerbated by law enforcement raids; that year, brokers scrambled to find whatever they could, even immature leaf and stem with no buds at all.

Their rendezvous location was out in the gulf, toward Vietnam. Bob Martin traveled to Hong Kong to prepare the boat for the voyage. The sixteen-meter black-hulled schooner with red sails was nearly invisible at night. The decorated combat veteran was not worried about pirates because "We were the pirates." Before they left Hong Kong, Martin wanted to gut the brand-new boat's interior to make room for the load, but his partner, who was getting the boat after the scam, was reluctant to destroy the teak interior.

Ritter captained one of the two Thai fishing boats carrying the pot to the mother ship. He easily made visual contact in calm seas and also saw a trail of teak debris as Martin's crew gutted their boat to make room for the pot. "As I came close to Bob's boat, he jumped into the water and swam over to us. His crew was ripping the last of the boat's beautiful wood interior out and tossing it into the sea to make room for our cargo. There was a line of jetsam of hand-wrought shelves, bookcases, bunks, etc., floating in the placid gulf waters." Ritter grabbed a bookshelf for Lek as a souvenir. The trawlers tied up to both sides of the sailboat and marijuana bales began to rain down on it. Once the pot was transferred, the boats went their separate ways, the only evidence of the encounter a trail of teak. The sailboat was packed so full of pot that even the galley and cockpit had bales stacked from bow to stern. It took Bob Martin eight days to fit the one-kilo aluminum bags into the sailboat like a jigsaw puzzle, with only a small foxhole for sleeping in the fo'c'sle that you had to enter through a top hatch.[21]

The black sailboat had taken the Great Circle route back to the United States and was a few days out from California when he contacted his partner, Bob Clark, who told him that the DEA had rented a house five kilometers from their offload spot. Although Clark was camping on a cliff in the redwoods with every radio known to man, his best intelligence was coming from a mole working in the Coast Guard office. Because the DEA had four boats patrolling the offload area, the smugglers decided to take out an insurance policy: they would pack as much pot as possible in the inflatable and Martin would make a kamikaze run through the surf. First he did visibility tests at sea with the Zodiac. "I'd go to where I see the boat but it was real small and [they'd say], 'No, we can't see you.' And I just kept on the radio with them and then got closer and closer and, man, I was right next to them, they couldn't see me." Once they got within sight of the California coast and the deep blue sea turned brownish green, Bob Martin knew it was time to load the Zodiac. Just as the sun was setting, he donned his wetsuit and launched the marijuana-packed inflatable. As he was making his way toward shore, Martin saw a police helicopter take off. "He went pretty close. Again, it was a black Zodiac with a black tarp over it; I knew they couldn't see me," the smuggler said. "All my experience offshore, you think somebody's looking at you, but they are looking past you. It's hard to see objects in the water."

When Martin finally reached the rendezvous spot, nobody was there. He radioed his partner, who told him to abort the mission because there were too many police around. "Hell no, man! We're doing this!" Martin barked into the radio as a DEA patrol boat came over a swell and was now one hundred meters away. "They were just idling. These guys, you can't see, looking from the cabin with the lights on," said the smuggler. "They were obviously doing their job, their eight-hour shift. I don't think they were tipped off. I watched them go by." Bob Martin continued down the coast until he ran out of gas and dropped the hook 16 meters from shore. He called his partner on the radio, but the batteries were dying and the signal was fading. His heart sank; after crossing the Pacific, he was now a sitting duck just off shore, "the worst thing that can happen to you after crossing the ocean and all that. I go, 'Fuck this. I've got a joint.'" When the smuggler lit the joint, the radio cracked to life: his partner said, "Oh, I see it."

Bob Clark had recruited his offload crew that night from a local red- neck bar. He picked out guys with beards and long hair, "local lumberjack characters. He recruited like fifteen guys and three or four pickups that night in the bar, to unload us. Everybody's like they're having a party. They're all drunk, having a great time." When Martin saw his partner on the beach, they embraced and began to jump up and down. "We were so stoked." They unloaded the Zodiac, and Martin went back out and suc- cessfully brought in the rest of the pot. "I was so proud of myself that I had found this spot," said Martin, "driving from the Philippines, driving the Zodiac to the right spot." By the time the sun came up, all of the pot was off the mother ship and Martin had dumped the outboard into the ocean and cut the Zodiac into pieces. Finally, Clark handed each truck driver a huge bag of pot, way more than they had expected. More than newfound wealth, Martin was struck by his sense of relief, "the biggest feeling of accomplishment in my life, and that seems to be the biggest deal, finishing those ventures, making the money and truly knowing that money isn't everything."[22]

9

MULTITONS AND
MOTHER SHIPS

More, larger loads of Thai marijuana were coming into beaches and bays from California to the Pacific Northwest. Typically, Oregonians don't need a reason to hate Californians, but the Californian who bought the New River Ranch in Bandon inflamed his already hostile neighbors by posting a popular fishing spot with "no trespassing" signs. When a local official visited the ranch to try to convince the new owner to allow residents to fish his stream, he grew suspicious of the city slicker with soft hands, clean fingernails, and ironed creases in his blue jeans.[1] Over the next few weeks, there were more anomalies at the New River Ranch: guard dogs, untended land, even tire tracks that vanished into the sea. The DEA and local police put the ranch under surveillance. On New Year's Eve 1977, signal lights began to flash from shore and a trawler offshore responded.

A six-wheeled, amphibious navy troop carrier (DUKW) made its way through the shore break and out to a mother ship called the *Cigale*. Filled with aluminum containers, the DUKW made it back to shore, and when it drove up the beach, the offload team cheered. The celebration was cut short by a Coast Guard helicopter that took off from behind a dense tree stand, swooped down, and lit up the offload site. There was a brief flurry of gunfire, and many of the smugglers fled in all directions. Police found one man a few hundred meters down the beach, covered in seaweed, who told them he was "bird watching." The crew tried to scuttle the mother ship, but the Coast Guard was able to salvage six tons of prime Thai in 581 aluminum containers. "The kind of stuff headed for ski resorts and football stadiums. It was for the middle and upper class—not some little street hippies," said one police officer. Although the hypothermic owner of the ranch was captured the morning after the raid, "The next day an off-duty deputy gave a ride to a grubby hitchhiker near the farm who later was tentatively identified as Brian Peter Daniels," wrote longtime federal agent Charles Fuss Jr.[2] Ritter's old associate Tim Nicholson* and Daniels had also been importing pot into the United States inside the cylinders of helicopter engines that they shipped to San Francisco, where Brian's brother John picked them up. Daniels also began shipping larger loads in plywood boxes. "Brian was good at packing things. He was probably the best at controlling packaging and weights and things like that, really good at it. But he pissed everybody off; nobody liked him, including the Thais," said Nicholson.[3]

As the size of the loads continued to grow, simpler methods of smuggling, like false-bottomed suitcases and small sailboats, were no longer sufficient. Because Thai and American police were getting wiser, smugglers diverged into two schools of thought. Some, like Abdul, moved into commercial shipping, while others, like John Parten, stayed true to their hippie roots and did smaller, high-quality bro deals. Parten did not smuggle contraband in shipping containers, cargo ships, or airplanes because the only way to do those scams was to pay bribes and associate with criminals who could ensure safe passage into harbors and private docks. Instead he personally handpicked and packaged smaller loads of the finest pot that were transported on friends' boats and offloaded in remote locations by experienced watermen who relied on skill and wits rather than bribes. "When I started doing this, I saw that my niche was going to be the yacht thing. It was a lot more soulful, for one thing, because you weren't dealing with anybody who owned a gun, basically. That, to me, was the way I wanted to go. I didn't want to get involved with the criminal element," he said.

The majority of John Parten's associates refused to work with gangsters; the vast majority were surfers who still expected total honesty. His partner was one of his best friends, and nobody was ever shortchanged: "It was just, 'Oh yes, I forgot to tell you that I got an extra hundred thousand there, so here's yours.' Things can get confusing when you've got a lot of money going around, but everybody was just totally honest and we didn't have any jealousies that could cause a lot of friction like that, where people take things." By the late 1970s, Parten had a well-established reputation for smuggling only the best pot and being meticulous about his packaging. His loads were highly anticipated and usually presold—a closed cell among the brothers. At the time, Ritter considered him a bit aloof and arrogant, but he respected him as a skilled scammer.

Parten's cool under fire was tested when one of his boats arrived in Thailand with the cash for the final payment, so that he didn't have to carry money through Thai customs. Parten met the sailboat a few days later, and as he was leaving the dock with $60,000 in a bag, "A little mini-platoon of police guys jumped out and stopped us. They're surrounding us, they've got machine guns, and we had this bag of money, sixty thousand dollars in hundred-dollar bills." Dom and his Thai associates jumped into the fray and began negotiating furiously. The smuggler cringed when the police captain opened the bag and saw the cash inside. "We're going, 'Oh shit. Now what are we going to do? We got to get sixty thousand dollars more.' We figure this is it, he'll let us go, but he's going to keep the money." Much to their amazement, the policeman took one bundle of hundred-dollar bills—five thousand dollars—and handed the Americans back the rest. "Everybody shook hands, and that was that."[4]

Like John Parten, Mike Ferguson and Craig Williams continued their small, unaccompanied baggage scams until they "lost one of their nine lives" at Hong Kong's Kai Tak Airport. The pair left Bangkok with two large Halliburton suitcases filled with Thai sticks. When they got to Hong Kong, the transit baggage storage counter, where they usually checked their bags, was closed. Before they could even consider their options, they were standing at the head of the customs line with pot-filled suitcases. When Ferguson saw the Buddhist monk in front of them in line get his bags torn apart over a tin of tea, he began to think that the game might be over. As he lifted his suitcase up to the inspection counter, there was a yell from across the room. It was time for a shift change, and the head customs lady waved the Americans through without opening their bags. After this close call, Ferguson and Williams decided that if they were going to continue taking such risks, they would make some real money.

Mike Ferguson contacted his travel agent and fixer in Hong Kong and told her that he needed some introductions. He knew that this would be no problem for the cagey young Chinese-Thai woman who was the favorite girl Friday for gangsters, mercenaries, and Air America pilots. She introduced him to Andrew "Tiger" Li, a Chinese underworld leader with connections in the Thai national police and the military. Li had worked for the American military during World War II and served as an instructor at the Kuomintang military university in China, where he trained many of the Chinese generals who now ran the Golden Triangle. When Ferguson met the nondescript, middle-aged Chinese general, he handed the American a 20-pack of prime Thai sticks to sample and told him that the price was $10,000 a ton. Next, Tiger introduced him to his new Thai handler, a retired boxer/street thug named Somsak, and put his arms around both men and said, "You are my sons, you are my Thai son, you are my American son, now we work together." From that day forward, Somsak or his men followed Ferguson and Williams at all times and made sure they were protected. Mike Ferguson quickly realized that if he was to work with the gangsters, things would be done their way. "He's got things in the fire you don't even want to know about, he's gonna get there, but you can't tell him how to do it. Not only did the Thais have their own way of doing things, they also had their own order of doing things."

After a few successful loads, Ferguson and Williams approached Tiger with an ambitious proposition. "We wanted to grow it ourselves when it started getting more expensive. We found that we could grow it better, have better quality control." The general contacted one of the region's high-ranking political officials, who agreed to set up a logging operation as cover for their pot farm. They used the timber company's heavy equipment to cut a road from southern Thailand, near Prachuap Khiri Khan, into Burma and had a faction of the Mon ethnic tribe guarding the operation. Tiger's men cleared some of the forest and built a village and sawmill; farmers from Nakhon Phanom planted seeds. Ferguson handled the growing operation while Williams prepared their boat for the voyage back to the United States. Both were present at the plantation when they harvested their acres of lime-green buds and handled quality control. All of the pot was put in vacuum bags, given a shot of nitrogen, heat sealed, and graded: 1X, 2X, 3X, and the best of the best, MKK, short for "*Mi kong kai*," meaning feather duster in Thai. A total of 12,000

The Americans' pot plantation in Thailand. Photo: Michael S. Ferguson

The load leaves for the coast: Mike Ferguson. Photo: Michael S. Ferguson

kilos were loaded into an armed convoy of 10-wheeled military transport trucks that drove from Burma to the Thai coast, where they waited for the mother ship to arrive.

The Americans' 50-meter ocean supply boat left Florida for the Panama Canal, but got too close to a disputed island off Nicaragua and was intercepted by a Nicaraguan gunboat. Because they had so much electronic gear on board and were sending computerized flash messages by satellite, the Nicaraguans were convinced it was a spy boat. "They fucking tortured and knocked all the teeth out of the captain. They fucked everybody up really good and confiscated the boat," recalled Williams. When they informed Tiger Li about the delay, he said that he needed more cash immediately. The Americans were trying to keep him on a short financial leash and were unsure when his demands for cash were legitimate. "We figured Tiger was crying wolf again," said Ferguson, "but didn't realize how serious the situation was." By the time the Americans got a second boat traveling, the Thai had sold their magnificent pot to a group of Australians, and they never saw a dime for all their labor. [5]

Tiger Li had put part of a load together for another American, Lynn Mizer, who was the advance man for Donald Steinberg, one of the largest marijuana smugglers in the United States. Steinberg's "company" brought Colombian loads as big as 36,000 kilos into southern Florida and did not sell it by the ton—they sold addresses to pot-filled houses. However, by the late 1970s, because the DEA had cut the supply of Colombian pot in the United States more, big-time smugglers like Steinberg were looking for big suppliers in Thailand. However, they did not understand the Thai trade. "We called him 'Megabucks,' some Florida guy," said Ferguson, who described Lynn Mizer as a scrawny, disheveled American "on a mega trip, he had to be the biggest." In Bangkok, Mizer bought as much pot from as many people as he could. "They were stupid, they had more money than sense. They were throwing money at a whole bunch of different people at the same time and getting all kinds of stuff and all kinds of heat."[6]

After the load was secure, Mizer sent his captain to Singapore to buy a mother ship; he settled on *Euphoric*, a 32-meter oceangoing tugboat. Once the outfitting was complete, the ship steamed deep into the Gulf of Thailand near the Burmese border and loaded 10 tons. The pot was not vacuum bagged or even in heat-sealed bags; it was haphazardly thrown into burlap sacks. This would have sufficed for a short voyage from

Colombia and Florida, but the trip from Thailand to the United States could take months.[7] The *Euphoric* headed to the Philippines, took on fuel, and continued west. Two hundred kilometers northwest of Palau, the tugboat lost all electrical power and was adrift for two weeks before someone rescued them and towed them back to the Philippine port of Cebu for extensive repairs. By the time the mother ship met the fishing boat that would take the load the rest of the way to California, *Euphoric* had been at sea for 110 days. Although the pot was successfully offloaded, when Mizer arrived at the safe house in Marin County, he found that most of it was both dry and moldy; what was not completely worthless was no better than commercial Mexican. "They had big bales rotting in the hold, they did not package their product correctly. Unlike sailing a Colombian load into South Florida, the transpacific crossing was a major undertaking," said Mike Ferguson.[8]

Because Mizer's load was such a financial disappointment and Craig Williams had been delayed, Tiger Li did not get paid in full. He was in a financial pinch, and when an Air America pilot contacted him about a heroin deal, he agreed to do it. The pilot was a police informant and set Tiger up, but luckily for the general, most of the "heroin" was laundry soap. Ferguson and Williams visited him in Lao Yard Prison, where the guards did "everything but click their heels and salute." Not only did the general have his own small hut, he received groceries each week.[9]

Another big Florida scammer who showed up in Thailand looking for giant loads was Ross "The Fatman" Hobson. When Mike Boyum was in Singapore, he met Hobson's advance man, who was looking for an ocean-going tug to tow a pot-filled barge across the Pacific. Hobson, a 300-plus-pound New Jersey native, was anything but a surfer scammer; the Fatman was a true criminal, a sign of the times in the rapidly changing Thai marijuana industry. By the time he got to Thailand, Hobson had already smuggled hundreds of thousands of kilos into southern Florida, and when he was finally busted in 1981 during "Operation Sunburn," prosecutors called his organization "the largest organized pot ring ever uncovered by federal authorities." The Fatman bought a 42-meter seagoing tug called the *Doctor* that was capable of going anywhere on earth. When Mike Boyum saw it in Singapore, he thought it was the most impressive vessel he had ever seen. Hobson was willing to pay $100,000 per ton and ordered 10 tons from Abdul.[10]

With luxurious houses in Bali, Bangkok, and Tahiti, Abdul entertained lavishly. When pro surfers Jeff Hakman and Bruce Raymond attended a party at his giant house in Papeete, Tahiti, they entered a walled court-yard filled with the most exotic beauties the pair had ever seen. The mix of French and Tahitian sometimes resulted in high-cheekboned blondes with cocoa skin and blue eyes. When Abdul's gay friend Marcel noticed that the Australian surfer was smitten by a particularly beautiful woman named Terri, he put his arm around her waist and said: "'Terri has a beau-tiful pussy, exquisite.' And he gently pushed her skirt up, her panties down and planted his hand between her legs, opening her labia for inspection. Terri beamed with pride." Even the pro surfers, who were anything but innocent, sensed that they had entered a new world of Dionysian excess.[11]

For people like Abdul, who had lived outside the States for over a decade, it was difficult to realize how much things had changed—above all, the laws regarding smuggling. Many scammers acted as if it was still 1969 and erroneously assumed that police needed to catch you on the beach with the load. "I wasn't really aware of the conspiracy thing—being able to be caught like that," he said. "Actually we started getting lazy." Because he had made so much money so quickly, he began contracting others to do the dangerous work and just put up the capital. Lek and Jo would get the load from the farmers in Isan, then pack and ship it.

Everything was running smoothly until the day Abdul and his part-ner boarded a flight to Singapore. One stewardess offered the first-class passengers complimentary flutes of champagne, while another fanned out a selection of world's newspapers. When his partner took a copy of the *Straits Times,* his jaw dropped and the blood drained from his face. "What's wrong?" Abdul asked. His partner pointed to a front-page pic-ture of their pot-filled shipping container surrounded by dogs. The head-line read, FOUR NATION HUNT ON FOR DRUG MASTERMINDS. "It's up, man, and we're going to Singapore now. Fuck!" his partner said and began to panic. "Look here, read the article. It says they're looking for the masterminds!" said Abdul. "They don't even know who it is. It says some-body sent that thing out. We had nothing to do with it, you know. Those guys never met us—the guys that ratted that load out." When the smug-glers landed in Singapore's Changi Airport, they were waved through customs without opening a bag. Their first container made it to Mexico, but the DEA received special permission from the Mexican government to enter the country and intercept it. Abdul was out eight tons of pot, the container era was over, and he would now need to consider other options.

Although Abdul had distanced himself from the operational details of the pot trade, it was hard to miss the loud, handsome, long-haired surfer traveling around the world first class, tipping lavishly, always with a beautiful Thai or Tahitian girl on his arm. When he rented a house on the first tee of the Mafia-owned Rancho La Costa Country Club in Carlsbad, California, he quickly became known around the resort, and it wasn't for his tennis or golf game. Abdul loved to gamble, and it did not take long for him to meet former tennis great and aging hustler Bobby Riggs, who also lived at the resort. Best known for losing a tennis match to Billie Jean King in 1973, the former tennis legend had bet on himself to win the singles, doubles, and mixed doubles at the 1939 Wimbledon championships. After he defeated Elwood Cooke in singles, Charles Hare and Frank Wilde in men's doubles, and Frank Wilde and Nancy Brown in mixed doubles, his $500 bet matured into a $100,000 payday.[12]

"He was like a little hustler up there," said Abdul. "I had told Bobby that if he could drum up some business, I'd give him a percentage of whatever I won." One night, Riggs called and said that he was downstairs with his friend "Jim," who wanted to play high-stakes backgammon. When the smuggler got down to the lobby, Riggs was standing next to a dark-haired man with a neatly trimmed beard and moustache in a maroon velour jogging suit. "This is my friend Jim, he's a jet setter, he flies all over the world. He's got lots of money, and he'll play you if you want," said Riggs. Abdul was leaving for the airport in a few hours and got right down to business; he pulled $5,000 cash from his pocket and said, "I don't know you, so if you really want to play, it's got to be cash, no checks, none of that. See, I've got money here, I can play. I've got more if I lose." Jim told Abdul that he didn't want to play right now, but maybe some other time, and left. Little did Abdul know that Bobby Riggs had just introduced him to DEA agent Rich Gorman.[13]

Gorman was part of a central tactical unit (CENTAC) created in the mid-1970s to move up the criminal chain of command and catch kingpins rather than couriers. It took law enforcement many years to realize that marijuana smugglers, unlike the heroin lords and the cocaine cowboys, were nonviolent and usually trafficked only in marijuana. Scammers represented a departure from the stereotypical smuggler in terms of motivation, lifestyle, and drugs of preference. Initially, among those who most misunderstood the Thai marijuana trade were American law enforcement agents, who refused to believe that no one person controlled it. "It wasn't like in South America, where you could meet somebody and get a bunch of weight. There just wasn't that much there," said Abdul. Although there were some increasingly powerful individuals getting involved (like Thai businessman and politician Thanon Siriprechpong), police incorrectly assumed that if they just kept going up the ladder, they would eventually find one Mr. Big.[14] Although law enforcement agents like Gorman and Jim Conklin were getting closer to some of the major Thai players, smugglers like Mike Ritter and Abdul did not perceive them as any more of a threat than the weather or pirates, one of many floating variables that were out of their control.

One day Abdul was at the quay in Papeete where he met another young, idle, rich Southern Californian who became fast friends with Abdul and his neighbor, Brotherhood member David Hall. The trio fished, surfed, and played golf together. Although he claimed to be a real estate developer, when Abdul mentioned that that he lived in Thailand part of the year, the Californian told him that he was a pot smuggler and that his group, the Coronado Company, had just brought their first load of Thai into Northern California. Although the 2.5 tons earned them $8 million, they were unhappy with their Thai connection and asked Abdul if he could help them get pot in Thailand.[15]

Compared to the leaders of this smuggling operation, Abdul possessed the humility of a Buddhist monk. Home to the Navy SEALs, Coronado Island is a thin strip of land located outside San Diego Bay, just 20 kilometers north of the Mexican border. It was also home to one of the most successful marijuana smuggling rings of the 1970s, the Coronado Company, also known as "Corco." Ed Bridgely*, lifeguard and the captain of the CIF champion 1968 Coronado High School swim team, was drawn into Corco by an old surfing buddy who asked him if he was interested in making $1,000 in one night. "'Who do I have to kill?' He says, 'No, no, no, no.' He says, 'I've just been watching you swim out there, and I would just like to have you swim from the Tijuana bull ring to Imperial Beach.'" Another tall, blond surfer with a sturdy build from long-distance swimming, Bridgely had no problem doing a 10-kilometer swim towing a duffle bag in 3 hours. When his buddy handed him a jar containing $1,000, the young surfer was amazed. "I remember my first thousand dollars I made. It was just one thousand dollars, fifty twenty-dollar bills rolled up in a little jar. I thought I was in hog heaven. I thought I was shitting in tall cotton. You know, this was as much money as I made all year working as a lifeguard, and I made that in one night, and I was in awe of the amount of money, the rapid pace that that money was made, and the power that that money wielded." The lifeguard compared himself to a gambler who hit it big at a young age and couldn't stop chasing the big payoff.[16]

Bridgely's swims across the border became a regular milk run. However, one night there was a huge swell running and his bag of pot was ripped from him by a big wave. The smuggler made it to shore and when he walked up to the bag in the shallows, he saw the silhouette of a U.S. Border Patrol jeep and the glow of a cigarette cherry. The border patrol agents did not see him as he crawled on his stomach to the bag and crawled back to sea. Just as he got through the surf and resumed his swim, a fin popped up next to him. "So here I am, I got the border patrol in the beach, and I've got a dorsal fin circling me. I'm going, 'Oh, shit. Do I get eaten by a shark here, or do I go in and get busted?'" Even though it turned out to be a dolphin, when Bridgely finally got to shore and handed off the pot, he decided that was his final swim.

Shortly thereafter, Bridgely and his friends formed the Coronado Company and divided the labor into their respective fields of expertise. One person procured the load, another smuggled and offloaded, and a third handled sales. They established a militarylike hierarchy complete with lieutenants, second lieutenants, specialists, and offloaders. Lieutenants got a percentage of the profit, and specialists made more than the beach labor. "I could not do the whole thing myself. No one could do it without my expertise; I couldn't do it without other people's expertise—it was a team unit." They began to move 300- to 600-kilo loads using the Navy SEAL's favorite boat, the Zodiac Mark V, and their motto remained "amphibious assault." Corco used probabilities: they never worked during the summertime, because the coast was too crowded; they never went near a bay or harbor and only brought their loads through the surf. They would secure a beach, bring in their Zodiacs, unload quickly, and get the boats back out to sea. "Well, it was working great for the SEALs and special forces, so I knew it would work good for us," said Bridgely. By the mid-1970s, their fleet expanded to include an 8-meter Sea Ray and a 14-meter

Chris Craft, and they were now moving tons of commercial Mexican. The biggest problem for the Corco partners was communicating with their Mexican supplier. They needed a translator, so they contacted their old high school swimming coach and Spanish teacher.[17]

Lou Villar was a handsome, streetwise Cuban from New York who made quite an impression the first time he pulled his red Corvette into the parking lot of Coronado High School. It did not take Villar long to lose his teaching license for having sex with a student. The Corco partners offered him $50 to go down to Tijuana to talk with their Mexican supplier about the pricing structure. Thanks to Villar's perfect Spanish and diplomatic skills, in short order, the young Californians were dealing directly with the well-known Peltron crime family. Soon they were sending fishing boats down to mainland Mexico to pick up multiton loads on beaches guarded by *federales*. Very quickly, Lou Villar, "the man with the golden tongue," became a key player in the Coronado Company. The downside to the Cuban playing such a central role in all negotiations was that he was the only person who could truly communicate in Spanish. Although he told his American partners they were paying $50 a kilo, they were only paying $40 and Villar was skimming the difference. "He was a real shark and a snake. I don't think he knew any better," said Bridgely. "I think maybe it was his Cuban upbringing. He had to be rough and tough, and that's just the way he was. They don't know any better. They have to take more than their fair share, and that caused a lot of problems."[18]

Bridgely was now offloading boats near his northern Malibu beach house. The 5-hectare property on the beach side of Highway 101, just south of Leo Cabrillo Beach, had only one private access road that ran from the beach to the highway. Corco put up a chain-link fence and had guard dogs patrolling it. The mother ship would loiter just outside the kelp beds and Bridgely would ferry the pot to shore, one ton at a time. When Corco offloaded their largest load to date in Malibu in 1977, the 20 tons of Mexican was delivered by none other than Mike "Charley Tuna" Carter, the skipper of the *Ancient Mariner*.[19]

Corco got their start in Thai pot after one of their classmates from Coronado High School contacted Bridgely to tell him that Thai sticks sold for $3,000-$4,000 per kilo and that a Thai foreign exchange student he was attending college with could put together a load. Bridgely quickly did the math in his head and was floored: a ton that cost $50,000 in

Thailand resold for $3,000,000 in the United States. They bought a 18-meter sailboat called *Painui* in 1976, sailed to Thailand, and loaded 2.5 tons of prime Thai sticks.[20] The *Painui* sailed the Great Circle Route to Northern California, where their offload team was waiting in a small, desolate cove north of Fort Bragg. When they received word that the boat was a day out, his team secured the beaches and placed lookouts with radios at chokepoints on the roads.

The smugglers had purchased an amphibious DUKW and added a pop-riveted deck, more prominent bow and hatch covers. They marked the channel back to the beach by placing chemical lights inside of Ajax bleach bottles that were anchored just underwater. When they saw *Painui*'s signal lights, the DUKW plowed through the shore break and into deep water. They loaded the entire 2.5 tons and followed the channel markers to shore. "I could just head in to the beach and spot the glowing green light in a bottle. It would just be bobbing there on the surface, a little green light. Coming in and out, you could see our path that we had made. It was our landing lights, so to speak, the lineups," said one Corco offloader. When the DUKW drove up the beach, the lookouts announced that the coast was clear, and Bridgely pulled the pot-filled landing craft onto the highway and drove to their safe house 8 kilometers away.[21]

One of Corco's principals was arrested in 1978 and turned state's evidence. Although 27 of the organization's members were indicted by a grand jury and most surrendered, Ed Bridgely and Lou Villar remained fugitives, living fantasy lives under false identities. Bridgely outbid Goldie Hawn for a 100-year old redwood house in Ross, California, and paid the $550,000 in $9,500 cashier's checks. He also bought $250,000 worth of prerelease French wine, started playing polo, and reinvented himself as Edward James Morgan, the polo-playing great-grandson of J. P. Morgan. He admits that he was "kind of a snotty, arrogant person." To those who asked what he did for a living, he replied haughtily, "I mind my own business. What do you do?" To Bridgely, life as a fugitive was simple: fill in the blanks and people's curiosity is gone. "I learned that at a young age. If you can fill in the blanks—if it's bullshit, it's bullshit; but do not ever leave a blank empty." Although Bridgely and Villar were fugitives, their lawyer, Phil DeMassa, was trying to negotiate a plea bargain with the feds. The DEA wanted Bridgely to go to Colombia to buy cocaine and find the processing labs. The Corco leaders rejected this risky offer and continued to run their criminal enterprise.[22]

While Bridgely was content to sit back and enjoy his newfound wealth, Lou Villar wanted to diversify. Villar's brother-in-law had recently been to Morocco on a surfing trip and claimed that he knew somebody there who could put together a large load of hash. Corco bought and outfitted a 25-meter albacore boat for the scam and sent it across the Atlantic to the Canary Islands. Bridgely flew to Morocco expecting to confirm the weight and quality of the load, but instead found his advance man drunk in a seedy hotel room; not only did he have no hash, he had lost all of Corco's money. The Americans traveled to the Ketama Valley, deep in the Rif Mountains, to try to make a deal with the heads of the Berber village that grew the pot.

Called "the land of insolence" by the sultans and Spaniards who failed to occupy the region, the Rif Valley was and is one of the largest marijuana-growing areas in the world. The Berber elders who controlled the trade agreed to supply Corco with the load of hash they were presently making. Meanwhile, the smugglers lived without electricity and running water in a room above the village courtyard and subsisted on mostly greasy mutton and rabbit.[23] Six weeks later, when the load was ready, the Berber elders said that one of the Americans had to remain in the village as collateral until they were paid, so Villar's brother-in-law stayed behind.

Bridgely successfully loaded the albacore boat, and it crossed the Atlantic without incident and brought the hash into Machias, Maine, where Corco had recently purchased a hunting lodge above a remote bay. In the lodge's basement, their engineer anchored the same kind of giant winch and cable system (a yarder) used by loggers to haul timber. They drilled two holes through the wall and ran cables out to a pulley that allowed them to lower four-wheel-drive pickup trucks down the cliff to the ocean. Because the biggest exposure while offloading was the radar signature of the loitering mother ship, Corco built a 5 x 13-meter Kevlar barge so they could offload without stopping. Once the barge was filled, the smugglers would tow it to shore at the highest tide possible so that when the tide went out, the barge sat high and dry on the rocks. After the trucks were lowered down the cliff; they drove up to the barge and were loaded, then winched back up. The entire operation was done at night, and it was "very, very precise. You've got a lot of energy going now, yeah, adrenaline, energy—you've got the whip and it's gotta be crackin'. Twenty people," recalled Bridgely.

After all the money, time, and trouble, the Moroccan hash was second rate and difficult to sell. The Berbers were expecting their money within a month, and it had been six weeks when Bridgely received a collect call from Villar's brother-in-law in Morocco.. "Are you ever coming back?" he asked nervously. He was no longer allowed to leave his mud hut, and the village leaders were threatening to stone him to death if they were not paid soon. Six weeks later, when Bridgely finally returned to the Rif Mountains with the money, he found his friend in the corner of a mud hut, wrapped in a blanket. "He was shaking and didn't even hardly know who I was," said Bridgely. "He is tweaked, his mind is gone, he's gone, and they were going to kill him. The women were going to stone him because the money goes to the village." The Corco leader picked him up and carried him away.[24]

One of the Corco leaders contacted Abdul and asked if he could supply their next Thai load. Although Abdul was noncommittal, Brotherhood member David Hall was there and said that he could provide as much as they wanted. "He was trying to snake in there and be their supplier. It was one of those things where David says he can do this, but he doesn't even know how," Abdul said. "He didn't have a connect; Lek was my connection." Abdul agreed to get them 10 tons, and Corco sent a 25-meter albacore boat called the *Finback* to Thailand. As they were going through the Luzon Strait, two American crew members got into a fistfight. When one of the combatants drew a gun, the other grabbed a big orange fishing buoy, tied his suitcase to it, and jumped overboard. Although he was 22 kilometers off the Philippine coast without a passport or money, the crewman managed to paddle to the beach and make his way to the American embassy, where he was debriefed by the DEA. Although Corco was hugely successful financially, they were leaving large footprints for law enforcement.[25]

When the *Finback* arrived in Thailand, Abdul had five trucks full of pot waiting. Lek had struck a deal with the village headmen, police, and power brokers in Krabi: for $25,000, he owned the town for a night. All of the townspeople were off the streets when the 10-wheeled trucks drove out of the dark and down to the docks. Police with automatic weapons slung over their shoulders were patrolling the streets on motorcycles by the time Bridgely and Abdul drove into town. When they began to load the boat, Abdul handed Lek a big wad of cash, told him to go to the nearby Thai Navy base, start a high-stakes card game, and lose it all. "Then the navy guys would just stay in there," explained Abdul. "They didn't want to go out on patrol because they were making all this money just playing cards." When Bridgely got on board the deckless Thai ore carrier that would ferry the pot to the mother ship, the crew was huddled around the small clay pot they were cooking over. "There's no compass; there's no satellite navigational aid; there's no radar; there's nothin'. My life is in these Thais' hands. Me and the Thais."

The pot was transported to the mother ship and it was successfully offloaded in Maine. Although Abdul was not there during the offloading, he went to New York City to collect his money at the Waldorf Astoria hotel. The Corco leader told him that he owed David Hall $250,000 and began to complain about Abdul getting 50 percent of the load. Disgusted by their "sniveling and crying," Abdul told him that he would pay their boat crew and give them another half ton, but added, "I never want to work with you guys again." For Abdul, it was a small price to pay to be rid of David Hall, who would follow the Corco leaders to Santa Barbara. "He was older and he would egg you on. He would want to share in the profits but he wouldn't want to share in the risk. Sometimes he would take stuff to be shipped in Thailand, but he would never do the pickup end. David would always be there for his share, but his involvement was never equal."[26]

Abdul was considering other options when Mike Boyum, his neighbor and sometimes nemesis in Bali, approached him with a proposition to buy a mother ship capable of hauling massive loads to the United States. Despite their long-standing animosity, Boyum knew that above all, Abdul was a businessman and the project would appeal to him. "He came up there and did a hard sell on this boat that was so good that he could fix it up and we could send our own boats back," said Abdul. "We didn't need to contract with anybody." Abdul agreed to buy and refit a decommissioned 30-meter Japanese fishing trawler called the *Shanghai Trader* and hired a Singaporean fixer to oversee the repair of the engines, pumps, and generators and even reweld the hull and superstructure. Although the ship was berthed near the oil company warehouses in the industrial section of town, Mike Boyum rented an apartment downtown and lived lavishly on Abdul's money; he wore tailor-made suits, Italian leather shoes, and a Swiss watch. When he gorged himself on bluefin tuna belly at the Mandarin Hotel, home to the best sushi restaurant in Singapore, he tipped the Japanese chef at least $100 per visit. Abdul contracted Tim Nicholson to supply and deliver a load to the *Shanghai Trader*. Given Abdul's financial backing and Nicholson's ability to get things done in Thailand, it seemed like a pretty simple scam. However, the minute Mike Boyum got involved, he began to scheme with a sociopath's predictability.[27]

10

THE DEA
GAINS GROUND

When Mike Ritter learned about the Abdul–Boyum partnership he was "stung with envy" because he believed that he knew the Thai business better than most. "So how was it that I was broke and out of a job, and Mike Boyum was in charge of a ship with a million-dollar budget?" To make it even worse, Lek was supplying the load through Ritter's connection, Tim Nicholson*. Ritter doubted that Boyum could manage the pickup and delivery of a load across the Pacific: "I found it hard to believe Abdul would grant him that much responsibility for a job that he knew nothing about, or even that Abdul would consider doing business with the person who had ripped him off in Bali."

Mike Ritter hadn't spoken to Abdul since he had stolen his girlfriend, Dang, but he was still in touch with Mike Boyum. The next time Ritter passed through Singapore, he visited the shipyard where they were outfitting Abdul's boat, the *Shanghai Trader*. The decommissioned Japanese fishing vessel had a narrow beam and high bow; it was built for heavy seas and extended voyages and looked similar to a North Sea trawler. The wheelhouse and superstructure sat on the stern and there was a giant, refrigerated fish hold at midships, a beautiful thing to a marijuana smuggler. "Many otherwise successful smuggles ended in disaster due to moldy weed," wrote Ritter. If the pot was not fully cured or if any moisture got into a bag, the product could spoil in the long hot months from packaging to delivery. If you could refrigerate your marijuana, like any other agricultural product, it would arrive fresh.

Mike Boyum told Ritter that his cover was that he was running a charter boat business that took wealthy surfers to remote destinations around the world. Ritter was impressed until Boyum showed him some of the luxury features he had added to the *Trader*. Not only was there a sauna to loosen up tight muscles from long surf sessions, there was a sushi bar built out of wood imported from Japan. Although his stateroom was full of radios and state-of-the-art navigation gear, when Ritter asked about the engines, he knew nothing and replied dismissively, "Oh, that's up to someone else." "Typical Mike—he's focusing on how to make himself comfortable and losing sight of the mission," said Ritter. "I thought, and felt the foreboding of another Boyum disaster." Mike Boyum and Abdul's relationship reminded Ritter of the fable of the scorpion and the frog: "Even as the frog is providing the scorpion a ride on his back across the river, the scorpion cannot prevent himself from stinging the frog, bringing disaster to both of them."[1]

Just before the *Trader*'s rebuild was complete, some of the crew traveled to Bangkok, where Abdul took them out for a night on the town. At dinner, one of them asked, "It sounds so easy, we're just going into Mexico, but the part that I don't understand is why we got to go into Hawaii before we go to Mexico?" A stop in Hawaii had never been part of Abdul's plan. "What do you mean, go into Hawaii?" he asked, stunned. "Oh yeah, the plans are to go in and drop off a couple of tons in Hawaii and then go on to Mexico," replied the crew member. Intentionally or not, Boyum's plan to steal part of the load had been revealed. "Hey, how would you like to make all the money that Boyum was going to make on the trip?" asked Abdul. All the crewman had to do was push him off the boat in the middle of the ocean and the money would be his.[2]

When, the *Shanghai Trader* finally left port and began to steam for Thailand to pick up the pot, the trip was cut short by a horrible vibration in the propeller shaft. They limped into the sanctuary of Manila harbor and the smugglers checked into the Manila Hotel, General MacArthur's headquarters at the end of World War II. When Boyum opened his curtains the next morning, he saw a Philippine customs boat tied up to the *Trader*. Even worse, there was a white guy on board who looked like a DEA agent, and he was very curious about the fishing boat with no fishing gear on board. Not only had Boyum failed to get the boat in working order, she was now on the DEA's radar and useless as a mother ship.

Back in Thailand, nobody had bothered to tell Tim Nicholson that the *Trader* had returned to port; he and Lek had brought the load down to the coast, and when they sent the first boat full of pot out, it ran aground on a sandbar and a police boat captured the crew, including an American friend of Nicholson. After a Thai-style interrogation of the crew, the police learned the location of the rest of the pot and confiscated it all.

The *Shanghai Trader* debacle created bad feelings all around: Nicholson had lost an entire load, his friend was in jail, and Abdul felt ripped off. There was only one thing everyone could agree on—they had all been played by Mike Boyum. By now, even his brother Bill had given up on "living the dream," to him the world of scamming was a world of lies that was growing "sleazier all the time." While most Thai pot smugglers refused to traffic in cocaine, they were not above using the drug. Nothing did more to get scammers to break from their hippie roots than the widespread use of "weasel dust." "Our program was pretty clean at first. But we sabotaged it. A little marijuana turned into lots of cocaine," wrote Bill Boyum.[3]

Abdul was not the only smuggler having a run of bad luck. When the Coronado Company's 40-meter oceangoing tug reached Maine with 10 tons of Afghan hash on board, they were met and boarded by U.S. Customs. The tug was covered with a layer of ice that made it difficult to search the boat, and although customs agents couldn't find the hash, they told the captain to follow them back to their dock. Because the cutter was in the lead, there was a blind spot between the two boats, and the smugglers jettisoned the entire load during the 20-kilometer voyage. Although law enforcement was only able to recover 350 kilos, washed up on shore or later retrieved from the sea, it was enough for the DEA to gain more ground on Corco.

The leaders of the Coronado Company sent the *John L. Weston*, a 40-meter supply vessel, to Thailand to do a makeup load. They successfully loaded 8 tons, and because they had offloaded in Northern California so many times and Maine was now hot, they decided to try something new.

They hired an air force reserve helicopter pilot who could check out helicopters for the day. With their huge lift capacity, the choppers could carry tons at a time. Corco engineers built giant, four-sided, hinged baskets out of chain-link fence to hold the bales of pot. The mother ship radioed when they were a day out; the helicopter was standing by and the trucks were waiting 45 kilometers inland at a loading zone in the woods when a bank of thick fog rolled in. The pilot could not take off, and after three days of waiting, Corco went to plan B: they hired local salmon poachers from a nearby Makah Indian reservation in Neah Bay, Washington. The poachers used the Waatch River mouth to run their boats out to the open ocean. However, they were used to hauling a few hundred kilos of fish through the surf, not tons of pot, and flipped their heavily laden boats when coming in through the breaking waves.

Corco's beach crew salvaged much of the pot and packed it into a rental truck that they drove off the beach just before sunrise. As it was making its way up a muddy road, the overloaded truck lost traction, slid off the road, and rolled onto its side. The driver was not an experienced scammer, so when the cargo door jammed, he panicked and ran for his life, leaving $20,000,000 of prime Thai behind. "They just peed down their leg, is what happened," said Ed Bridgely*. Although the majority of the load was lost, another vehicle managed to get out with a ton, which earned $5,000,000, enough to pay all the salaries and make a small profit. However, not only did the police find the pot-filled truck, they found the license plate from a car that one of the offloaders had rented under his real name.[4]

After Corco's disaster at Neah Bay, they needed yet another makeup load, so they sent a 25-meter bait boat called the *Robert Wayne* to Thailand and loaded 8 tons without a hitch. As they made their way up the South China Sea, a massive typhoon hit and the ship's bow began to go down the short-interval swells at such an extreme angle that the propeller began to cavitate, and the tons of thrust on the shaft's 8 centimeters of cold steel sheared the prop clean off. The *Robert Wayne* was now dead in the water with no propulsion, no windows, and 8 tons of pot in the fish hold. Finally, the captain managed to get a CB radio working and put out an SOS on the distress channel 16. The closest vessel, a U.S. Navy destroyer escort, arrived first on the scene. "By God, look at all these broken antennas. You guys look like a bunch of smugglers," were the first words out of the Navy captain's mouth. The smuggler laughed it off, said they were fishermen, and went aboard the military ship; their radio operator patched him through to Bridgely's mansion in Monterey, California.[5]

It was 8 o'clock at night in Monterey, California, and Ed Bridgely was watching a movie when the phone rang. "I'm talking to my captain that has this thirty million dollars' worth of pot on the boat. He's out in the middle of the ocean with a sheared-off propeller and the military sitting there, right alongside." Bridgely pulled out a nautical chart, saw that there was a nearby island, Chichi-jima, and told the captain to have the military tow them there. Although they were boarded by Japanese customs at the island, the load was well concealed in the main hold beneath a small mountain of fishing nets. When a Japanese customs agent moved toward the door to the hold where the pot was, a fast-thinking crew member told him it was a fuel bunker and, scrambling up a ladder, said, "If you open that door, we're going to die, and I'm outta here!" Luckily his ruse worked and the customs agent followed him.[6]

Ed Bridgely got on the first flight possible to Japan and contacted an American prostitute he knew in Tokyo with Yakuza crime syndicate connections. The six-foot-tall California blonde was totally blind and so distinctive looking that she got $1,000 a night just to be seen in public with men. She introduced Bridgely to a Japanese gangster called Kawasaki, who was missing two fingers. "Now, these guys are pretty serious fellows. I mean, if you make a mistake in that organization, you have to cut off your finger, the tip of your finger, and you have to surrender it to the head honcho. If he accepts it, that means you're back in the club; if he does not accept it, that means you cut your finger off for nothing, and you are pretty much shunned, outcast throughout the whole organization."

Kawasaki had a fishing boat tow the *Robert Wayne* to a friendly shipyard where they transferred all the pot onto a Japanese fishing boat and fixed the windows, radios, and propeller shaft. Three weeks later, the *Robert Wayne* left dry dock, rendezvoused with the Japanese fishing boat, transferred the load, and headed for Northern California. "We got our load back. I mean, we got every bag, everything back, one hundred percent," said Bridgely. The Japanese wanted one American to stay behind as collateral and $250,000 after the load landed in the United States. Kawasaki called every three days and asked the same questions: "Any problems? Have you heard from the boat?" "We just heard from the boat," Bridgely would reply. "The boat's going to be in, in the next forty-eight hours."[7]

Corco's offload team was assembled in a safe house near Bear Harbor. One of its members was Jim Lawton*. After eighteen months in a Vietnamese jail, Lawton had returned to Santa Barbara and resumed his work as a commercial fisherman. Some of his friends were offloading for the Coronado Company, and when he expressed interest, they invited him to a barbeque at Lou Villar's Montecito mansion. The Corco leaders used to hold these informal cookouts to audition perspective employees. Lawton watched Corco bosses drink expensive French wine, smoke Thai sticks, and snort cocaine. "Coke! They had coke all the time. They had college girls. Tassels on their penny loafers! It was kind of gross at times to the beach crew guys. They were living in big mansions on Park Place," said Lawton. "The whole thing with polo ponies—not one, not two, a stable full! A couple Cobras, matching ones, red ones on a trailer—just this type of extravagant stuff."

The fisherman was especially unimpressed by Lou Villar. To him, Villar was a caricature of a drug dealer. "They called him 'Poppers.' He was supposed to be like the Godfather—Poppers, the dad, the big daddy," recalled Lawton. "They'd all just go goo-goo over all their fame and fortune and stuff." What was missing to the surfer smuggler was "that hippie vibe that we'd had when we were working independently, just doing a handful of things and doing our own core loads, Ma and Pa operations." While it was clear that Ed Bridgely and Lou Villar were in charge of the operation, Lawton didn't want to know more than was necessary to do his job. "We didn't care what they called themselves. We didn't even know that they were really called the Coronado Company. To me they were just a bunch of high-line rich guys with big egos and treated people like shit, really, for the most part."

Lawton and his fishermen friends launched their inflatables from Bear Harbor, ran out to a big black trawler, and stacked pot bales on the Zodiacs. "I'd have to stand up on the edge of the boat and look over a giant pile to navigate it back into the shore. Then there were rocks in this cove where we had to navigate in—it was kind of a channel, the place where you wanted to go between the wash rocks." The smugglers followed their underwater light sticks channel back to the beach, where body-lifted four-wheel-drive trucks with camper shells were waiting. Once the boats landed, the beach crew set up supermarket roller ramps that went from the boats to the trucks' tailgates.

Even though there was a public access road into Bear Harbor, the trucks went up a steep firebreak trail to the ridge line. "They just had these four-wheel-drive trucks with little shell campers and big V-8 engines and big knobby tires, and they'd roar these loads up and get them out of town before dawn."[8] Corco posted one man dressed in a forest service uniform, complete with Smokey the Bear hat, name tag, flashlight, and law enforcement belt and key ring. His vehicle looked identical to a U.S. Forest Service truck and was posted on the main road. The "ranger" knocked down a tree with a chainsaw, so even if someone got past him, there was still the tree to get over. The few times he encountered campers, the fake ranger told them there was a rabid skunk on the beach or that the police were searching the area for a dangerous fugitive. After the 8 tons were successfully offloaded and sold, Bridgely flew back to Japan with a leather suitcase that held $250,000 cash under the false bottom. "They got a quarter large and they were laughing. Everything worked out. We had no problems. They just said, 'Next time you want to, come back.'"[9]

Although Corco seemed to have dodged another bullet, the DEA was getting closer thanks to broader interpretations of the Racketeer Influenced and Corrupt Organizations Act (RICO), the Continuing Criminal Enterprise Statute (CCE), and the Controlled Substances Act, new federal laws that gave law enforcement wider latitude. DEA Agent Jim Conklin teamed with a gun-toting IRS agent named Jim Nielson, and the pair began to push the boundaries of asset forfeiture. During the 1970s, the law made it very difficult to seize drug dealers' assets because the informant had to see the suspect sell the drugs, take the money, and spend the money, but now the IRS agent could apply a "net worth theory" to show that although the smugglers had a great deal of money, most of them hadn't filed a tax return in years.[10]

"There was a guy, a DEA agent, by the name of [James] Conklin, and Conklin wanted to catch us dirty," recalled Bridgely. "They didn't want to get us just for conspiracy, but they wanted to catch us with possession, on the beach." Someone Jim Conklin had arrested led him to the mansion of a "big Thai marijuana kingpin" in Montecito, California. Although the smuggler had moved out, they found a forwarding address, "a woman whose name was Bambi Merryweather, and when I ran that in the computer, it lit up." Merryweather was the ex-wife of *Endless Summer* star, smuggler, Brotherhood associate, and surfing icon Mike Hynson.[11] As

Conklin pointed out, money caused the biggest problems. Conklin also found a carpenter who had repaired Corco leader Lou Villar's house in Hilton Head, South Carolina. Villar had bragged to the young carpenters that he was a big pot smuggler and told them that their pay was invested in his next load. "When it comes in, instead of the eighty grand, you know, I wanted to style you guys out. I'll give you four hundred thousand dollars for having invested in my thing." Two months later, after the load got busted, Villar told them matter-of-factly: "You can't get your money back; that's the way it is. If you gamble that you're gonna make big profits, you've got to suffer the losses. If you lose, you lose. Nobody's gonna pay you back your money."[12] After getting stiffed, the carpenters went to the DEA

Jim Conklin flew the contractors out to California, and they led him to the Corco leaders' houses. He was amazed when he pulled up to a beautiful mansion owned by one of the leaders. "It wasn't the drug; it was the assets. The assets started to become a big, big issue," he said. "These guys would have ten houses, and they were all beautiful." For the first time, the DEA agent realized how much money was being made in Thai marijuana. "Having worked Mexican marijuana before, I realized how much more Thai marijuana was worth. I think in those days it was selling for about two thousand dollars a pound. We were used to Mexican grass, which was maybe a hundred bucks a pound. Probably a drug trafficker could make more money in Thai marijuana than any commodity in the world, more than gold, more than anything," said Conklin. "I remember it was three million dollars a ton and these guys are bringing over ten tons at a time, so you're talking thirty million dollars. It was staggering in the eighties."[13]

By the late 1970s, Thai authorities were also making big gains and wrapping up many of the first generation of hippie and surfer scammers. When scammer and Bali surf pioneer Ray Lee was arrested by Thai authorities 10 kilometers off the coast aboard the sailboat *Ingrid*, police found 800 kilos of marijuana, an M-16, and 3 illegal walkie-talkie radios. Later that night, when police took the handcuffed American to the customs pier at Klong Toey to retrieve his belongings, the surfer grabbed one bag, jumped into the Chao Phyra River, and swam for his life. Two police officers jumped in and swam after him; when they caught Lee, they found four large packages of heroin in his bag. Thanks to a new Thai law, possession of more than 500 grams was now punishable by death. The next day, Thai police arrested his cohort, original Pattaya surfer scammer Dick Petit, and found a small amount of heroin on him. Like the American soldiers during the Vietnam War, scammers like Lee, Petit, Buddy Boy, and many others fell victim to Thailand's cheap, plentiful, and pure heroin.[14]

Thai police busted another member of the hippie old guard in 1980 when they caught longtime American smuggler Robert "Todd" Temler* with three tons of perfectly packaged marijuana in Bangkok. One of the original hippie smugglers, Temler was mentioned in a 1973 FBI report on the Brotherhood of Eternal Love. When police raided the house of his accomplice, Thai army captain Somchai Siripong, he was loading boxes of pot into a Volkswagen van. After Somchai was interrogated at police headquarters, he led the authorities to a warehouse where they found another two tons. Temler's associates in Thai Customs and airport ground crews were also arrested for false air freight and declaration bills. The Thai government was embarrassed by the fact that the pot was being stored at the Thai Army's 11th infantry base in Nonthaburi Province. The American's claim that he was an English teacher who had lost his passport was rejected by a Thai court before they sentenced him to forty-five years in prison.[15]

After the *Shanghai Trader* disaster, both Abdul and Mike Boyum retreated to Bali to nurse their respective wounds. Although Boyum studiously avoided him, the day before Abdul left for the United States, he drove out to his house in Kuta and confronted him. "'Hey, you got the money? Do you have a chunk of money?'" he asked. "I got some money here," Boyum said as he wrote a check for $1,500. "'Man, fifteen hundred dollars,'" said Abdul. "'I told you six months ago, you got to have something substantial, man.' And then I said something to him like, 'Enjoy the rest of the waves you can ride, however many you can.'"

Boyum knew that Abdul was flying back to the United States the next day, so he called the DEA office in Jakarta and told them that a fugitive was flying from Java the next morning. When the smuggler got to the airport in Jakarta, he glanced down at the embarkation list and was stunned to see his real last name, which he had not used in decades, beneath his alias. "Who's that, another late passenger?" he asked the customs agent. "Is that you?" the agent replied icily. "No man, I'm Monroe, you got my passport." The Indonesian said nothing, but when Abdul sat down in the departure lounge, the same guy was peeking at him from behind a pillar.

Abdul flew a circuitous route from Indonesia to New Caledonia to South America and then Mexico, thinking it would throw any pursuers off his trail. When he landed in Tijuana, he saw border patrol cars and fed-looking Ford Crown Victorias lined the runway. He picked up his bag and walked to the curb, where his parents were waiting in his brand-new Mercedes sedan. Abdul got into the car and they drove to the U.S. border a few minutes away in San Ysidro. A female U.S. Customs agent asked his father the usual questions: "Where've you been in Mexico? Do you have anything to declare?" Although his father masterfully batted back the answers, the smuggler's heart sank when the agent said, "I'm just going to walk you over to secondary, I'll put my hand on top of the car and you follow along with me."

When they reached secondary inspection, the agent asked for his ID, and he replied unconvincingly that it had been stolen. The agent took his mother into a room alone. Ten minutes later she came out and whispered to Abdul, "They searched me. [Asking,] who were you? I told them you were my sister's son, that I hadn't seen you in ten years." Next they took his father into the interrogation room; he was out in minutes, loudly demanding a lawyer. When they searched his mom a second time, they found Abdul's passport. He was taken into another interrogation room; inside sat six or seven plainclothes agents. "Why don't you tell us about yourself?" asked an investigator from the Treasury Department sitting at a desk. "You're coming from Asia, what do you do over there?" "I've got a snack company, I make snack food—tortillas and stuff like that," the smuggler explained. The evasive conversation went on a few minutes until an agent looking over Abdul's shoulder shoved a copy of his original California driver license in his face and said, "Okay, James, that's enough bullshit, we know who you are. We know all about you." Abdul felt like he was "dying right there."

As they were putting Abdul in the car that would take him to jail, Richard Gorman, the CENTAC agent who had hunted down top drug traffickers like Cuban exile Alberto Sicilia-Falcon, turned to him and said, "Remember me? I met you a long time ago." Although Abdul denied meeting him, he racked his brain to recall the familiar face, and it came to him! Gorman was the "jet-setting gambler" tennis legend Bobby Riggs had introduced him to at the Rancho La Costa Country Club. Thanks to Mike Boyum's tip to the DEA, eight regional offices were coordinating the surveillance, from Bali to New Caledonia to Mexico. Although he was only charged with making false statements when applying for a U.S. passport, the DEA was working overtime to reindict him for smuggling while they had him in custody.[16]

Thanks in part to the information provided by Lou Villar's unpaid carpenter, the DEA had the Corco leaders' houses under surveillance and their phones bugged. Agents were waiting when Ed Bridgely and two other Corco principals pulled up to a horse ranch in Montecito. Just as Bridgely was about to turn his Mercedes into the driveway, he saw a guy sitting in a Chevy Vega drop his newspaper and pick up a radio. The smuggler floored the powerful sedan, but as he came around the corner, a pickup truck blocked the road. Before he could turn around, an under-cover policeman pulled alongside and he was staring down the barrel of a pistol. Three more agents arrived on the scene and handcuffed the Corco leaders. "Your name is Ed Bridgely," said one of the cops. "No, no, you have the wrong guy," he replied, as he handed him a California driver license in the name of James Norris. The officer called the license in and someone on the other end of the radio spat: "I don't care what that guy's name is, who he says he is, you bring him down here NOW!" Inside the briefcase, they found two more California driver licenses with the same photo and a binder filled with notes about Corco's smuggling activities.[17]

Bridgely's bail was set at $5,000,000, and multiple indictments were issued after the initial arrests. Cooperating witnesses named everybody from the truck drivers to the offloaders, even the guy in the fake forest service outfit. Offloader Jim Lawton was one of the men caught in Agent Conklin's dragnet. "They were like slap-on-the-back yes-men, and every-thing's groovy and we're so cool, tennis courts and bottles of wine and sweaters wrapped around their necks," said offloader Jim Lawton. "They did not even bother to pay lip service to the old ideals of trust or loyalty; these guys didn't have that."

In an attempt to distance himself from the Coronado Company, Law-ton and his friends dubbed themselves "the Santa Barbara Five." When the fisherman saw Agent Conklin at Joe's Restaurant on State Street in Santa Barbara, he smiled at him. "It was just like friendly cops and rob-bers. He knew he wasn't chasing somebody who was going to shoot him, it wasn't a restaurant in Chicago where he was sitting at this table and we were sitting at the next one by chance and there was going to be a shootout. He knew we didn't have anything more than a smile." Lawton saved his harshest words for the Corco leaders. "They turned us in, that was really the lowest thing," he said. "And they rubbed it in our faces and got us into it, then they had the nerve not to pay us fully."

All of the smugglers and their lawyers were dragged into court in San Diego. Lawton pled guilty to the federal conspiracy charges and refused to talk: "It was the simple, clean way out, going through the whole thing. So bingo, I just said, 'Okay, I can do that. I don't need to talk about anybody. I'm not going to tell you anything. I'll tell you what I did.'" The offloader was sentenced to a year in Lompoc Federal Prison; compared to Vietnamese jail, it was easy. Not only was he allowed letters and visitors, by the time he got there, everyone had heard about his case. "I smoked just as much weed at Lompoc or at MCC [Metropolitan Correction Center, San Diego] as I would on the street," he said. "We were treated as celebrities whenever we went anywhere, because everybody knew the story of the Coronado Company in jail—that we'd done these huge loads of Thai weed and like that, and that we were heroes and the guys had snitched us off." [18]

Of all the people indicted, Jim Lawton felt sorriest for his old friend Abdul. Although he had been an associate of Corco, law enforcement erroneously assumed he was one of their leaders. "No, he was actually on their fringe, but his flamboyance and the way he associated with people, he left an impression that he was definitely right there at the top. His traveling and passport and records of traveling to the East so much aroused their suspicion quite a bit." After he was arrested crossing at the Tijuana border, Abdul was sentenced to 18 months for passport fraud. Weeks before his release, six guards came into his cell, handcuffed him, and started to take him to solitary confinement. "Hey man, I haven't done anything wrong. What's the deal?" he asked. One of the guards told him that he had been reindicted and because his bail was so high, they couldn't risk having him in the yard. The next day, the U.S. marshal informed Abdul that he had been charged with conspiracy to import and intent to distribute more than 20,000 pounds of marijuana, and his bail was set at $1 million. [19]

After Abdul's lawyer, Phil Demassa, was kicked off the case because he too was indicted, the famous defense attorney Tony Serra took over his defense. Abdul's parents were horrified by the hippie lawyer in the knit skullcap and baggy Indian shirt—until they saw him perform in court.

During the week, Serra lived with Abdul and his now wife, Dang, in Southern California. Each day on the drive home from court the lawyer and his client would smoke a fat joint. One day Abdul asked his lawyer why he was only charging $20,000 when all the other lawyers were asking for hundreds of thousands. "Look, man. I am not a lawyer to make, like, tons of money and have fancy cars and all," said Serra. "You're a marijuana smuggler, right. Well, I like to smoke marijuana."[20]

After Lou Villar was convicted and sentenced to ten years, he decided to cooperate with the feds and even took the stand during Abdul's trial. Although the district attorney claimed that Abdul had been in Maine when one of the loads landed, the smuggler denied it vehemently. "I never met the guy before," said Abdul. "They got somebody that said he saw me somewhere where I wasn't; I could prove that I wasn't even there—I had stamps in my passport that I was in Europe." After the fourth day of jury deliberations, Tony Serra was certain they were hung and would declare a mistrial. When they returned with a guilty verdict, the veteran criminal defense attorney was stunned. "He couldn't believe it. I remember I saw tears in his eyes because he felt that he really let me down. He was real close; by that time he'd been living with us for a month and a half. He was really close with Dang and I."

Abdul appealed the verdict, lost the appeal, and was sentenced to eight years. He started in California federal prisons (Lompoc, Terminal Island, the Metropolitan Detention Center [MDC] in Los Angeles, the MCC in San Diego), did a tour of Arizona's (Tucson, Phoenix, Stafford, and Florence), and managed also to serve time in Springfield, Missouri; El Reno, Oklahoma; Terra Haute, Indiana; and Midland, Michigan. After having the world at his fingertips, prison came as a shock: "Everything taken away—a whole lifestyle, not just your life there in the States, an international-type lifestyle—it was tough. Being so free, so rich, calling all the shots, then having that happen—it was a different reality for sure." Abdul learned a completely new sense of time in prison. "One day in there is like three days out here. Everything is just dragging on. You try not to think about it, like how many days you are doing." After a few months, he stopped counting the days; when one of his cellmates put a calendar up on the wall, he asked him to hang it inside his locker.[21]

11

CONFIDENTIAL
INFORMANT

Just as Corco and Abdul were falling, Mike Ritter was rising. Now he had a 707 with a cargo door ready to fly in a giant load. Ross "the Fatman" Hobson offered Ritter $1,000,000 to bring it in to a landing strip on an island called Norman's Cay in the Bahamas. This famous smuggling outpost, controlled by Colombian cocaine dealer Carlos Lehder, had a 1,000-meter runway and was the Medellin cocaine cartel's key trans-shipment point (featured in the movie *Blow*). While it sounded good, Ritter was wary of the East Coast gangster and decided to work with his old friend, a Vietnam veteran, instead. He said he could provide a safe landing in Montgomery, Alabama. The plane would leave Thailand fully loaded, head to the United Arab Emirates, and continue to the United States with paperwork for scheduled maintenance. It was common for overseas-owned, U.S.-built aircraft to return for repairs, and they were subject to minimal customs inspections. However, once the weed was packed and waiting, the retired Taiwanese Air Force pilot who was supposed to fly the plane got cold feet, and Ritter decided to move it by ship.[1]

Kitty, the same Chinese hustler who'd found Ritter his pilot, said he had a ship that could haul the pot and asked Ritter to meet the owners at his lawyer's office in Singapore. In a legal environment where chewing gum was forbidden, spitting on the sidewalk got you a $150 fine, and drug trafficking was punishable by death sat this den of thieves. The gang's leader was a steely-eyed hood named Allen who could look you straight in the eye and lie through his teeth. He had worked on a big-budget Hollywood film shot in Singapore and as a result, considered Americans dumb rich kids who could be conned out of their allowance, if not their gold fillings. Allen had been briefed, and although he appeared relaxed, as if this was business as usual, his piercing eyes taunted Ritter.

His lawyer, Mak, was the son of a Chinese man and a Kenyan woman; he had a dark complexion and a big afro that was oddly juxtaposed to his obvious Chinese features. He sat behind a desk covered with files. A lawyer's gown hung on a rack next to a framed photograph of a small cargo ship. Ritter silently speculated on what her cargo might have been. Allen's favorite scam, one that he had successfully pulled off three times, was to buy ships on their way to the scrap yard, forge invoices for valuable consumer goods, and insure the make-believe cargo. Once the weather got nice and calm, he would scuttle the ship in the deep ocean off the Philippines and radio the helpful Americans at nearby Subic Bay for help. By sunset Allen would be enjoying a hearty meal, compliments of the U.S. Navy, and anticipating collecting his insurance money.

When the Chinese took Mike Ritter to the Singapore harbor to see their boat, he excitedly scanned the hundreds of anchored vessels, everything from state-of-the-art oil tankers to rusting hulks that looked like they had been anchored since the days of Sir Stamford Raffles. When they pointed to a riverboat that looked like something Lord Jim might have navigated to a forgotten upriver village, Ritter was shocked. The *Rusty Bucket*'s shallow keel, low bow, and forward bridge deck were fine for navigating rivers, but totally unsuitable for storm-tossed open-ocean conditions. Even worse, it was late in the season, so there would be weather in the South China Sea. Ritter doubted the ship was capable of the voyage from Thailand to meet the mother ship off of the Philippines. Allen assured him she was seaworthy, and certainly nobody could beat their rock-bottom price of $100,000 due after delivery. Ritter hired American Rod Kelton, an experienced "warrior captain," who already had sailed a couple of successful loads from Thailand. The Chinese went to Clifford Pier, where able-bodied seamen assembled every morning to sign on to a ship. Within hours, the *Rusty Bucket* had an Indonesian crew who were told that they would be hauling "contraband." When Kelton arrived in Singapore and began installing navigation gear, Ritter's doubts turned to optimism.

Mike Ritter returned to Thailand, and by the time he got to his pirate partner Sa's pier, the pot was already loaded onto a Thai fishing trawler. Once they left the protection of the coast, the trawler began to pound horribly in the steep, short-interval swells. The Thai captain was visibly nervous because his little boat was not built to take this kind of abuse. The wind and waves built all night and after one especially violent drop-off, a large wave, there was an audible crack, two hull planks split, and they began to take on water. The captain ran to the leeward side of a nearby island where they dropped anchor and surveyed the damage. Everyone agreed they could go no farther, so Ritter radioed Sa and told him he needed another boat fast. A few hours later, a larger trawler appeared in the distance. The new vessel was the strongest and most seaworthy Thai boat Ritter had ever used.

They drove hard through the mounting seas far outside the Gulf of Thailand, where they found the *Rusty Bucket* after nightfall. Because of the severe swell surge, the two boats could not tie up alongside. Instead, the *Rusty Bucket* crew strung a cargo net across the top of her hold and when the trawler rose up on the 3-meter swells, Ritter's crew tossed bales into it like they were shooting hoops. When a big set of waves approached, the boats would pull apart. Ritter's captain, an expert seaman, was enjoying himself. "It became a game, and the trawler crews tried to outperform each other," said Ritter. They loaded all seven tons in just two hours. There was no time for the customary hugs and friendly chitchat before the long sea voyage ahead, so they waved farewell and the *Rusty Bucket* quickly vanished in the large swells.

Back in Bangkok, Ritter called the *Rusty Bucket* every night from a makeshift radio station at Surin's house. The respected Hindu-Thai police captain with the permanent grin on his round face had been Lek and Jo's guardian angel for many years, and they turned to him when their marijuana business problems needed solving. Ritter had been using a simple code and duplicate dictionaries to communicate with the *Rusty*

Bucket, and as he began to decipher the American captain's transmission, his heart sank. The Indonesian crew had not been told they were going to be hauling marijuana, they had assumed that contraband meant cigarettes or electronics. However, after they saw the pot, they demanded to be paid more for their silence. There was no way Ritter could meet their demands; furthermore, if there was no rendezvous, there was no more money. Kelton said he would try to explain the situation and call the next day. When they spoke the next day, the situation had grown even more dire. Ritter was so alarmed that he told his captain to forget the code and speak directly. Although they were still on course, the crew was threatening to mutiny if they were not paid more money. "I felt like I was speaking to the radio operator of the *Titanic,*" said Ritter. "The project was sinking and we both knew it."

Kelton did not respond to radio calls the next day and Ritter assumed the worst. As he found out later, after one of the Indonesian crew members discovered two handguns in the American captain's stateroom, he told his crewmates that they were going to be killed and thrown in the sea after they delivered the pot. The crew took the American prisoner and tied his hands to the top of the shower stall. The crew jettisoned the pot, steamed back to Menado, their home port on the northeast tip of Indonesia's Celebes Islands, and vanished. A week later, Allen, the Chinese gangster, phoned Ritter and informed him that the *Rusty Bucket* was in Menado, where an Indonesian boarding party had found Rod Kelton tied to the shower stall and covered in his own excrement. Ritter and Allen flew to Indonesia, and when they found Kelton, he was still in a state of shock. When the gangster complained about the loss of his ship, Ritter laughed. He was out seven tons of pot.[2]

After two years of watching Mike Ritter and Tim Nicholson* load boats with very little profit to show for their risk and effort, their mutual friend Mike Linman* proposed a scam. His group included an Air Force Academy graduate and a couple of boat-savvy Floridians who had been among the first to run shrimp trawlers full of weed from Colombia's Guajira Peninsula into southern Florida. Physically tough, with both the strong build of a former wrestler and an iron constitution, Linman reminded Ritter of Danno from *Hawaii Five-O.* "He could eat any food and not get sick and had that strange ability to be able to sleep anywhere under any conditions, noisy or whatever, if he wanted," said Ritter. The American had studied

Thai and Lao at the University of Hawaii's East-West Center before moving to Laos to work as an intelligence officer during the Vietnam War. He grew disillusioned with the military, resigned as a captain and moved to Bangkok. By the time he showed up in Bali, he had made a significant sum of money in an early Colombian pot scam. That money allowed him to maintain a credible front in Bangkok as a businessman.

Mike Linman had entertainment value and a fantastic memory: he could regale people with war stories about tank battles in Vietnam or describe a hit movie in exquisite detail. Although it was unclear if he had seen the movie or been in a tank battle, "he could make it appear as if he had been there, and that his presence was central to the event," said Ritter. Linman also liked to foster the impression that he was connected to the embassy, maybe the intelligence section; though he certainly had friends in the State Department and DoD from his air force days, according to Ritter, "he couldn't produce any intelligence of much value other than who he was with in the Patpong bar the night before."

Ritter and Nicholson agreed to provide seven tons of pot at $100,000 per ton. When Linman returned to Bangkok with the money, he had a new, "Now that I'm in charge, we'll get things done right" attitude. Ritter's doubts grew after he asked for the operational, offload, and contingency plans and Linman produced a spreadsheet detailing the division of profit down to the last penny. "Whenever I saw someone figuring that way," said Ritter, "I immediately knew they didn't understand the business. If there was one thing you could be sure of in the Thai trade, the unexpected was always ready to ambush you. You had to be ready to change tack at any time." Ritter was resigned to the fact that he needed huge cash reserves to cover unanticipated problems.

Although he realized that Linman was out of touch with Thai reality, he was pleased with his large bankroll and the 27-meter oil rig supply ship that was supposedly en route to Asia. Nicholson got Ritter some of the best pot to leave Thailand that year, and the season had just begun. This was no small feat; by now, Thai marijuana of all grades arrived on the Pacific Coast. American pot growers anticipated the springtime influx of Thai "with the same enthusiasm Detroit automakers reserve for Japanese imports," wrote *High Times* Magazine.[3]

After a month of excuses, Mike Linman told Ritter and Nicholson that there had been a problem and he no longer had a boat. A lot of effort and trust had gone into securing the pot, promises for bonuses had been made, and many were already counting their money. Ritter needed another boat fast, so he agreed to load 1,000 kilos onto a tiny 10-meter sailboat, whose know-it-all American captain he did not like. One 10-wheeled truck easily carried the packages from the warehouse to Sa's private dock near the Cambodian border. As usual, they departed late at night and arrived at the rendezvous point the next morning. Once they made visual contact with the sailboat, Ritter had the Thais drop anchor. He radioed the sailboat's captain and told him to wait until the fenders were down before tying up. The impatient captain pulled alongside just as a swell lifted the heavy wooden fishing boat, and it came down on the small sailboat with a violent crash. When the boats pulled apart, they saw that the sailboat's rail and hull planking were damaged. The American captain was so shaken that he refused to load anything and returned to Singapore with no pot. Ritter was upset because he had lost face in front of the Thais; not only was the sailboat small and unimpressive (the Thais were always anticipating a large ship), "the captain appeared cowardly and foolish. I had to return to shore in the trawler with the load still on board—not a very comfortable thing to do."

At roughly the same time, American scammer John Stansberry was in Thailand with a boat and no pot. He found Ritter and begged him for pot but had no money to put down. Stansberry claimed that all of his money was invested in a stoutly built, double-ended ketch called the *Orca* and swore that no matter what happened, he would send $50,000 when he returned to California. Ritter put a ton and a half on Sa's trawler and headed out to sea. Just as the sun was rising, the boat's rudder post snapped. Although the American wanted to fix the problem immediately, the Thai crew, well aware of the miserable work ahead, took a break for a game of cards. "After the hassle I had caused by not loading the first time," said Ritter, "I decided I better leave it alone. There was nothing I could do about it anyway." After their card game, the crew made a splint for the rudder out of PVC pipe; a man went overboard and lashed it to the post with a length of cheap plastic rope, and the trawler was in open water by sundown. When they met the *Orca* the next evening, Ritter took his usual position on top of the trawler's pilot house with mechanical counter in hand and clicked off the bales as they flew into the boat.

A month or so later, the *Orca* was 3,000 kilometers southwest of Kodiak Island, closing in on Alaska, when the Coast Guard cutter *Boutwell* noticed her riding low in the water and decided to board the *Orca* for a routine safety inspection. When one of the Coast Guard lieutenants moved a sail bag, he saw an opaque aluminum foil package with green particles stuck to the outside. Although the *Orca*'s captain claimed that the 642 identical sealed aluminum bags contained dried fruit, the Coast Guard took the crew into custody and put the sailboat under tow. The *Boutwell* was en route to Dutch Harbor when the cutter suddenly lost all power and electricity. Crewmen raced to the engine room and found that the main oil line had been cut, the service generator drained, and the wires to the emergency gas turbines removed. Several Coast Guard crew members were interrogated; one admitted disabling the ship in an attempt to sail away with the pot in the *Orca*. They repaired the damages and got back under way to Dutch Harbor. One week later, as the *Boutwell* was closing in on Kodiak, another Coast Guard crewman donned a survival suit and tried to slide down the 30-meter towline to the sailboat in a second attempt to sail away with the pot. However, he got tangled in the towline and although the crew could hear him screaming, by the time they found his body, he was frozen nearly solid.

For Mike Ritter, the *Orca* was another disaster: not only had the entire load been captured, he had fronted the pot to John Stansberry. When Ritter met Stansberry in Singapore, he had no money and said earnestly that he had spent it all on the crew's legal expenses. Ritter believed him, until Stansberry added disingenuously, "There will always be more money, but you can never replace your friends."[4]

Ritter was still sitting on a large amount of pot in Thailand. Later that summer, he agreed to load Brotherhood member David Hall's boat *Kotitti II*. Like his other sailboat, the *Sea Tiger* that had been captured by the Vietnamese, this one was also tiny and poorly equipped. When Ritter, in a Thai trawler, pulled alongside the 10-meter sailboat to load the pot, the crew already looked "underfed, worn-out, and desperate, and they had not even begun their transpacific crossing." The smuggler gave the sailors his satellite navigator, an extra radio, and whatever food the Thais could spare; he "felt bad and there was little I could do, but I was amazed Hall would send another poorly provisioned boat across the Pacific after the *Sea Tiger* disaster." Furthermore, it was September, so they were guaranteed to face the huge winter storms coming down from the Aleutian Islands.

By the time the *Kotitti II* got 1,000 kilometers from their rally point off the Oregon coast, they were taking on water and sinking fast. David Hall rushed to Coos Bay and found a gruff pirate captain who was reputed to be a black marketer, expert knife fighter, and all-around badass. He agreed to find the sinking sailboat and transfer the pot onto his wooden schooner. He set sail from Coos Bay with only a directional finder and managed to locate the sailboat in the open ocean, transfer all of the pot, and scuttle the sailboat.[5] When Mike Ritter arrived in Coos Bay to help with the offload, he did not like what he saw: a bunch of suntanned Southern California scammers staying in a dreary motel, practically lining up to use the pay phone. When Hall's Mexican brother-in-law began talking about what he was going to buy when he "hit," Ritter grew worried. "I thought of Mike Linman with his neat list of numbers representing the money each participant would receive. I had a similar premonition of disaster; such talk meant taking your eye off the ball. I did not want to expose my identity to this collection of loose cannons and left immediately."[6]

For the next ten days, David Hall and his offload team sat by the ham radio, waiting to hear from the pirate schooner that now had their pot. When the radio finally burst to life, the captain said that he was just offshore and demanded that they offload immediately. "If this shit is not off tomorrow," he warned, "I am going to feed it to the crabs." Hall had a house on a coastal cliff and planned to offload using a tow truck with a crane and cargo nets. Large surf foiled that plan; not only was there thumping, double-overhead shorebreak, giant waves were breaking across the harbor mouth of the now closed port. The offload team put on their wet suits, blasted through the shorebreak in their inflatable, and although they got absolutely battered, managed to get to the mother ship and bring in over a ton without losing a boat or a life. However, an innocent bystander saw the men standing in wetsuits on the beach with their heavily laden inflatable and reported the suspicious activity to police. The next day the seas were even bigger, and there was no way to get out to the mother ship. True to his word, the pirate captain dumped the rest of the pot into the ocean.

When the *Kotitti II*'s three-man crew checked into the Thunderbird Motel after 90 days at sea, they looked like members of the Manson family. The already suspicious motel staff grew even more suspicious about the guests who paid for everything in cash with large bills. When one of the smugglers asked the motel's front-desk clerk for $35 in quarters and the employee called the police.[7] The next day, David Hall drove south in a rental car and the pot traveled in a rental van behind him. When two undercover police cars began to chase them, the van's driver jumped out and tried to escape on foot but was caught in a Holiday Inn parking lot with the van's keys in his pocket. After a high speed car chase, Hall managed to escape and checked into another motel in Eugene. The next morning, as he was pulling out of the parking lot in the pouring rain, he noticed two guys wearing sunglasses in a Dodge sedan. When they began to follow him, Hall did everything he could to evade them. The powerful, rear-wheel-drive police car was sliding all over the wet road, and when Hall momentarily got out of sight, he pulled the rental car into the driveway of a suburban house and ran through yards until he found good cover under a low hedge. For the next seven hours he watched police cars go up and down the street in the freezing rain. When it got dark, he left his hiding place and called an associate, who came and picked him up.

Although David Hall managed to escape, police found his passport in the trunk of the rental car. After more than two decades of smuggling, the jig was up; he surrendered to police and offered to cooperate. One of the first people to interview him was DEA Agent Jim Conklin.[8] A recently arrested prisoner had a very limited shelf life and had to make very difficult decisions quickly. "They get so upset and so discombobulated; it's really hard for them to think. You try and convince them to do exactly what their attorneys have told them not to do," said Conklin. "All their dope-dealing lives, the attorneys said, 'Don't say nothin'. You're trying to tell them, 'Say everything. Don't pay attention to that attorney. Just tell us everything you know.' I can't even say, 'You'll get out of jail.'" The DEA agent put prisoners between a rock and a hard place, because their value was so fleeting. Many times, he would spend entire nights recording confessions. "I'd sit there till six o'clock in the morning listening to these guys' stories, getting this all down, because if he didn't cooperate at that moment, he went to jail, and the word would come up the guy had been in jail; people wouldn't sell him a marijuana cigarette."

After being debriefed, the newly turned informant was released at dawn and the arrest was kept quiet. The only thing Agent Conklin could promise was that he would make Hall's cooperation known to the U.S.

attorney, who would inform the sentencing judge. Part of the reason for Conklin's success was the high currency of his word. "I never screwed one of them. I told people exactly what was going to happen, and that's the way I go for it. I never let a guy cooperate and then put him in jail afterwards," he said.[9]

The many Coronado Company cases were nearly finished, and between the DEA and the IRS, they had seized $12 million in assets, at the time one of the biggest asset cases ever done on the West Coast. Now Jim Conklin wanted to go to Asia to speak with Japanese, Thai, and Indonesian police, as well as a Hong Kong banker and some newly turned confidential informants. When the DEA approved the trip, Conklin's first stop was Tokyo and a Roppongi bar called Maggie's Revenge, where he found the blonde American prostitute who had introduced Corco to the Yakuza.[10]

In Hong Kong, Conklin got a better sense of how loose banking laws allowed smugglers to move money between nations. In Thailand, he traveled to Isan to see where the pot was grown and then on to Bangkok to interview confidential informants. Finally, in Bali, the DEA agent checked out Abdul's house and sat in on an interrogation conducted by Indonesian police. "It may seem like a waste of money to send a DEA agent over to these foreign countries, but I think you really get to look at it from the other side. I think I got to understand the drug traffickers a lot better when we got to these countries and saw how they operated. You really can understand how people do things," said Conklin. "You learned that Asia was a place where you could get things done with money. The laws aren't as strong as in this country. The enforcement is very corrupt. It's a different kind of lifestyle that they led."[11]

Jim Conklin realized that the scammers' greatest liability was how disconnected they were from the political and legal changes in the United States. Ronald Reagan was now well into his presidency, and all hopes for the legalization of marijuana were gone. "They didn't realize how the drug world was changing as they lived overseas," said Conklin. "The sixties-era Americans became the yuppies driving their SUVs and are now antidrug, you know. But they were all smoking grass in those days and very liberal. But like anybody else, when they age they get more conservative." Conklin had two new informants who would play key roles: Ritter's old friend, Mike Linman, and Tim Nicholson.

When Conklin asked the DEA for a transfer to Thailand, it was granted. In less than five years, Agent Conklin, with Nicholson and Linman's help, would wage one of the most successful campaigns against a specific drug, Thai marijuana, in DEA history.[12]

CONCLUSION

The final blow to the Thai marijuana trade came in 1988, after DEA Agent Jim Conklin's confidential informants Tim Nicholson* and Mike Linman infiltrated Brian Daniels' organization. When Daniels' mother ship, the *Encounter Bay*, neared its offload location in the Pacific Northwest, the *Boutwell*—the same Coast Guard cutter that had been disabled by its crewmen while towing the pot-filled *Orca* in 1982—was waiting.

When the Coast Guard spotted the stoutly built former oil rig supply vessel on the afternoon of June 10, 1988, the smaller ship attempted to flee. The *Boutwell* easily caught up to the smugglers and pulled alongside, and Coast Guard Captain Cecil Allison warned over a public address system that "disabling fire" would commence if they did not stop. The *Encounter Bay*'s captain, Army Special Forces veteran Sam Colflesh, accused Allison of "piracy on the high seas" and continued to run. Machine-gun rounds tore the *Encounter Bay*'s steel hull before a blown engine brought the chase to an end. After securing the uniformed crew, the Coast Guard boarding party noticed a mobile crane and several large shipping containers on deck; all had been painted the same color as the ship's false deck.

The large hinged doors of the first container creaked open to expose a cargo of gray, blue, and brown tote bags. Inside each were eight 1-kilo heat-sealed bags of Laotian marijuana, each with a logo sticker and a tax stamp. The Coast Guard recovered 144,000 pounds of high-grade marijuana from the 8,152 identical boxes inside the containers and below the false decks—wholesale value $200 million, street value $400 million. The *Encounter Bay* was the Pacific Coast's largest single marijuana seizure, one of eight mother ships captured by the Coast Guard in 1988, for a total haul of 463,000 pounds of Southeast Asian marijuana.

Agent Conklin met Brian Daniels in a Swiss jail shortly after his arrest. Not only did Conklin want the smuggler to cooperate, he also wanted him to surrender $30 million that had vanished after the *Encounter Bay* bust. Daniels responded with a counteroffer: "I'll tell you about the Vietnamese government. I'll tell you about the Laos government, no problem there. As far as testifying about my history, I'll tell you what I've done, but I'm not going to talk about my friends. I flat out will not tell you about my partners." The smuggler paused and made the DEA agent a very tempting offer. "You want that thirty million? I'll give it to you. You let me walk out of here and I'll give that money to you." When Conklin refused the bribe, Daniels asked for ten minutes alone to consider his plight. When the DEA agent returned, the Swiss guard informed him that Daniels was gone; he had asked to be taken back to jail. Both men held to their respective codes: the cop refused the bribe and the smuggler refused to talk.

Even though it took American law enforcement agents and prosecutors most of the 1980s, they shut down the export Thai marijuana trade. By the early 1990s, the Thai marijuana fleet had been mothballed, and the DEA's campaign against Thai pot can be counted as one of the few unequivocal victories in the War on Drugs.[1] Irrespective of their successes, every narrator you have met in this book was caught, and most were incarcerated.

Although he exported at least 100 tons of Thai pot and hundreds of millions of dollars passed through his hands, James "Abdul" Monroe* did not save a dime. Today the retired smuggler lives comfortably, and prefers his present, more humble lifestyle to his years as a jet-setting fugitive. "I just felt like the whole thing could crumble. There was an element of insecurity then, you didn't feel totally comfortable all the time," he said. "I mean, a cop could come along in the old days and just turn my life upside down, you know." After he was released from prison and off parole, Abdul moved back to Asia and has no plans to return to the United States. He looks back philosophically on his years as a pot smuggler and compares his time in prison to *Hogan's Heroes*—"Like we were in a prisoner-of-war camp," he said. "I felt I was a prisoner of the marijuana wars. A lot of the people I hung out with were like that too, you know. We were like war buddies in there because it was us against the feds."[2]

To Jim Lawton*, his years as a pot smuggler were "a Boy Scout adventure." More than the money, today he misses "the thrill of watching an airplane take off and fly over your head with the engine roaring and carrying the weight of a whole bunch of weed back to California; the spray in your face in the night, blasting into a foggy night with no radar, coming up the coast with a load of Mexican weed." Lawton is proud of his past and considers himself a standard bearer, one of the "guys who were brave enough to go and ride the wild range, the sea, the air, by whatever underground means of concealment and connivance and illusion that we could produce." He bears no grudges toward Jim Conklin or any of the other law enforcement agents who put him behind bars. "There's the cops and there's the robbers; they're the opposing political sides, and they're soldiers that go to war."[3]

Before guidelines and minimum mandatory sentences, it was possible for a smuggler to keep his mouth shut, spend a few years in jail, and keep his money. "A lot of these guys didn't look at themselves as being crooks, they thought of themselves as being hippies. Marijuana was sort of a way of life. It was going to change the world and the way they thought," said DEA Agent Conklin. "When they went to jail, they couldn't handle it, they really couldn't do it; they weren't hardened criminals." When John Parten's associate John Stansberry was finally arrested, he became the government's star witness and helped to convict twenty-three of his former associates. While his offloaders, drivers, and mechanics went to prison, Stansberry, the organization's leader, went to law school. "The elephants were set loose on the ants," said defense attorney Lew Geiser at the time.[4]

After amassing close to $10 million, John Parten retired in 1982 and lived the dream, dividing his time between skiing in Sun Valley, Idaho, and surfing Viti Levu, Fiji. He shared a tax attorney with Michael Jackson, and a decade after his final scam, he figured that the statute of limitations had run out and he was home free. In early June 1993, after an awards ceremony at his daughter's school in Ketchum, Idaho, the proud father was walking toward his car in the school parking lot when six U.S. marshals jumped out of nowhere with guns drawn and arrested him. Shortly thereafter, police in flak jackets arrested his mother and charged her with being part of her son's conspiracy. Everybody on Parten's team was arrested and most cooperated. His 100-count indictment and the three superseding indictments charged him with money laundering, conspiracy, and a combination of RICO and CCE charges. In discovery, he learned that the ex-wife of a coconspirator had gone to the DEA because she was unhappy with her divorce settlement. "There was a code in the beginning, 'Everybody's brothers and you don't turn anyone in,'" the smuggler said. "Our code was, 'If you do the crime, be prepared to do the time.'"

Parten was intent on fighting his case until his attorney told him that not only was he facing twenty-five years to life, his mother had already been indicted, his wife might be indicted, and his kids might end up in foster homes. When John Parten weighed it all, his family was the most important thing; the thought of his mother going to prison and his children growing up without him was too much to bear. "I look like an asshole with my friends because they think I turned everybody in. Fortunately for me, I was at the top of the pile here," said Parten. "Everybody had already testified against everybody, but I had to talk about it."

When John Parten finally testified in front of an Idaho grand jury, he provided a window into the mind of the surfer scammer. "I grew up in Southern California, and my passion was surfing," he explained. "My dream was to travel and ride these waves in various parts of the world, and that's exactly what I did. It would support my traveling and the food and the money I needed for the air tickets."

> John Parten: "It was called doing a scam then."
> District Attorney: "And your travel took you to—besides Morocco and South Africa, it took you eventually to Fiji?"
> John Parten: "Yes, it did."
> District Attorney: "Bali?"
> John Parten: "Yes."
> District Attorney: "Australia?"
> John Parten: "Yes."
> District Attorney: "Thailand?"

John Parten: "Yes."

District Attorney: "Where else?"

John Parten: "Basically, all over the world."

District Attorney: "You surfed everywhere?"

John Parten: "Surfed everywhere."

District Attorney: "Pretty much a surfer's dream at that point in your life?"

John Parten: "Yes. It was a common thing for people to want to do this, but a lot of people didn't take the initiative to do it. I guess the fact that I was successful at smuggling marijuana, it enabled me to accomplish the dream I set out to do."

When Parten walked into court on his day of sentencing, the prosecutor told him, "You know, I'm going to be like a defense attorney today." In the end, the smuggler was sentenced to time served, and although the government took his money, they could not take his memories of surfing the world's best waves before the arrival of crowds and cameras. Today, John Parten is content working as the maintenance manager at a condominium complex in Sun Valley, Idaho, where his biggest concerns are trash day and getting his kids through college. "I don't really think ahead. There's not a lot of places I really want to go or things I need to do. I'm enjoying the moment right now."[5]

According to DEA Agent Jim Conklin, "stand-up crooks," the guys who will not talk, are extremely rare, and he feels the sorriest for them because those whom they refuse to talk about almost always testify against them. After Mike "Charlie Tuna" Carter was arrested in Kenya and extradited to the United States, the district attorney offered to reduce his sentence if he would testify against a crooked financier who had ripped him off. "If you want me to go punch his eyes out and break his knees, I'll do that," said Carter. "But you know what? I just can't be a witness against him, that's against my rules. I'll do anything else, and I hope you get him, but I can't do it." The smuggler, who estimates that he moved 100 tons in his career, was sentenced to 11 years and served 7. Like Jim Lawton, he never viewed law enforcement as an enemy, only one of many adversaries. To him, smuggling was never a moral issue. "I've thought about it many times," said Carter. "I think that this is not something that is necessarily a great and proud thing, but it's something that happens, and it's something that shows the potential of what people can do if they want to do it and what the potential of the government is to restrict you from doing things that you find no problem with." Mike Carter still lives in Northern California and is trying to regain the simplicity he had when he was a commercial fisherman. Like so many other pot smugglers, he believes that money was not his only motivation. "I miss the adventure, I miss the camaraderie," Carter said. "I miss working with that type group of people and getting something done, way above my head." The retired smuggler believes that marijuana's virtual legalization in California has made "it all a big joke."[6]

Unlike "stand-up crook" Mike Carter, the Shaffer brothers surrendered and shrewdly negotiated a plea deal. Bill Shaffer turned himself in, pled guilty, got his brother to surrender, and agreed to help recover assets for the government. Although one Shaffer brothers scam during the 1980s allegedly netted close to $60 million, when they presented the government with a cashier's check for $1,025,000, they were hailed as heroes who had learned their lesson. During sentencing, the courtroom atmosphere was "so full of goodwill one could almost forget the punitive purpose of the proceedings," wrote Peter Lewis in the *Seattle Post-Intelligencer*. "The federal prosecutor was complimenting the defendants, the defendants were complimenting the government, and everybody was appropriately deferential toward U.S. District Judge John Coughenour." The irony was not lost on the reporter, who reminded his readers that this was, after all, the "sentencing of the ringleaders of the largest marijuana-smuggling organization ever prosecuted in Western Washington." Although Chris and Bill Shaffer were sentenced to 13.5 years and 12 years respectively, both were released after 6. In 1998, the *Hollywood Reporter* announced that just 8 months after their release, the Shaffers had recouped most of the $1,025,000 they'd surrendered to the feds after New Line Cinema allegedly bought a screenplay of their life stories for one million dollars. The Hollywood trades breathlessly announced that Brad Pitt was set to star in *Smuggler's Moon*, a film that was never made.[7]

Judge Coughenour, who had showed such generosity to the Shaffer brothers, was not so kind to Brian Daniels. The smuggler was extradited to the United States to face federal drug smuggling charges in Reno, San Diego, and Seattle. A "stand-up crook" to the end, Daniels refused to cooperate or talk about any of his coconspirators. Although Coughenour praised Daniels for admitting his guilt and "resisting the temptation to get involved in the cocaine heroin business," he sentenced him to twenty-five years in 1990. Daniels was not released until 2009. Agent Conklin expressed mixed feelings about the Daniels sentence. "I felt sorry for him because all the guys that he didn't talk about eventually were all arrested, they all cooperated, they all talked about him. But he wouldn't give up a word and he got twenty-five years, which I always thought was too much time."[8]

Today, retired DEA Agent Jim Conklin works as a private eye in Las Vegas and looks back on his years working the Thai marijuana trade as the high point of his career. Compared to the heroin kingpins he had investigated in New York City and the meth dealers he had busted in San Diego County, the Thai marijuana cases were fun. "These guys were all smart, they were interesting to talk to, they had a lot of fun life experiences, they're all a lot of fun, and they weren't violent. I mean, you don't gotta worry about these guys pulling a gun on you," he said. "I can't think of an instance." Over the years, the agent came to respect the Thai smugglers because "they really did a great job" and never had any personal animus toward them; in fact, quite the opposite: Agent Conklin believed that anyone who could put together a successful Thai marijuana scam had the potential to "organize any major corporation in the country." Above all, he believed that there was a great deal of camaraderie between the smugglers and the police who pursued them. "These drug guys were doing this because it was very interesting, very exciting to them," said Conklin. "And the cops are doing the same thing."

Mike Ritter and I were finishing up the last of our research in 2002 when DEA and customs officials in Hawaii contacted Jim Conklin to inform him that they had reopened their criminal investigation of Mike Ritter. "They came to me, these Hawaiian guys: 'Hey, old retired guy, can you help us out, can you provide us these informants that know Ritter,'" recalled Conklin. "I remembered Ritter, we had worked on him years ago, but we never had quite enough to indict him. It was a smaller case, so it was kind of put on the sidelines and we really never put it together." The Hawaiian law enforcement agents suspected that Ritter was involved in an ongoing conspiracy with Tim Nicholson. Given my numerous research trips to Thailand and Cambodia since 1994, they also had questions about me. The retired DEA agent was most taken aback by their borderline hostile treatment. "They brought Tim [Nicholson] over, they treated him poorly," said Conklin. "They were talking bad to me. In the old days, you wanted to form a little team, we are all in the same boat. . . . I was very disappointed in that, because it was a very hard thing for Tim."[9]

During the summer of 2003, Mike Ritter received a phone call from an old associate warning that DEA agents in California were asking questions about him. Ritter was not particularly worried; over the years, he had periodically cleaned out his files and had been careful to throw out address lists, promissory notes, and anything else that would link him to his overseas bank accounts. A few weeks later, he got a call from his old friend Tim Nicholson, who said that he was on Maui with a group of Thai businessmen and wanted to get together for lunch. Ritter knew that Nicholson had become one of Agent Conklin's most effective confidential informants, and although he didn't approve of that decision, they remained friends.

The smuggler made no connection between Nicholson's surprise visit to Maui and the warning he had received a few weeks earlier. There was something odd about his friend's story, though: why would a group of rich Thais stay at a cheap hotel in Kahului? Ritter shaved, put on his best aloha shirt, and drove down to the seedy hotel. The front desk clerk directed him to Nicholson's room; he knocked on the door, and as it opened, he knew something was wrong: "It reminded me of a scene from the movie *Goodfellas*. Joe Pesci is to become a 'made man.' Beside himself with excitement, he dresses in his slickest suit and goes to what he thinks will be a party in his honor," wrote Ritter. "Entering the house, he is greeted by an elder Mafioso who sticks a gun to the back of his head and pulls the trigger. Tim had set me up." Instead of a gun to the back of the head, two federal agents handed Mike Ritter a search warrant and said they had evidence he was a marijuana smuggler and had been following his offshore money transfers for two years.

Like many former smugglers who believed they were immune from prosecution because they had been out of the business for so long, Ritter had failed to realize how the events of 9/11 fundamentally changed the rules of the game. When he reached his house in Kula, it was swarming with agents from U.S. Customs, the IRS, and the Maui Police Department's vice squad. The police immediately confiscated his computers and began to scrutinize every scrap of paper they could find. As the search went on, the police grew frustrated because they could not find any financial records and threatened to break open the walls. By the time the sun had set, much of our historical research was boxed and tagged—"evidence" in the case of *U.S. v. Michael Keith Ritter*. "Surprisingly," said Ritter, "I was more concerned about losing our research than I was about impending financial loss. It was more important to me to validate my past than to secure my future."[10]

I was driving by Waimea Bay the next morning when my phone rang and Ritter informed me that the feds had confiscated his copies of our research. I called my wife in New York City; she and a trusted colleague boxed up my copies of the interviews and got them out of our apartment. First, I called the Columbia University Oral History office to ask if they would hold our tapes. Ron Grele had retired and the new director, although sympathetic, feared the legal problems we might bring and said that she could not help us. Our greatest support came from a criminal defense attorney I knew through my academic work. Death penalty and terrorism cases were his daily bread, and he was unfazed by my request. Although he was willing to store our tapes in his office, he offered some sobering advice about our limited options and told Mike Ritter that he should be very grateful that nothing more had happened. His tone and response conveyed the message that, in the wake of 9/11, the federal government was capricious and had unlimited power. This new breed of law enforcement agents even considered many of their DEA predecessors as "bent" due to their lack of evangelical zeal.

A week after his house was searched, Ritter and his lawyer, Phil Lowenthal, sat down with U.S. Attorney Chris Thomas, U.S. Customs Special Agent Frank Okamura, and IRS Special Agent Kevin Shimoda. Thomas seemed like an earnest Mormon trying to move up the career ladder, while Shimoda reminded Ritter of John le Carre's antihero George Smiley and the muscle-swollen, gun-toting Okamura played the tough guy. After three days of negotiations, Ritter realized that the federal prosecutor was not concerned with the details of his old smuggling operations; they only wanted money. The prosecutor made it clear that Mike Ritter's freedom was riding on the forfeiture of a large sum of cash and led him to believe that if he met the terms of a vague, unwritten agreement, he would keep his home and serve no jail time. When the retired smuggler told his attorney that he wanted the terms of his deal in writing, Lowenthal scoffed at him and said the feds "were honorable people who could be trusted on their word."

Like most defendants in federal cases, Ritter waived his Constitutional right to a trial and pled guilty. U.S. Attorney Edward Kubo made the most of the public relations opportunity on the front page of the *Honolulu Advertiser* and claimed that the case proved "we are very serious about forfeiting the ill-gotten gains of drug dealers." Kubo went on to say that Ritter had played a role in at least a dozen large shipments of marijuana from Thailand and was facing twenty years in prison.

Although Mike Ritter had pled guilty, he had not been sentenced, and now the real negotiations began. After he signed the document admitting his guilt and forfeited $450,000, the feds moved the goalposts—now they demanded an even million. According to Ritter, U.S. Attorney Chris Thomas led him to believe that if he surrendered a million dollars, he would not go to jail or lose his house. Although Ritter eventually sold his house to come up with a million dollars and met the terms of the verbal agreement, Judge Susan Oki Molloway sentenced him to 24 months in federal prison. The judge threw him a bone and recommended Ritter for an intensive, in-prison drug treatment program. Although he had not smoked marijuana in two years, Ritter agreed to drug rehab because it would reduce his sentence by a year.[11]

Three days after spending a leisurely Fourth of July with his family, Mike Ritter stood at the gate of the Florence Federal Correctional Complex in Colorado, a facility with prisons of several security levels. The Florence "super max" is the most secure prison in the United States and has housed famous criminals like John Gotti, Unabomber Ted Kaczynski, Terry Nichols, John Walker Lindh, and other members of America's criminal elite. After being handcuffed, searched, photographed, and fingerprinted, Ritter was issued a green polyester jumpsuit and a pair of Herman Munster boots and assigned a bunk. He was one of 550 inmates housed in the low-security "camp" at Florence. The pair of two-story buildings had small dorm-style rooms with bunk beds, small lockers, and desks. Breakfast was served at 7:00, lunch at 10:45, and dinner at 4:30. Ritter worked the swing shift at the powerhouse from 3:00 p.m. to 11:00 p.m. It took him only five minutes each hour to check the gauges, and he sat around for the rest of the time. The leisurely job left him plenty of time to work out and drink coffee with his new friends.

The inmates were a mixed bag; most were incarcerated for drug and financial indiscretions. Ritter's best friend was a young NASA scientist who had been arrested for stealing and selling rocks from the moon. Although he found the guards unpleasant and eager to hassle prisoners for the slightest infractions of the rules, Ritter was surprised by how considerate inmates were to each other. "I have seen no fighting or even verbal altercations. Inmates hold doors open for each other, patiently wait in line, share smokes and conversation," he wrote from prison. "We are all doing time and everyone dreams of getting out." Worse than the food and the regimented life were the hours Ritter spent in his bunk, as images from his past would appear in his mind like random snapshots, only to fade away and leave him with a bone-grinding sense of loss.

After a year in prison and six months in a halfway house, Mike Ritter took a job as a desk clerk at a Waikiki hotel before he returned to college. The 64-year-old graduated from the University of Hawaii in December 2012 with a double major in physics and astronomy and a minor in mathematics, and a 3.7 grade point average. Although he has not smoked marijuana for the better part of a decade, he looks back proudly on his career as a marijuana smuggler. Today, Mike Ritter feels fortunate to have lived through "a very special time in history" and has no ill will toward the feds who busted him. Like Abdul, Ritter feels a great sense of relief at not having to conceal the truth about his past anymore: "Human beings are social creatures, and we like to share tales of our challenges, sacrifices, triumphs, and failures with our fellow humans."[12]

Although the U.S. government shut down the Thai marijuana trade, what did they actually win? There was no reduction in either the supply or the demand for marijuana; in fact, quite the opposite. By the mid-1980s, marijuana was the number one cash crop in the United States thanks to a huge demand and an artificially high price. As everyone from economist Adam Smith to the Thai politicians who were pressed by the U.S. government to crack down on pot has pointed out, political laws will always be less powerful than the economic law of supply and demand. The illegal marijuana industry is one of the best examples of Smith's "Invisible Hand" in action. Ironically, today the biggest opponents of marijuana legalization are not law enforcement agents but some of the black market growers and smugglers, because their pricing structure would collapse.

The worst blowback effect of law enforcement's successful efforts against marijuana is that in the places they were most successful, Hawaii and Thailand, marijuana got so expensive that users simply replaced it with cheaper, far more destructive smokable methamphetamine. Despite a 40-year War on Drugs that has given the United States the largest prison population on earth, Americans are more drug-addled than ever. With less than 5 percent of the world's population, Americans consume 80 percent of the world's opioids and 99 percent of the hydrocodine (the opiate in Vicodin). Although painkillers are responsible for more deaths than crack and heroin combined, Vicodin, oxycodone, cocaine, morphine, and amphetamines are Schedule II drugs in the DEA's hierarchy, while marijuana and heroin remain Schedule I—classified among the most dangerous illegal substances. Today America is led by a president who was once a habitual pot smoker, but his DEA head administrator refused to admit that heroin and methamphetamine were worse for a user's health than marijuana. A 2013 Pew Research poll showed that for the first time in 40 years, more than 50 percent of Americans (52 percent) favored the decriminalization of marijuana, yet the door to "The Cannabis Closet" remains closed and locked. Our hope is that this book can help crack open the door so that generations of Americans can come out of the closet.[13]

NOTES

INTRODUCTION

1. Tom Wolfe offered his view of the "surfing lifestyle" in *The Pump House Gang* (New York: Farrar, Straus & Giroux, 1968). Surfers were not impressed by the East Coast author's attempt to document their culture. Lance Vargas, "Surf and destroy: WIndanSea's [*sic*] secret society," http://www.lancevargas.com/meda.php. "Though Wolfe brought the group international appeal, he is not thought of as a sage or prophet among the Windan-Sea locals. 'Tom Wolfe is a dork!' was once spray-painted on the pumphouse he named his story after."

2. William Langewiesche, *The Outlaw Sea: A World of Freedom, Chaos, and Crime* (Berkeley, Calif.: North Point Press, 2005), 1. Stan Pleskunas, e-mail to author, December 21, 2012.

3. After decades of petty larceny and small-time scams, Dora was arrested for credit card and check fraud. Although he was the son of a Hungarian aristocrat, Dora's life was changed forever when his mother remarried Gard Chapin, one of the pioneers of California surfing. Prior to World War II, surfers were not widely admired and viewed as bums or eccentrics. Surfing was born in Hawaii, but Southern Californians played a huge role in spreading both the sport and the subculture. Chapin was a hard-drinking, musclebound woodworker "considered by many to be California's most talented and least-liked Depression-era surfer." C. R. Stecyk III and Drew Kampion, *Dora Lives: The Authorized Story of*

Miki Dora (Santa Barbara, Calif.: T. Adler Books, 2005), xxii–xxiii; Stan Pleskunas, e-mail to author, December 21, 2012: "It was a time when the gremmies learned by watching and swimming for their boards. You had to pay to play. There were no cords. That meant the most experienced and talented got the best waves. . . . Some would say surfing culture is as broken as the Apache's way of life. Some would see the changes as a trail of tears."

4. Although he was not a surfer, actor Rob Lowe offered this observation about growing up in Malibu during the 1970s: "Malibu was populated by a wonderful mix of normal working-class families, hippies, asshole surfers, drugged-out reclusive rock stars and the odd actor or two. . . . Parents were rarely seen in Malibu. The kids lived *Lord of the Flies* style, running their own programs without apparent interference from an adult— ever." Rob Lowe, *Stories I Only Tell My Friends* (New York: St. Martin's Griffin, 2011), 37, 44.

5. Although actor Sean Penn grew up surfing Point Dume, he could not easily surf Trancas Point, only two miles north. "I was out at Trancas Point one day, surfing there— which is me not being local, and localism was a big thing: you don't surf other people's beaches. A guy I never liked much, Doug Jones, pelted my car with rocks as I left, and I nearly lost control of the car." Richard Kelly, *Sean Penn: His Life and Times* (New York: Cannongate, 2004), 47.

6. In the introduction to Dr. Don James's book *Surfing San Onofre to Point Dume: 1936–1942* (San Francisco: Chronicle, 1998), C. R. Stecyk III described many of the subjects in Don James's photographs of pre–World War II surfers as "a colorful cast of Runyonesque characters. Ten years earlier, rum runners had come ashore at Paradise Cove during Prohibition, and organized crime bosses anchored gambling ships offshore from the Santa Monica Pier in order to be beyond federal and state jurisdictional limits. . . . A decade before, during Prohibition, many a beach boy profited by delivering surf-splashed Canadian whiskey to the appreciative stars who congregated along Santa Monica's golden coast" (12). Not all surfers were pot smokers; many were adamantly opposed to drug use, and surfing underwent a culture war during the 1960s. Surfers who had come of age during the 1950s, like Fred Hemmings, made their disdain for drug use known. However, so ubiquitous was pot smoking within the surfing culture by the 1970s that Sean Penn wrote: "I remain today the only living surfer of that age who doesn't smoke pot." Kelly, *Sean Penn,* 43.

7. Bernard Jackson, interview with author, Venice, California, 1996. Born in 1963, months premature, KK suffered from fetal alcohol syndrome, heroin addiction, and a heart murmur. He was not expected to live, but after close to a year in an incubator, he went to live with his grandparents in Oakwood because his parents were both heroin addicts and career criminals. KK's Uncle Bernard stabbed and killed a man outside a Santa Monica restaurant in 1964 but was acquitted. According to the press accounts of the Guerico murder, there was a struggle and the gun went off. According to Uncle Bernard, there was no struggle: he and his partner cornered the man and demanded his money. "Walter was pointing a .38 at him. Walter was wearing gloves, he lost grip of the hammer and the gun went off and he shot him in the head." For more on the murder, see *People*

v. Lee, 249 Cal. App. 2d 234, Crim. No. 11343, Second Dist., Div. One, Mar. 7, 1967; "2 Couples Linked to Guerico Killing," *Evening Outlook*, February 6, 1965.

8. For more on Carl Jones, see Mike Sokolove, *The Ticket Out: Darryl Strawberry and the Boys of Crenshaw* (New York: Simon and Schuster, 2004).

9. David Chandler speculated about the American prisoners' connections to U.S. intelligence in *Voices from S-21* (Berkeley: University of California Press, 1999), 112.

10. Quoted in Joseph Earl Dabney, *Mountain Spirits: A Chronicle of Corn Whiskey from King James' Ulster Plantation to America's Appalachians and the Moonshine Life* (Ashville: Bright Mountain Books, 1974), xvi. "Indeed, in legal terms, moonshining has been defined by federal law as *malum prohibitum*, which means that it is bad because there is a law against it, not bad in itself. . . . Hence he is a tax violator rather than a criminal, whose crime is defined as *malum per se*, or *malum in se*, bad in itself." Horace Kephart's observations in his study *Our Southern Highlanders* could also apply to the early Thai marijuana smugglers. "The little moonshiner . . . fights fair, according to his code, and singlehandedly against tremendous odds. He is innocent of graft."

11. E .P. Thompson, *The Making of the English Working Class* (New York: Vintage, 1966); Alessandro Portelli, *The Death of Luigi Trastulli and Other Stories: Form and Meaning in Oral History* (Albany: State University of New York Press, 1991); for more on Portelli's methodology, see Betsy Brinson, "Crossing Cultures: An Interview with Alessandro Portelli," *Oral History Review* 28, no. 1 (Winter/Spring 2001).

12. For the victorious policeman's perspective, see Paul Eddy and Sara Walden, *Hunting Marco Polo: The Pursuit of a Drug Smuggler Who Couldn't Be Caught by the Agent Who Wouldn't Quit* (New York: Little, Brown, 1991); James Mills, *The Underground Empire* (New York: Doubleday, 1986). For the smugglers' perspective, see Robert Sabbag, *Smokescreen: A Misadventure on the Marijuana Trail* (New York: Little, Brown, 2002); Phil Sparrowhawk with Martin King and Martin Knight, *Grass* (London: Mainstream Publishing, 2003); A. R. Torsone, *HERB TRADER: A Tale of Treachery and Espionage in the Global Marijuana Trade* (Woodstock, N.Y.: Woodstock Mountain Press, 2009); Joseph Pietri, *The King of Nepal: Ice Wars Edition* (self-published, 2006); George Wethern and Vincent Colnett, *A Wayward Angel: The Full Story of the Hells Angels* (New York: R. Marek Publishers, 1978).

1. SURFERS, SCAMMERS, AND THE COUNTERCULTURE

1. In the introduction to Dr. Don James's book *Surfing San Onofre to Point Dume: 1936–1942* (San Francisco: Chronicle, 1998), C. R. Stecyk III wrote: "There was no lifesaving profession to speak of, and those who dedicated their lives to ocean centricity were viewed with contempt, or at best with heavy suspicion, by society at large. . . . Times were hard, and these resourceful native sons adapted with distinction" (12). Gerry Lopez bluntly described how socially unacceptable surfers were in his book, *Surf Is Where You Find It* (Santa Barbara, Calif.: T. Adler Books, 1996). Stan Pleskunas described the antisurfer

sentiment best in an e-mail to author, December 21, 2012: "In our day, if your daughter was going to date a surfer or a biker, as a parent, you would have preferred the biker. At least a biker had some mechanical ability. Surfers were seen as the lowest, laziest, most useless dogs of society." For more on Duke Kahanamoku, see Sandra Kimberley Hall, *Duke: A Great Hawaiian* (Honolulu: Bell Press, 2004); for more on Tarzan Smith, see Dorian Paskowitz, "Tarzan at Waikiki," *The Surfers Journal*, Summer 1993; Malcolm Gault-Williams, "Tarzan Redux: Chapter Fill-ins from the Life of Gene Smith," *The Surfers Journal*, Spring 2004, http://files.legendarysurfers.com/surf/legends/ls09z_tarzan.html.

2. 24 F.3d 1059, 40 Fed. R. Evid., Serv. 936, UNITED STATES of America, Plaintiff-Appellee, v. Daniel James FOWLIE, Defendant-Appellant, No. 91-50383, United States Court of Appeals, Ninth Circuit, Argued and Submitted April 6, 1993; Linda Fuller, "Lord of the Ring," *Orange Coast* (December 1991); http://www.thefactsaboutdan-fowlieandpavones.com/en/index.php; for more on Bridgeman, see http://papanuisays.blogspot.com/2009/02/bill-bridgeman-surfer-aviator-test.html. Craig Williams, interview by Mike Ritter, Maui, Hawaii, October 1998.

3. A 1964 *Time* magazine article, "Shooting the Tube," compared surfing to "going on hashish." For more on hash and pot-filled surfboards, see *People v. Superior Court* (1973) 33 CA3d523; "Beyond the Reefer," *Honolulu Star Bulletin*, January 8, 1969. Jerry Kamstra, *Weed: Adventures of a Dope Smuggler* (Santa Barbara, Calif.: Santa Barbara Press, 1983). Bunker Spreckels, surfing's "divine prince of decadence," offered this observation: "Drugs and surfing sort of go hand in hand in the sense that it's the kind of lifestyle with which drugs are more or less an occupational hazard, like in the world of rock music."

4. David Ortiz, interview by Mike Ritter, Santa Barbara, California, October 1999, July 2007; and various telephone conversations.

5. Craig "Owl" Chapman, conversation with author, Sunset Beach, Hawaii, 2004.

6 Craig Williams, interview by Mike Ritter, Maui, Hawaii, October 1998. Mike Ferguson, interview with author, Pupukea, Oahu, June 2004. "Three Get Month for Using 'Pot,'" *Bangkok Post*, September 26, 1969; "GI Here Mailing Pot to US?" *AP,* October 12, 1969; "APO System 'Being Abused,'" "Agents Find Marijuana In GI Mail," *AP,* August 9, 1969; Charles Durden, *No Bugles, No Drums* (New York: Viking, 1976). Durden described one GI scam in his novel, *No Bugles, No Drums*. Flying home after his tour, a soldier dropped a duffle bag at the feet of his comrades and said, "Grade-goddamn-A Thai grass. One thousand dollars a pound, whole-sale." Qtd. in John Clark Pratt, ed., *Vietnam Voices: Perspectives on the War Years 1941–1982* (Athens: University of Georgia Press, 2008), 448.

7. Terry Dawson*, "The Road to Anaraxta."

8. Michael McPherson, *Rivers of the Sun* (Hilo, Hi.: South Point Press, 2000), 13–14.

9. Dawson, "The Road to Anaraxta." In an anonymous e-mail to the author, one of Baxter's Maui associates wrote: "Ralph asked me to go to a party of Brotherhood guys up on the hill and give his aloha to BL. I did, but Brian, who was a dear old friend to me, looked at me like I'd gut-shot him, like really scared I'd shoot him again. I didn't know what had gone on between them, so I put my hand on BL's shoulder and said, 'No, really, he likes you.' That's how those guys took messages from Mr. Baxter."

10. Ned Jones*, interview by author, Pupukea, Oahu, June 2004; Mike Ferguson, interview by author, June 2004; Herb Torrens, *The Paraffin Chronicles: A Surfer's Journey 1960–1971* (Victoria, Canada: Trafford, 2003), 72. David E. Kaplan and Alec Dubro wrote in *Yakuza: The Explosive Account of Japan's Criminal Underworld* (Boston: Addison-Wesley Longman, 1986), that in addition to Hawaii's geographic position in the mid-Pacific, "the islands hosted the right elements in which organized crime could flourish: machine party politics coupled with a tough labor movement; a hedonistic culture with widespread acceptance of prostitution, gambling, and drugs; and a massive tourist industry that each year gathered millions of visitors from around the world and turned them loose on Honolulu streets" (xviii).

11. *Roach Haleiwa* II, no. 3, March 23–April 6, 1969; "2 Sentenced in Murder," *Honolulu Star Bulletin*, November 9, 1970; "Leave North Shore, Arrive Lahaina: Maui 'Mellow So Drug Ring Moves In,'" *Honolulu Star Bulletin*, April 20, 1972; "'Narcs' Have Their Eye on Maui Ring," *Honolulu Star Bulletin*, April 19, 1972; "Maui Officials Eye Drug Ring," *Honolulu Star Bulletin*, April 22, 1972.

12. Terry Dawson, interview by Mike Ritter, Boulder, Colorado, February 1999; Dawson's claim that he sold the Golden Voice to the Hell's Angels is bolstered by Hell's Angel George Wethern and Vincent Colnett, *A Wayward Angel: The Full Story of the Hells Angels* (New York: R. Marek Publishers, 1978).

13. *Rainbow Bridge,* dir. Chuck Wein (Los Angeles: Transvue Pictures, 1972). Pezman's discussion of Leary and surfers can be found in Andrew Kidman's 2006 surfing film *Glass Love*: "Leary saw surfers as the throw aheads of mankind versus the dregs of mankind versus the irresponsible sector of mankind. He described the highest destiny of man on earth as a form of existence in the universe as evolving towards an aesthetic state. That was the highest possible goal that man could attain as a species. They were the living example of man to be emulated. He said surfers were the perfect example of 'be here now.'" Drew Kampion, "When the Smoke Cleared," *The Surfers Journal* 2, no. 1 (Spring 1993).

14. Kampion, "When the Smoke Cleared" Nick Schou, "Mike Hynson, Star of 'The Endless Summer,' Resurfaces With Tales of the Brotherhood," *Orange County Weekly*, July 9, 2009. Both Hyson and Merryweather had prominent roles in *Rainbow Bridge*. "We were the hotshot surfers of the day, they knew us from the beaches we ruled. A lot of the surfers were adventurous and they liked to smoke weed," said surfer Gary Chapman. "People started to figure out that if they could find the source, it was cheap and there was quality control. The next thing you know everyone wanted it. So if you can get it and everyone wants it, it kept escalating. Even if they weren't surfers they were water people." Gary Chapman, interview by author, Sunset Beach Hawaii, February 1996.

15. Terrence Maitland and Peter McInerney, eds., *The Vietnam Experience: A Contagion of War* (Boston: Boston Publishing Co. 1982), 7; Godfrey Hodgson, in *America in Our Time: From World War II to Nixon—What Happened and Why* (New York: Doubleday, 1976), described California as "America raised to the nth power, the superlatively American part of America. . . . They take it for granted that the way they live is a preview of the new society that must come to birth" (288); Todd Gitlin, *The Sixties: Years of Hope, Days of Rage* (New York: Bantam, 1987), 13; Tom Wolfe, *Mauve Gloves & Madmen,*

Clutter & Vine (New York: Farrar, Straus & Giroux, 1976), 116; Cynthia Palmer and Michael Horowitz, eds., *Shaman Woman, Mainline Lady: Womens' Writings on the Drug Experience* (New York: William Morrow, 1982).

16. Wolfe, *Mauve Gloves & Madmen.* Sheltered from calamity, Tom Wolfe described these baby boomers as "Superkids" who knew only "the great payoff."

17. Ritter's mother, Hilde, explored alternative religions. Although she was impressed by the Indian philosopher Paramahansa Yogananda, she and her father joined the Self-Realization Fellowship and later became Christian Scientists. Later she would stress the importance of education to her children because it was "something they can never take away from you." Mike Robles*, essay, 2011. Art Robles* grew up in Los Angeles during the 1950s and described similar fears of nuclear war in an August 17, 2012 e-mail to author: "The erosive effect of that weekly, city wide, air raid siren 'test' was murderous on the fragile minds of kids raised in the golden glow of the late 50's; where white bread, 'abundance is your right' and 'God is on our side', were both preached, and accepted, as gospel. We didn't know any better. We were just following orders." As historian Todd Gitlin pointed out, "The affluent society was awash with fear of the uncontrollable." Gitlin, *The Sixties,* 22.

18. Myra McPherson, *Long Time Passing: Vietnam and the Haunted Generation* (Bloomington: Indiana University Press, 1984), 92; Gitlin, *The Sixties,* 412. As Harvard scientist James Q. Wilson noted, for a decade that began with such optimism, it ended "in an agony of bitterness and frustration." Quoted in Godfrey Hodgson, *America in Our Time: From WWII to Nixon—What Happened and Why* (New York: Doubleday, 1976), 11–12; Art Robles, e-mail to author, August 17, 2012.

19. Robles, e-mail to author, August 17, 2012. The Bixby Ranch is approximately 3,200 hectares while the Hollister Ranch is 5,700; together they comprise close to 45 kilometers of coastline; http://www.surfline.com/surfing-a-to-z/the-ranch-history_927/. Not only was the beach a favorite for surfers, in the coming years, the Hollister Ranch would become a favorite offload spot for smugglers. DEA agent Jim Conklin said, "Every doper in Santa Barbara had one of those parcels, I seized three myself."

20. Many in the counterculture who considered the New Left "square and hypocritical—middle class kids comforting themselves with plans for the future while supporting themselves with checks from Mommy in their dull-eyed present." Gitlin, *The Sixties,* 225.

21. Wolfe, *Mauve Gloves & Madmen,* 151, 163, 165; Camille Paglia, "Cults and Cosmic Consciousness," *Arion* 10, no. 3 (Winter 2003). British historian Godfrey Hodgson put it best: "Young Americans who could not conceivably be persuaded to read Milton or Pascal pored with scholarly patience over theses on the Druidic cults at Stonehenge. Their eyes watered with excitement over wild hypotheses about the legend of Atlantis." Hodgson, *America in Our Time,* 311. "It all started in California," Ken Kesey would later write, "went haywire in California and now spreads out from California like a crazy tumor under the hide of the continent." Quoted in Martin Torgoff, *Can't Find My Way Home: America in the Great Stoned Age, 1945–2000* (New York: Simon & Schuster, 78).

22. Gordon Kennedy, *Children of the Sun: A Pictorial Anthology from Germany to California 1883–1949* (Ojai, Calif.: Nivaria Press, 1998), 135–43.

23. Kennedy, *Children of the Sun,* 165–81.

24. Mike Ritter, essay, 2011. Camille Paglia made a similar point: "The psychedelic 'trip' into inner space replicated the shaman's magic journey, from which he returned with secret knowledge for his tribe." "Cults and Cosmic Consciousness," 89.

25. Lawrence Schiller, "A Remarkable Mind Drug Suddenly Spells Danger: LSD," *LIFE* magazine, March 25, 1966; Wolfe, *Mauve Gloves & Madmen*, 151.

26. Richard Davenport-Hines, *The Pursuit of Oblivion: A Global History of Narcotics* (New York: Norton, 2002), 333.

27. "Pot and Parents," *Time Magazine,* January 26, 1968.

28. Mike Ritter, essay, 2011; David Hall, phone conversation with Mike Ritter, December 2008.

29. By far the best book on the Brotherhood of Eternal Love is Nic Schou's *Orange Sunshine: The Brotherhood of Eternal Love and Its Quest to Spread Peace, Love, and Acid to the World* (New York: St. Martin's Griffin, 2011); for more on the Brotherhood's formation as a church, see 50–51. See also Stewart Tendler and David May, *The Brotherhood of Eternal Love: From Flower Power to Hippie Mafia, the Story of the LSD Counterculture* (London: Panther Books–Granada Publishing, 1984), 65; Wolfe, *Mauve Gloves & Madmen*, 163.

30. Robert Greenfield, *Timothy Leary: A Biography* (New York: Harcourt Trade Publishers, 2007), 329; Tendler and May, *The Brotherhood of Eternal Love*, 63; "Timothy Liar," *LA Weekly,* May 31, 2006; "John was sinewy and hirsute. He had a round head and soulful eyes that drooped a little at the corners. He had a wry smile and a short beard of wiry black." The core members of the Brotherhood were not college students or revolutionary poseurs; most were the "blue-collar sons of the World War Two generation, whose transplanted parents had helped to create the Southern California dream of suburbia. . . . They were the tract kids raised among the hollow echoes of formerly meaningful cultural icons which had lost their pertinence and persuasiveness within the conditions of the shallow and speedy materialism which was generated in the postwar reshuffling of society." Dion Wright, unpublished manuscript; see also Joan Didion, *The White Album* (reprint, New York: Farrar, Straus & Giroux, 2009), 47. "We were seeing the desperate attempt of a handful of pathetically unequipped children to create a community in a social vacuum. Once we had seen these children, we could no longer overlook the vacuum, no longer pretend that the society's atomization could be reversed. This was not a traditional generational rebellion. . . . These were children who grew up cut loose from the web of cousins and great-aunts and family doctors and lifelong neighbors who had traditionally suggested and enforced society's values." For more biographic material on John Griggs, see Schou, *Orange Sunshine*, 11–15.

31. Dion Wright, unpublished manuscript; for more on Griggs's first acid trip, see also Schou, *Orange Sunshine*, 21–22.

32. Tendler and May, *The Brotherhood of Eternal Love*, 63; Dion Wright, unpublished manuscript. For more on the Brotherhood's early group acid trips, see Schou, *Orange Sunshine*, 36–38. Acid chemist Owsley was not overly impressed by the Brotherhood and dismissed them as a "bunch of loose cannons on a ship of fools" (*Orange Sunshine*, 61).

33. Jim Lawton*, interview by Mike Ritter, Santa Barbara, California, July 1999; Gary Chapman, interview by author, February 1996.

34. Craig Williams, interview by Mike Ritter, Maui, Hawaii, October 1998; Green-field, *Leary*, 330–32; Tendler and May, *The Brotherhood of Eternal Love*, 70; Joe Esterhaus, "Strange Case of the Hippie Mafia," *Rolling Stone*, December 1972. For more on the early Brotherhood pot loads, see Schou, *Orange Sunshine*, 73.

35. Lawton, interview by Mike Ritter, Santa Barbara, California, July 1999; Esterhaus, "The Strange Case of the Hippie Mafia." According to their archenemy, Laguna Beach detective Neil Purcell, "trying to surveil the area was an impossible task. They had what was known as a bicycle patrol . . . every time they saw someone who looked like a police-man, they would blow the whistle and the whistle would be heard throughout the colony there, and after a while it sounded like a bunch of crickets in there with those whistles." For more on the police and Laguna Canyon, see Schou, *Orange Sunshine*, 105–6.

36. Jim Lawton, interview by Mike Ritter, Santa Barbara, California, July 1999.

37. "Intergalactic Union Dopogram," *East Village Other*, July 1968.

38. Hashish Smuggling and Passport Fraud: "The Brotherhood of Eternal Love." Hearing before the Subcommittee to Investigate the Administration of the Internal Secu-rity Act and Other Internal Security Laws of the Committee on the Judiciary, United States Senate, 93rd Cong., 1st sess., October 3, 1973 (Washington, D.C.: U.S. Govern-ment Printing Office, 1973), 4–6; "Intergalactic Union Dopogram." In his book *Flash-backs*, Leary would describe the Brotherhood members as a "group of uneducated young couples, all children from that swarm of Okies who filled up the valleys stretching out from LA. . . . They had been groomed to be gas station attendants or wives of gas station attendants" (226).

39. Ned Jones, interview by author, Pupukea, Hawaii, June 2004.

2. THE HIPPIE TRAIL

1. Richard Neville, *Play Power: Exploring the International Underground* (New York: Random House, 1970), 134; Mike Ritter, essay, 2011.

2. Mike Ritter, essay, 2011. "GIs Sending Marijuana to Pals at Home," *Bangkok Post*, September 7, 1967.

3. Mike Ritter, essay, 2011.

4. "New Death on Leary's Ranch—Tests Planned," *Oakland Tribune*, August 4, 1969; "Leary on Trial Today in LSD Death of Girl," *UPI*, December 1, 1969; "Hippie 'High Priest' Sought After Girl's Death," *UPI*, July 26, 1969. For more on Griggs's death, see Nic Schou, *Orange Sunshine: The Brotherhood of Eternal Love and Its Quest to Spread Peace, Love, and Acid to the World* (New York: St. Martin's Griffin, 2011), 191–92.

"The Brotherhood threw a jolly wake in Dodge City. I wouldn't go to it. The darkness was closing in on me, and I thought the Brothers were fools not to understand the disas-ter that had befallen them," wrote Dion Wright (unpublished manuscript). Bob Latch* described the shift in the Brotherhood in an April 2001 interview with Mike Ritter, Maui, Hawaii. "The beginning of it was a lot different; it got very hard-core, very cold. Things changed around 1970, it got more competitive and mean." To Latch, a fisherman from Northern California, the Brotherhood members of the 1970s were "way too cool," quint-essential Southern Californians: "They were very glamorous. . . . They were the rock and roll stars, but I was rocking and rolling before they were even around. Maybe that's one reason I didn't like them."

For more on the end of the 1960s, see Joan Didion, *The White Album* (reprint, New York: Farrar, Straus & Giroux, 2009), 47; D. C. Munro, "The Children's Crusade," *American Historical Review* (October 1913).

5. Terry Dawson*, "The Road to Anaraxta," x. Todd Gitlin expressed a similar senti-ment a few days after the Rolling Stones Altamont concert in an article for an under-ground paper entitled, "The End of the Age of Aquarius": "If there is so much bad acid around, why doesn't this contaminated culture, many of whose claims are based on the virtues of drugs, help its own brothers and sisters? Why do the underground papers leave it to the media narcotizers to deplore the damaging possibilities of bad drugs?" Quoted in Gitlin, *The Sixties: Years of Hope, Days of Rage* (New York: Bantam, 1987), 406.

6. David Ortiz, interviews by Mike Ritter, Santa Barbara, California, October 1999, July 2007, and various telephone conversations. Stewart Tendler and David May, *The Brotherhood of Eternal Love: From Flower Power to Hippie Mafia, the Story of the LSD Counterculture* (London: Panther Books—Granada Publishing, 1984), 125.

7. *Rainbow Bridge,* dir. Chuck Wein (Los Angeles: Transvue Pictures, 1972). Ecology, drugs, fluoride in the water, world peace, and their regular interactions with "the space people" are just a few of the issues raised. For more on the Brotherhood, Jimi Hendrix, and the making of the film *Rainbow Bridge*, see Schou, *Orange Sunshine*, 217–27.

8. Jules Witcover, *The Year the Dream Died: Revisiting 1968 in America* (New York: Warner Books, 1997), 366–67; "Richard Nixon Address," Anaheim Rally, September 16, 1968, Nixon Library, Speech File, Box 4, File 11. According to historian Alan Brinkley, the success of socially conservative Republicans like George Wallace and Richard Nixon was a clear statement that the country was "against the antiwar movement, against the counterculture, against violence and for law and order."

9. Richard Reeves, *President Nixon: Alone in the White House* (New York: Simon and Schuster, 2001). The president implored his aides to "Make it 'out' to wear long hair, smoke pot and go on the needle. Make it 'in' to indulge in lesser vices, smoking (cigars preferably non-Castro) and alcohol in reasonable quantities" (196).

10. Elaine Shannon, *Desperados: Latin Drug Lords, U.S. Lawmen, and the War Amer-ica Can't Win* (New York: Penguin,1989), 47; Kate Doyle, "Operation Intercept: The Perils of Unilateralism," *The National Security Archive*, online journal published by George Washington University, posted April 13, 2003; "Alarming Rise in Dope Traffic," *US News and World Report*, September 2, 1968; "Mexico's War on Marijuana," *US News and World Report*, December 29, 1969; "Pot: Year of the Famine," *Newsweek*, September 22, 1969; Special Presidential Task Force, Document 9: Memorandum to Bud Krogh From Tom Whitehead: Task Force Report: Narcotics, Marijuana and Dangerous Drugs—Findings and Recommendations, 6 June 1969. Tom Whitehead at this point was Special Assistant

to the President (Nixon). The Budget Bureau's addendum reads like a dissenting opin-ion; the main point was prophetic: "it suggests the possibility that our policy in this area may have more political costs than benefits and may backfire." All Nixon administration drug debate documents from folder: "Ex FG 221-28 Narcotics, Marijuana and Danger-ous Drugs [1969–70]," Box 5, FG221 Task Forces, WHCF, Nixon Presidential Materials Staff, National Archives. Charles Fuss Jr., *Sea of Grass: The Maritime Drug War 1970–1990* (Annapolis: Naval Institute Press, 1996), xv.

11. Richard Neville, *Play Power: Exploring the International Underground* (New York: Random House, 1970), 21; Robert Connell Clarke, *Hashish!* (Los Angeles: Red Eye Press, 1998), 97; Joe R. Pietri, *The King of Nepal* (Indiana Creative Arts, 2001), 10–11. Twelfth-century Persian religious leader Shayk Haydar (1155–1221) is said to have introduced can-nabis and its various preparations to the Muslim world: "God has granted you the privi-lege of knowing the secret of these leaves," he wrote. "Thus when you eat it, your dense worries may disappear and our exalted minds may become polished."

12. Mike Ritter, essay, 2011; Bob Jones, interview by Mike Ritter, Carlsbad, California, 2001.

13. Ed Gardner, interview by Mike Ritter, Maui, Hawaii, December 1999. As Joe Pietri pointed out to the author, by the 1960s most Afghan hash was made using sieves.

14. Clarke, *Hashish*, 137.

15. Ned Jones*, interview by author, Pupukea, Oahu, June 2004. Amanullah Tokhi told one smuggler, "Just put your car here and we'll take care of everything." For more on the Tokhi brothers, see Schou, *Orange Sunshine*, 88–89.

16. William Graves, "Bangkok: City of Angels," *National Geographic*, July 1973; Phongpaichit and Chris Baker, *Thailand: Economics and Politics* (Oxford: Oxford Uni-versity Press, 2002), 218–19; Rong Syamananda, *A History of Thailand* (Bangkok: Chul-alongkorn University, 1986), 116–17.

17. Graves, "Bangkok: City of Angels"; Mike Ritter, essay, 2011.

18. Mike Ritter, essay, 2011; John Burdett, *Bangkok 8* (New York: Knopf, 2003). Nov-elist John Burdett made an important and overlooked point about the Thai sex trade in an author's preface: "The sex industry in Thailand is smaller per capita than in Taiwan, the Philippines, or the United States. That it is more famous is probably because the Thais are less coy about it than many other people."

19. "Greener Grass—Grimmer Jails," *Newsweek*, June 15, 1970.

20. Jim Conklin, interview by Mike Ritter, Las Vegas, Nevada, July 2000.

21. American Robert Koke established the Kuta Beach Hotel in 1936. Because Koke had surfed in Hawaii, he imported surfboards and tried to establish an Indonesian Waikiki; Louise Koke, "Our Hotel in Bali," http://balisurfstories.wordpress.com/2010/09/27/balis-first-surfer-and-first-expat-squabble-and-first-pommie-surfer-too/.

22. Donna and Gilbert Grosvenor, "Bali by the Back Roads," *National Geographic*, November 1969.

23. Mike Ritter, essay, 2011.

24. Mike Ritter, essay, 2011. Pietri, *The King of Nepal*, 31–32.

25. Mike Ritter, essay, 2011.

3. KUTA BEACH

1. Bob Martin, interview by Mike Ritter, Maui, Hawaii, March 2001; Thomas Abercrombie, "Morocco—Land of the Farthest West," *National Geographic*, June 1971. After Spain assumed suzerainty over northern Morocco in 1912, it took 14 years to defeat Berber chieftain Abd el Krim et Khattabi, who declared a jihad against the invaders. His guerilla army killed 16,000–20,000 Spaniards in 1921 at the Battle of Annual, and after he surrendered in 1926, it took 300,000 French and Spanish soldiers to bring "The Land of Insolence" under their control.

2. Bob Martin, interview by Mike Ritter, Maui, Hawaii, March 2001.

3. James "Abdul" Monroe*, interviews by Mike Ritter, Indonesia and Andaman Islands, March and May 1999.

4 Joseph Pietri, *The King of Nepal* (Indiana Creative Arts, 2001), 18–22. "Kathmandu was the ultimate hippie paradise in those days. People smoked openly without fear, as it was legal. Hippie vans, most of which were sold in Nepal or shipped back to the west full of hash, were in abundance" (18–19).

5. Laurence Cherniak, "Great Balls of Nepalese Fire," *High Times,* January 1981.

6. James "Abdul" Monroe, interviews by Mike Ritter, March and May 1999; Pietri, *The King of Nepal*, 26–27; "Gains in the War on Against Drug Smugglers," *U.S. News and World Report,* June 21, 1971.

7. James "Abdul" Monroe, interviews by Mike Ritter, March and May 1999.

8. Nat Young, *The Complete History of Surfing: From Water to Snow* (Layton, Utah: Gibbs Smith, 2008). Bill Boyum, "Punching Out": "The concept of a professional surfer hadn't been conceived of yet. . . . We were what were then called 'soul surfers.' Loosely defined it meant we weren't interested in sharing what we had found with the rest of the world. These guys had stuck their necks out traveling and figuring things out on their own effort."

9. James "Abdul" Monroe, interviews by Mike Ritter, March and May 1999; Boyum, "Punching Out."

10. Phil Jarratt, *Mr Sunset: The Jeff Hakman Story* (Melbourne, Australia: General Publishing Group, 1997), 118–19.

11. Mike Ritter, e-mail to author, December 10, 2010; for more on "runners," see Pietri, *The King of Nepal*, 42–43.

12. "Singapore: Reluctant Nation," *National Geographic*, August 1966; The Burke Library Archives (Columbia University Libraries), Union Theological Seminary, New York, Missionary Research Library Archives: Section 4, Munshi Abdullah Papers, 1918, http://clio.cul.columbia.edu:7018/vwebv/holdingsInfo?bibId=4737108; "No mortal dared to pass through the Straits of Singapore," wrote early Malay historian Munshi Abdullah (1796–1854). "Jins and Satan even were afraid, for that was the place the pirates made use of, to sleep at, and divide their booty."

13. "We pride ourselves on offering good, fast service," one port official explained to a reporter. "There is probably less pilferage on our docks than anywhere else in the East." "Singapore: Reluctant Nation," *National Geographic*, August 1966.

14. "The trade and traders alike had an undeniable glamour. For if the risks were great, the profits were colossal," wrote Jack Turner in his book *Spice: The History of a Temptation* (New York: Vintage, 2005), 105. "From their harvest in distant tropical lands, spices arrived in the markets of Venice, Bruges, and London by an obscure tangle of routes winding halfway around the planet, serviced by distant peoples and places that seemed more myth than reality. For mystery meant profitability. . . . Hardly anyone involved in the trade knew who or what lay before the last transaction, and much the same held true all along the spice routes. . . . What was generally agreed was that spices came from a topsy-turvy world where the normal rule of European life did not apply" (5); Mike Ritter, essay, 2011.

15. Mike Ritter, essay, 2011.

16. James "Abdul" Monroe, interviews by Mike Ritter, March and May 1999. Bob Jones, interview by Mike Ritter, Carlsbad, California, May 2001.

17. Bob Jones, interview by Mike Ritter, May 2001.

18. Boyum, "Punching Out"; James "Abdul" Monroe, interviews by Mike Ritter, March and May 1999; http://www.surfersvillage.com/surfing-news/56397.

19. Mike Ritter, essay, 2011; Boyum, "Punching Out."

4. THAI STICKS

1. "Thai: The Dope of the Eighties?" *High Times*, May 1978.

2. For more on the boutique industry, see Peter Reuter, "Transnational Crime: Drug Smuggling," paper presented at conference on Transnational Crime, University of Cambridge, January 7, 2000; "Thai Sticks Newest Drug Threat," *Times Herald*, April 28, 1974. According to the reporter, Thai sticks were "three times stronger than regular marijuana."

3. Terry Dawson*, "The Road to Anaraxta." Joe Pietri makes a similar point about how marijuana traffickers rarely crossed paths with cocaine and heroin dealers in *The King of Nepal*. There was the obvious difference in price—a kilo of the finest marijuana cost no more than $2,000, while a kilo of heroin fetched $300,000—and in customers: "They were from two different worlds with two different sets of morals. The heroin users were a desperate group who would do anything to get the drug, including ripping off marijuana dealers. Cocaine was just too expensive" (3).

4. Dawson, "The Road to Anaraxta."

5. A photograph of the surfers' boxes was featured on the cover of the *Honolulu Advertiser*: "Marijuana Shipment Seized," *Honolulu Advertiser*, January 28, 1970.

6. Mike Ferguson, e-mail to author, April 9, 2003.

7. "Moscow Rules," a term used by spies operating in Moscow during the Cold War, was made famous by author John le Carré. The International Spy Museum in Washington, D.C., defines Moscow Rules as:

1. Assume nothing.

2. Never go against your gut.

3. Everyone is potentially under opposition control.

4. Don't look back; you are never completely alone.

5. Go with the flow, blend in.

6. Vary your pattern and stay within your cover.

7. Lull them into a sense of complacency.

8. Don't harass the opposition.

9. Pick the time and place for action.

10. Keep your options open.

"Super-marijuana is turning heads—even some old ones," *Honolulu Advertiser,* January 19, 1970. "It's called 'Colitas'—which means 'little tails.'"

8. Craig Williams, interview by Mike Ritter, Maui, Hawaii, October 1998.

9. Dr. Archana Upadhyay made the important point in his article "Dynamics of Smuggling in South East Asia": "The phenomenon of smuggling and the movement of contraband commodities in Southeast Asia has deep roots that reach to the very foundation of the region's historical experience. Sitting astride the land and sea routes that have traditionally connected Asia to the rest of the world, the region functions as a conduit between burgeoning Pacific economies and trading nations elsewhere on the globe." "Dynamics of Smuggling in Southeast Asia," *Dialogue* 5, no. 1 (July–September 2003). Eric Taliacozzo, *Secret Trades, Porous Borders: Smuggling and States Along a Southeast Asian Frontier, 1865–1915* (New Haven: Yale University Press, 2005); Pasuk Phongpaichit and Chris Baker, *Thailand: Economics and Politics* (Oxford: Oxford University Press, 2002), 218–19. Rong Syamananda, *A History of Thailand* (Bangkok: Chulalongkorn University, 1986), 116–17.

10. Ron Chepesiuk, *The Bangkok Connection: Trafficking Heroin from Asia to the USA* (Dunboyne, Ireland: Maverick House, 2011), 112; "In no other region of the world did so many governments promote mass drug abuse with such unanimity of means and moral certitude," wrote historian Alfred W. McCoy in *The Politics of Heroin in South East Asia* (New York: Harper & Row, 1977).

11. Jo, interview by Mike Ritter, Bangkok and Nakhon Phanom, Thailand, January 2002.

12. Jo, interview by Mike Ritter, Bangkok and Nakhon Phanom, Thailand, January 2002; Prateep Chumpon, *The History of Traditional Thai Medicine* (Bangkok: University of Bangkok Press, 2002, the author documented "kanja" as a traditional cure for sleeplessness and vomiting.

13. Hui Lin Li, "The Origin and Use of Cannabis in Eastern Asia: Their Linguistic and Cultural Implications," and Marie Martin, "Ethnobotanical Aspects of Cannabis in Southeast Asia," in Vera Rubin, ed., *Cannabis and Culture* (The Hague: Mouton, 1975), 64; Stanton Report on Drugs in Vietnam, December 1, 1970, The Vietnam Center and Archive, Item Number 2274210009, www.vietnam.ttu.edu/virtualarchive/items.php?item=2274210009. For more on Chinese knowledge and use of marijuana, see Martin Lee, *Smoke Signals: A Social History of Marijuana—Medicinal, Recreational, and Scientific* (New York: Scribner, 2012), 4–5.

14 Sambat Suthern*, interview by Mike Ritter, Bangkok and Nakhon Phanom, Thailand, January 2002.

15. Leaf Fielding, *To Live Outside the Law: Caught by Operation Julie, Britain's Biggest Drugs Bust* (London: Serpent's Tail, 2011), 182.

16. Sambat Suthern, interview by Mike Ritter, Bangkok and Nakhon Phanom, Thailand, January 2002; Peter White, "Hopes and Fears in Booming Thailand," *National Geographic*, July 1967. Self-sufficient and wary of a government that only seemed interested in taxing them, Thailand was a frontier society until the mid-twentieth century. Not only were malaria and cholera common, the jungles and forests teemed with wild elephants, tigers, crocodiles, too many poisonous snakes to name and bandits that operated with impunity as long as they were generous with the peasantry. In a 1913 article about the legendary bandit Ai Pia, *The Bangkok Post* wrote, "The common people of the country have been in no humour to assist the Police, for it is said that Ai Pia was a kind of Robin Hood, robbing only the rich and often helping the poor." From *Royalty and Commoners: Essays in Thai Administrative, Economic, and Social History*, ed. Constance Maralyn Wilson, Chrystal Stillings Smith, and George Vinal Smith (Leiden, Netherlands: Contributions to Asian Studies, 1980), 34.

17. Mike Ritter, essay, 2011.

18. Tim Nicholson*, interview by Mike Ritter, Bangkok, Thailand, January 2002; "Mary Jane in Action," *Newsweek*, November 6, 1967.

19. Jo, interview by Mike Ritter, January 2002; Sambat Suthern, interview by Mike Ritter, Bangkok and Nakhon Phanom, Thailand, January 2002.

20. As military historian John Keegan pointed out, the Vietnam War was "the first war in which drugs were plentiful" (qtd. in Myra McPherson, *Long Time Passing: Vietnam and the Haunted Generation* [New York: Doubleday, 1984], 53). William Novak wrote, "No account of marijuana use in the United States during the 1960s can fail to take Vietnam into account. At least half of the American forces in Southeast Asia sampled the local product, and this included large numbers of men from all classes and backgrounds. Vietnamese marijuana was potent, cheap, and unbelievably accessible" (*High Culture: Marijuana in the Lives of Americans* [New York: Knopf, 1980), 169.

21. Interview with Emil "Bud" Krough Jr., from *Frontline*, "The Drug Wars," October 9, 2000.

22. Samuel Lipsman and Edward Doyle, eds., *The Vietnam Experience: Fighting for Time* (Boston: Boston Publishing Co., 1983), 103, 114; "25 GIs Seized in Viet Raid," *UPI*, October 13, 1967; "In Vietnam: Mama-San Pushers v. Psyops," *Newsweek*, April 21, 1969; "Armed Forces: As Common as Chewing Gum," *Time*, March 1, 1971,

23. Quoted in John Clark Pratt, ed., *Vietnam Voices: Perspectives on the War Years 1941–1975* (Athens: University of Georgia Press, 2008), 262–63.

24. "Armed Forces: As Common as Chewing Gum," *Time*, March 1, 1971; Paul McMullen, "Marijuana Smugglers Detected," *Air Force Times*, http://www.vspa.com/k9/dm-2.htm; "Marijuana Receives USAF 'Approval,'" *Bangkok Post*, November 15, 1971.

25. "Statement of Dr. Joel Kaplan before the Senate Subcommittee to Investigate Juvenile Delinquency," March 24, 1970; Peter Brush, "Higher and Higher: Drug Use Among U.S. Forces in Vietnam," *Vietnam Magazine* 15, no. 4 (December 2002); "Thai-Based GIs Run Drug Ring," *Bangkok Post*, October 21, 1972; GI arrest statistics from Richard Davenport-Hines, *The Pursuit of Oblivion: A Global History of Narcotics* (New York: Norton, 2004), 423; "The Troubled U.S. Army in Vietnam," *Newsweek*, January 11, 1971; "The GIs'

Other Enemy: Heroin," *Newsweek*, May 24, 1971. No. 4 heroin was more refined than No. 3 heroin. .

26. The definitive study of the heroin trade in Southeast Asia remains Alfred McCoy's groundbreaking *The Politics of Heroin in South East Asia*. For more on the history of the KMT and the opium trade, see "Report of a Staff Survey Team of the Committee on Foreign Affairs House of Representatives: The U.S. Heroin Problem and Southeast Asia," January 11, 1973 (Washington, D.C.: U.S. Government Printing Office, 1973), 1–4, 13–19, 30–33; "Indochina's Heroin Traffic," *Time*, July, 19, 1971; "World Drug Traffic and Its Impact on U.S. Security: Southeast Asia," hearing before the Subcommittee to Investigate the Administration of the Internal Security Act and Other Internal Security Laws of the Committee on the Judiciary, United States Senate, 92nd Cong., 2nd sess., part 1, Southeast Asia, August 14, 1972, 16, 17, 22–39; Sadie Plant, *Writing on Drugs* (New York: Farrar, Straus, & Giroux, 2001), 258–59; "Heroin Ring Formed in Germany in 1955," *Bangkok Post*, August 14, 1976; Jack Anderson, "GI Drug Abuse Hushed Up," *Washington Post*, August 9, 1970; "CIA Shield for Thai Smuggler," *Bangkok Post*, July 19, 1975. When a Thai businessman was busted with 59 pounds of opium in Chicago, the Justice Department dropped the charges at the CIA's request. "According to a newsletter from Deputy Assistant District Attorney General John Kenney, the charges were dropped because the CIA said the situation could prove embarrassing because of Mr. Puttaporn's involvement with CIA activities in Thailand, Burma, and elsewhere"; "CIA Director William Colby has publically testified he intervened against prosecution in the case on grounds it could not be prosecuted without exposing CIA operations and employees." "CIA Dropped Drug Case to Save Name," *Bangkok Post*, July 31, 1975. Legendary CIA paramilitary officer Tony Poshepny accused Laotian Major General Vang Pao of "making millions 'cos he had his own source of, uh, avenue for his own, uh, heroin." *The Search for Kurtz*, dir. Adrian Levy (Non Fiction Films, 1999).

27. U.S. Congress, Senate, Committee on the Judiciary, Subcommittee to Investigate Juvenile Delinquency, Hearing on Drug Abuse in the Armed Forces, Part 21 (Washington, D.C.: Government Printing Office, 1971), testimony of Dr. Joel Kaplan, March 24, 1970; "GI Drug Use Rises Fivefold," *Bangkok Post*, October 14, 1972.

28. Lipsman and Doyle, eds., *The Vietnam Experience*, 104. Although only one American was killed by enemy fire at Cam Ranh Bay in 1970–71, fifteen American servicemen died from drug overdoses during that same period; "The New Public Enemy No. 1," *Time*, June 28, 1971; Murphy testified, "Unfortunately, the longer it takes to bring this under control, the more difficult it will be to control it in the United States," *Congressional Record*, April 27, 1971; "The Heroin Plague: What Can Be Done?" *Newsweek*, July 5, 1971; "New Withdrawal Costs," *Time*, June 7, 1971.

29. "Ex-ISM Student Dead in Soi," *Bangkok Post*, April 20, 1972; "Pot Luck for US Youths," *Bangkok Post*, April 7, 1972; "'Halt Drugs or Else,'" March 8, 1972, *UPI*; "New Unit to Probe Narcotics," *Bangkok Post*, October 7, 1972.

30. For the text of the Shafer Report see http://www.druglibrary.org/schaffer/library/studies/nc/ncmenu.htm; for more on the Shafer Report, see Lee, *Smoke Signals*, 128.

31. Jim Conklin, interview by Mike Ritter, Las Vegas, Nevada, July 2000.

5. PATTAYA BEACH GROUND ZERO

1. Lek, interview by Mike Ritter, Chiang Mai, Thailand, April 1999.

2. Pasuk Phongpaichit and Chris Baker, *Thailand: Economics and Politics* (Oxford: Oxford University Press, 2002), 37, 41, 273, 303; Peter White, "Hopes and Fears in Booming Thailand," *National Geographic*, July 1967.

3. "Pattaya Beach and Thailand," Liberty Information Guide, USS *Kitty Hawk*, U.S. Overseas Diplomacy Program; Mike Ritter, essay, 2011.

4. Mike Ritter, essay, 2011.

5. Tim Nicholson*, interview by author, Bangkok, Thailand, January 2006.

6. Dave Kattenburg, *Foxy Lady: Truth, Memory and the Death of Western Yachtsmen in Democratic Kampuchea* (Toronto: The Key Publishing House, 2011), 169. The Vietnam veteran was one of many who said that smuggling pot on sailboats during the 1970s "seemed like a Robin Hood sort of thing."

7. Michael Forwell and Lee Bullman, *Blowback* (London: Sidgwick and Jackson, 2009), 27–28; "Smuggling—the Emphasis Shifts," *Sydney Morning Herald*, February 3, 1970; "Build-Up of Drug Patrol," *Sydney Morning Herald*, November 3, 1974.

8. Sally Waugh*, telephone conversation with Mike Ritter, notes, July 1999.

9. Sally Waugh, telephone conversation with Mike Ritter, notes, July 1999.

10. Tim Nicholson, interview by author, Bangkok, Thailand, January 2006; Peter Hutton, conversation with author, Annandale on Hudson, New York, 2010; Mike Ritter, essay, 2011.

11. James "Abdul" Monroe*, interview by Mike Ritter, Indonesia and Andaman Islands, March and May 1999.

12. Mike Ritter, essay, 2011. Jo, interview with Mike Ritter, Bangkok and Nakhon Phanom, Thailand, January 2002. Beginning in 1961, Thailand allowed the United States to build bases and launch airstrikes; "The U.S. military establishment in Thailand initially consisted of five major air bases and eventually about 50,000 U.S. military personnel. The bases were located at Don Muang, the headquarters of the Royal Thai Air Force, adjacent the main civilian airport of Thailand, located 17 miles north of Bangkok; Korat, located at Thailand's third largest city by the same name, about 117 miles northeast of Bangkok; Nakhon Phanon [*sic*] in northeast Thailand, next to the Laotian border in a politically unstable area; Tahkli, about 160 miles northeast of Bangkok, the smallest town adjacent to a United States Air Force–occupied base; and Ubon, a Royal Thai airbase also in the northeast part of Thailand.... Most of the 50,000 U.S. troops were in Thailand to support the airbases and logistics network, but U.S. personnel also included counter-insurgency advisors, technical advisors, training consultants and professional consultants. To gain a military presence in Thailand, however, Uncle Sam had to agree to maintain a low profile." Ron Chepesiuk, *The Bangkok Connection: Trafficking Heroin from Asia to the USA* (Dunboyne, Ireland: Maverick House, 2011), 65–66.

13. John Parten, interview with Mike Ritter, Ketchum, Idaho, October 1999.

14. John Parten, interview with Mike Ritter, Ketchum, Idaho, October 1999.

15. John Parten, interview with Mike Ritter, Ketchum, Idaho, October 1999; "When he [Spreckels] finally allowed his inheritance to fall upon him, Bunker immediately established 'branch offices' around the globe. Hotel George V in Paris, Hotel Edward in South Africa, Yacht Harbor Towers in Honolulu, Kuilima Estates in Kahuku, Sunset Tower in Hollywood. . . . Surfing remained a passion, but the earlier simplicity of his monk-like existence was replaced with vengeful, spectacular excess." Art Brewer and C. R. Stecyk III, *Bunker Spreckels: Surfing's Divine Prince of Decadence* (Cologne: Taschen, 2007), 16, 77; Richard Neville, *Play Power: Exploring the International Underground* (New York: Random House, 1970), 129.

16. John Parten, interview by Mike Ritter, Ketchum, Idaho, October 1999; Abdul, interview by Mike Ritter, Indonesia and Andaman Islands, March and May 1999; Bob Jones, interview by Mike Ritter, Carlsbad, California, May 2001.

17. Phil Jarrat, *Mr Sunset* (Loxahatchie, Fla.: Gen-X Publishing, 1996), 134–35; Wayne Rabbit Bartholomew with Tim Baker, *Bustin' Down the Door: The Surf Revolution of '75* (Sydney, Australia: HarperCollins, 2002), 103; Young, *Nat's Nat and That's That*, 262–65. "Big and blond, Eddie loved the sun; the only protection he used was a small green leaf he moistened with spittle and stuck to his nose." Mike Ritter best remembered his bamboo flute and the loud out-of-tune notes that it produced. "I remember seeing Ed returning from the beach, cross-legged on top of the roof of a public bus, leaf on his nose, notes screeching from the flute," said Ritter. "When he finished blowing one of his obnoxious melodies, Ed would return a fat ugly roach to his lips, where it remained."

18. Abdul, interview by Mike Ritter, Indonesia and Andaman Islands, March and May 1999.

19. John Parten, interview by Mike Ritter, Ketchum, Idaho, October 1999.

20. "Nine Arrested in WA drug raid," *Sydney Morning Herald*, December 29, 1976.

21. Kenneth MacLeish, "The Top End of Down Under," *National Geographic*, February 1973; John Parten, interview by Mike Ritter, Ketchum, Idaho, October 1999.

22. "How the 'Full Moon Drug Syndicate' Eclipsed Mr. Asia," *Sydney Morning Herald*, August 17, 1985; "Riley the Prime Mover, Court Told," *Sydney Morning Herald*, July 4, 1978; "Second Raid Finds Drugs Worth $30m," *Sydney Morning Herald*, June 17, 1978; "Former Detective Jailed," *Sydney Morning Herald*, October 10, 1978; "Tait May Name Drug Syndicate Leaders," *Sydney Morning Herald*, May 25, 1979; "Riley Says He Lied About Drugs Role," *Sydney Morning Herald*, March 27, 1980; Kirk Owers, "Wasted," *Waves Magazine*, January 1, 2011.

23. David Ortiz, interview by Mike Ritter, Santa Barbara, California, October 1999.

6. THE GREAT CIRCLE ROUTE AND THE SEA OF GRASS

1. Craig Williams, interview by Mike Ritter, Maui, Hawaii, October 1998; Tim Nicholson*, interview by Mike Ritter, Bangkok, Thailand, January 2002; David Ortiz, interview by Mike Ritter, Santa Barbara, California, October 1999.

2. The Hollister Ranch became a favorite offload site for smugglers of all sorts due to the miles of private coastline. Not only numerous loads of marijuana were offloaded there by Ortiz and others; one surfer witnessed a boat pull up and several Asian men in suits with briefcases wade to shore.

3. John Parten, interview by Mike Ritter, Ketchum, Idaho, October 1999.

4. David Ortiz, interview by Mike Ritter, Santa Barbara, California, October 1999 and July 2007, and various telephone conversations.

5. John Parten, interview by Mike Ritter, Ketchum, Idaho, October 1999.

6. John Parten, interview by Mike Ritter, Ketchum, Idaho, October 1999.

7. Jo, interview by Mike Ritter, Bangkok and Nakhon Phanom, Thailand, January 2002. Lek, interview by Mike Ritter, Chiang Mai, Thailand, April 1999.

8. Tim Nicholson, interview by Mike Ritter, Bangkok, Thailand, January 2002. Lek, interview by Mike Ritter, Chiang Mai, Thailand, January 2002.

9. Tim Nicholson, interview by Mike Ritter, Bangkok, Thailand, January 2002.

10. Mike Carter, interview by Mike Ritter, Mendocino, California, September 2000.

11. Mike Carter, interview by Mike Ritter, Mendocino, California, September 2000. "In 1977, the Mexican government allowed the US government to spray their pot and poppy fields with the herbicide Paraquat. Although the effort was successful in both wiping out plants and scaring pot smokers, ultimately, smugglers simply found others markets, most notably, Columbia and Thailand. Soon pot smokers, used to the higher quality marijuana, no longer wanted Mexican." Charles Fuss Jr., *Sea of Grass: The Maritime Drug War 1970–1990* (Annapolis: Naval Institute Press, 1996), 51–52. The largest load ever seized by law enforcement was the 160 tons found aboard the *Don Emilio* in 1976 (37). For more on Lynn Mizer and Donald Steinberg's operation, see 38, 52. For more on Norman's Cay, see 60.

12. "Thai Marijuana Smugglers at the Hearst Ranch," *Valley Morning Star*, November 2, 1976.

13. Carter found a suitable cove with a large rock that sat just offshore in six meters of water. He paddled a large chain out on his boogie board, wrapped it all the way around the rock, shackled the ends together, and hooked them to a snatch block. A week before the load was due to come in, he set the anchors, tensioned the cable, and tested everything. Once he decided it was good to go, he slacked everything so that it was barely underwater but totally invisible. Initially, he used a clothesline system to offload; it consisted of a loop of line moved through anchored pulleys and was powered by a muffled engine. The mother ship would drop a stern anchor, fasten the pulley, and hook the sealed plastic bags full of pot to the clothesline that would carry them back to the beach.

7. THE GOLD RUSH

1. Mike Ritter, e-mail to author, July 23, 2010; for more on the Shaffer brothers, see Brian O'Day, *High: Confessions of an International Drug Smuggler* (New York: Other Press, 2006): "The younger brother, Chris, was a lady-killer. . . . The nautical end of the

Shaffer brothers' empire, a sailor-adventurer and the man with the foreign contacts. Bill was the slim, blue-eyed business Machiavellian, formidable if joyless. He had recently completed a year living in a tent on the roof of his mansion, smoking base brought up to him by hookers" (266–67).

2. The person arguing with Shaffer was longtime smuggler "Tahoe Tommy" Smith. Smith was involved in the extremely high-profile Claude Deboc case; see http://www .johnknock.com/images/OPR_Report_of_Investigation_11–5–94_john_marcello.pdf. "Ex-Agent's Death Leaves Questions," *The Gainesville Sun*, April 11, 2000.

3. Although most pot smugglers refused to smuggle cocaine, most were not against the recreational use of the drug. For more on the negative effect of cocaine use on pot smugglers, see Jason Ryan, *Jackpot: High Times, High Seas, and the Sting That Launched the War on Drugs* (Guilford, Conn.: Lyons Press, 2011), 96–98.

4. Mike Ritter, essay, 2011.

5. Tim Nicholson*, interview by Mike Ritter, Bangkok, Thailand, January 2002; Mike Ritter, essay, 2011; Lek, interview by Mike Ritter, Isan, Thailand, July 2000.

6. Mike Ritter, essay, 2011.

7. James "Abdul" Monroe*, interview by Mike Ritter, Indonesia and Andaman Islands, March and May 1999. California smuggler Roger "Chip" Frye smuggled 5–10 tons at a time in a bladder that fit inside fuel trucks that went to a leased oil yard in Carson, California, where the trailers were place on trains that went all over the United States. His border payoffs were one million dollars per month, and he would import as much as 25 tons a week. One of his former associates compared their organization to UPS: "I would get a phone call, we'd do 2 to 2.5 tons, put them on a flatcar, and ship them around the U.S."

8. Lek, interview by Mike Ritter, Isan, Thailand, July 2000; Jo, interview by Mike Ritter, Bangkok and Nakhon Phanom, Thailand, January 2002.

9. James "Abdul" Monroe, interview by Mike Ritter, Indonesia and Andaman Islands, March and May 1999.

10. Jim Lawton*, interview by Mike Ritter, Santa Barbara, California, July 1999.

11. Jim Lawton, interview by Mike Ritter, Santa Barbara, California, July 1999.

12. Stefan Eklof, *Pirates in Paradise: A Modern History of Southeast Asia's Maritime Marauders* (Copenhagen: NIAS Press, 2006), 5. "Cargo Ship Robbed in Pirate Attack," *Bangkok Post,* August 26, 1976; "20 Armed Robbers Hold up Foreign Tanker Captain," *Bangkok Post*, September 4, 1974; "Pirates Murder Ship's Captain," *Bangkok Post*, March 15, 1975; "Pirates Attack Refugees 4 Times in 8 Days," *Bangkok Post*, June 7, 1980; C. R. Boxer, "Piracy in the South China Sea," *History Today* (December 1980).

13. C. R. Boxer, "Piracy in the South China Sea," *History Today* (December 1980):19–22; Mike Ritter, essay, 2011; Eklof, *Pirates in Paradise*.

14. Eklof, *Pirates in Paradise*, 5.

15. Jim Lawton, interview by Mike Ritter, Santa Barbara, California, July 1999; for more on sailor smugglers, see Dave Kattenburg, *Foxy Lady: Truth, Memory and the Death of Western Yachtsmen in Democratic Kampuchea* (Toronto: The Key Publishing House, 2011).

16. James "Abdul" Monroe, interview by Mike Ritter, Indonesia and Andaman Islands, March and May 1999; David Hall, telephone conversation with Mike Ritter, tape

recording, December 2008; "Yacht Drama Off Vietnam Coast," *Bangkok Post*, October 14, 1977. Sally Waugh* and her two-man crew were also arrested by the Vietnamese; however, her father was a personal friend of Cyrus Vance and they were released after a month in custody. "Yachtsmen Towed to Saigon," *Bangkok Post*, October 15, 1977; "Brillig Crew Fined for Pot," *Bangkok Post*, January 12, 1978, "The sources said 600 kilos" (1,320 pounds); "Brillig's Crew 'Held for Drugs," *Bangkok Post,* November 10, 1977.

8. PIRATES AND PERILS

1. Mike Ritter, essay, 2011; for more on the history of the Khmer Rouge, see: David Chandler, *Voices from S-21: Terror and History in Pol Pot's Secret Prison* (Berkeley: University of California Press, 1999); Peter Maguire, *Facing Death in Cambodia* (New York: Columbia University Press, 2005). The Khmer Rouge's most harden killers were taken from their parents and indoctrinated. "They did not make good killers because of their class, they made good killers because of they were young and you could impress upon them what needed to be done," explained Khmer Rouge death camp commandant Brother Duch.

2. Dave Kattenbus, *Foxy Lady: Truth, Memory, and the Death of Western Yachtsmen in Democratic Kampuchea* (Toronto: Key Publishing House, 2011), 159–60, 229.

3. Ron Jackson*, phone conversation with Mike Ritter, July 2002, notes; all of the facts about Jackson's sailboat were confirmed in an e-mail by Camper & Nicholsons Boatyard.

4. Ron Jackson, phone conversation with Mike Ritter, July 2002, notes; John Hagee*, phone conversation with Mike Ritter, July 2000, notes; "Searching for Answers," *Cambodia Daily*, May 7–8, 2005.

5. Confession of Christopher Edward Delance, Documentation Center of Cambodia, Phnom Penh, Cambodia; Nek Long*, interview by author, Kompong Speu, Cambodia, May 2005; for more on the *Mayaguez*, see Ralph Wetterhahn, *The Last Battle*: *The Mayaguez Incident and the End of the Vietnam War* (Cambridge, Mass.: Da Capo Press, 2001). Two other American sailors, James Clark and Lance McNamara, were also attempting to smuggle Thai marijuana and were captured by the Khmer Rouge in 1977 and sent to S-21. According to Clark's "confession," he and McNamara were sailing the fiberglass sloop *Mary K* near an island off central Cambodia when a wooden fishing boat appeared in the distance and opened fire. The *Mary K* was hit and nearly sunk by a 20-mm cannon shell. Ung Pech, one of the S-21 survivors, recalled hearing an American prisoner cry out in pain as a teenaged guard dragged him across the prison's courtyard by his beard. He overheard the guards discussing their fate: "Those Americans brought here will be executed after interrogation." After weeks of torture and interrogations, Clark broke down and claimed to be working for the CIA, with drug smuggling only his cover. Shortly thereafter, James Clark and Lance McNamara were executed.

6. Sok Sann*, interview by author, Phnom Penh, Cambodia, May 2005.

7. Meng Try Ea and Sorya Sim, *Victims and Perpetrators: Testimony of Young Khmer Rouge Cadres* (Phnom Penh: Documentation Center of Cambodia, 2001), 7, 11.

8. Meng Try Ea and Sorya Sim, *Victims and Perpetrators? Testimony of Young Khmer Rouge Cadres* (Phnom Penh: Documentation Center of Cambodia, 2001), 7, 16; Marie Martin, *Cambodia: A Shattered Society* (Berkeley: University of California Press, 1994), 182.

9. Historian David Chandler points out that friendship "provided little or no security, and patronage could be withdrawn at any moment. Every act could be construed as political" (*Voices from S-21*, 87). Former S-21 head guard Him Huy admitted years later, "We were all spying on each other." Him Huy, interview by author, Phnom Penh, Cambodia, March 14, 1997.

10. Chandler, *Voices from S-21*, 8, 22, 25.

11. S-21 Prison Torture Manual, courtesy of Tuol Sleng Museum of Genocide, Phnom Penh, Cambodia; Chandler, *Voices from S-21, p. 110.*

12. Chandler, *Voices From S-21*, 24, 134.

13. Confession of Michael Scott Deeds, Documentation Center of Cambodia, Phnom Penh, Cambodia; Confession of Christopher Edward Delance, Documentation Center of Cambodia, Phnom Penh, Cambodia.

14. Confession of Christopher Edward Delance, Documentation Center of Cambodia, Phnom Penh, Cambodia.

15. According to war crimes investigator Craig Etcheson, "The Khmer Rouge leadership realized those Americans were hot potatoes, so they took special measures to dispose of their remains secretly—though we now know the secret." Interview by author, Phnom Penh, Cambodia, August 10, 2002; for Duch's testimony on Deeds and Delance, see also Heather Goldsmith, "Duch Remains on the Hot Seat," *Cambodia Tribunal Monitor*, April 2, 2012, http://www.cambodiatribunal.org/blog/2012/04/duch-remains-hot-seat.

16. Mike Ritter, phone interview by author, January 10, 2001; John Hagee, phone conversation with Mike Ritter, July 2000. Karl Deeds, interview by Peter Maguire and Mike Ritter, Molokai, Hawaii, March 31, 1998.

17. Bill Bell, letter to the *Los Angeles Times,* May 5, 2002. Dean Temper*, phone conversation with Mike Ritter, June 2000.

18. "After receiving photographs of the two Westerners in a cache of 1,427 anonymously donated S-21 inmate portraits last month, Documentation Center of Cambodia director Youk Chhang suspected the two were DeLance and former Phnom Penh French Embassy employee Andre Gaston Courtigne. To find out if one of the photos was DeLance, Youk reached out to author Peter Maguire, who researched the killing of Westerners at S-21 in his book *Facing Death in Cambodia*. Maguire told Youk he had confirmed from two independent sources that the photo shows the face of DeLance. Reached by the *Post* via email, yesterday, Maguire declined to comment about the case, citing respect for the families involved." Joseph Freeman, "Western Inmate Identified in S-21 Portraits," *Phnom Penh Post*, September 3, 2012.

19. Craig Williams, interview by Mike Ritter, Maui, Hawaii, October 1998.

20. "Panic Over Paraquat," *Time*, May 1, 1978. Charles Fuss Jr., *Sea of Grass: The Maritime Drug War 1970–1990* (Annapolis: Naval Institute Press, 1996), 61.

21. Bob Martin, interview by Mike Ritter, Maui, Hawaii, March 2001.

22. Bob Martin, interview by Mike Ritter, Maui, Hawaii, March 2001.

9. MULTITONS AND MOTHER SHIPS

1. "Strange Doings Led to 'Pot' Raid," *Los Angeles Times*, January 8, 1978; "Country Boy Outslicks Big-City Drug Smugglers," *Los Angeles Times*, February 21, 1979; "Elaborate Smuggling Plot Leads to Jail," *Los Angeles Times*, January 27, 1979.

2. "Raid Could Provide Clue to Nationwide Drug Traffic," *Los Angeles Times*, January 3, 1978; Charles Fuss Jr., *Sea of Grass: The Maritime Drug War* (Annapolis: Naval Institute Press, 1996), 56. There are some factual discrepancies (size of the boat and load) between the newpaper accounts and Charles Fuss Jr.'s version.

3. Tim Nicholson*, interview by Mike Ritter, Bangkok, Thailand, January 2002.

4. John Parten, interview by Mike Ritter, Ketchum, Idaho, October 1999.

5. Mike Ferguson, interview by author, Pupukea, Hawaii, June 2004.

6. Mike Ferguson, interview by author, Pupukea, Hawaii, June 2004; "6 Area Men Charged as Pot Conspirators," *The Miami News*, February 10, 1982.

7. James Mills, *The Underground Empire* (New York: Doubleday, 1986), 112.

8. Mills, *The Underground Empire*, 125; Mike Ferguson, interview by author, Pupukea, Hawaii, June 2004.

9. Mike Ferguson, interview by author, Pupukea, Hawaii, June 2004.

10. For more on Hobson see U.S. v. Antonio E. Bascaro, Patrick Waldrop, Russell Hobson III et al., 742 F2d 1335.

11. "'Sunburn' Trial Witness Details Drug Operation," *Palm Beach Post*, March 18, 1982. Law enforcement estimated the defendants imported 1.2 million pounds of marijuana into the United States between 1977 and 1981; Phil Jarrat, *Mr Sunset: The Jeff Hakman Story* (Los Angeles: General Publishing Group, 1997).

12. Tom LeCompte, *The Last Sure Thing: The Life and Times of Bobby Riggs* (Kent, Ohio: Black Squirrel Books, 2003), 112.

13. James "Abdul" Monroe*, interview by Mike Ritter, Indonesia and Andaman Islands, March and May 1999.

14. Abdul, interview by Mike Ritter, Indonesia and Andaman Islands, March and May 1999.

15. Abdul, interview by Mike Ritter, Indonesia and Andaman Islands, March and May 1999.

16. Ed Bridgely*, interview by Mike Ritter, Palm Springs, California, July 2000. Bridgely was not the only person swimming across the border; see "Seventh Swimmer Sought in Marijauna Smuggling," *UPI*, November 11, 1970: "Customs officials said Tuesday they are seeking a seventh suspect in connection with a marijuana smuggling operation that used ocean swimmers to bring the drug from Mexico."

17. Ed Bridgely, interview by Mike Ritter, Palm Springs, California, July 2000; "Millionaire Drug Dealer Makes Deal," *Los Angeles Times*, May 9, 1983. For more on the origins of the Coronado Company and original partners, see: 749 F.2d 581, 17 Fed. R. Evid. Serv. 447, United States of America, Plaintiff-Appellee v. Richard Virgil BIBBERO, Jr., Defendant-Appellant. UNITED STATES of America, Plaintiff-Appellee v. James Paul

Marshall, Defendant-Appellant, Nos. 83-5073, 83-5074, United States Court of Appeals, Ninth Circuit. Submitted Dec. 5, 1983. Decided Dec. 14, 1984.

18. Ed Bridgely, interview by Mike Ritter, Palm Springs, California, July 2000; "Millionaire Drug Dealer Makes Deal," *Los Angeles Times*, May 9, 1983.

19. Ed Bridgely, interview by Mike Ritter, Palm Springs, California, July 2000; "Millionaire Drug Dealer Makes Deal," *Los Angeles Times*, May 9, 1983.

20. Ed Bridgely, interview by Mike Ritter, Palm Springs, California, July 2000.

21. Jim Lawton*, interview by Mike Ritter, Santa Barbara, California, July 1999. Ed Bridgely, interview by Mike Ritter, Palm Springs, California, July 2000.

22. Ed Bridgely, interview by Mike Ritter, Palm Springs, California, July 2000.

23. Ed Bridgely, interview by Mike Ritter, Palm Springs, California, July 2000.

24. Ed Bridgely, interview by Mike Ritter, Palm Springs, California, July 2000; "Millionaire Drug Dealer Makes Deal," *Los Angeles Times*, May 9, 1983.

25. Jim Conklin, interview by Mike Ritter, Las Vegas, Nevada, July 2000. Ed Bridgely, interview by Mike Ritter, Palm Springs, California, July 2000.

26. Abdul, interview by Mike Ritter, Indonesia and Andaman Islands, March and May 1999. Ed Bridgely, interview by Mike Ritter, Palm Springs, California, July 2000.

27. Abdul, interview by Mike Ritter, Indonesia and Andaman Islands, March and May 1999.

10. THE DEA GAINS GROUND

1. Mike Ritter, essay, 2011. Mike Ritter, e-mail to author, May 5, 2011. The source of the fable is unknown, but a similar tale called "The Farmer and the Viper" appears in Aesop's Fables.

2. James "Abdul" Monroe*, interview by Mike Ritter, Indonesia and Andaman Islands, March and May 1999.

3. Boyum, "Punching Out." Although retired federal agent Charles Fuss Jr. concedes that pot smugglers rarely smuggled cocaine, he refuses to admit a qualitative difference between the two drugs. "Marijuana smugglers, as a rule, were not 'Cocaine Cowboys,' but they would soon be lumped with their cocaine relatives in the government's crusade against narcotics. . . . Many American grass smugglers wanted nothing to do with cocaine. They had no moral qualms about importing tons of pot but expressed revulsion at the idea of carrying a few kilos of coke, a dangerous drug!" Fuss, *Sea of Grass: The Maritime Drug War 1970–1990* (Annapolis: Naval Institute Press, 1996), 69.

4. Ed Bridgely*, interview with Mike Ritter, Palm Springs, California, July 2000; "Indictments Target Big Drug Operation," *AP*, February 24, 1983; "Millionaire Drug Dealer Makes Deal," *Los Angeles Times*, May 9, 1983. For more on the Neah Bay load, see: Garrett v. United States, 471 U.S. 773, 105 S. Ct. 2407, 85 L.Ed. 2d 764, Jonathan GARRETT, Petitioner, v. UNITED STATES, No. 83-1842. Argued Jan. 16, 1985. Decided June 3, 1985. Rehearing Denied Aug. 28, 1985.

5. Ed Bridgely, interview with Mike Ritter, Palm Springs, California, July 2000.

6. Ed Bridgely, interview with Mike Ritter, Palm Springs, California, July 2000.

7. Ed Bridgely, interview with Mike Ritter, Palm Springs, California, July 2000.

8. Jim Lawton*, interview with Mike Ritter, Santa Barbara, California, July 1999. Ed Bridgely, interview by Mike Ritter.,Palm Springs, California, July 2000.

9. Ed Bridgely, interview by Mike Ritter, Palm Springs, California, July 2000; "Millionaire Drug Dealer Makes Deal," *Los Angeles Times*, May 9, 1983. Jim Lawton, interview by Mike Ritter, Santa Barbara, California, July 1999.

10. Jim Conklin, interview by Mike Ritter, Las Vegas, Nevada, July 2000.

11. Ed Bridgely, interview by Mike Ritter, Palm Springs, California, July 2000; Jim Conklin, interview by Mike Ritter, Las Vegas, Nevada, July 2000; "Endless Bummer," *People Magazine,* September 19, 1994; Nic Schou, "Mike Hynson, Co-Star of 'The Endless Summer,' Resurfaces with Tales of the Brotherhood," *Orange County Weekly,* September 19, 1994.

12. Jim Conklin, interview by Mike Ritter, Las Vegas, Nevada, July 2000; "Millionaire Drug Dealer Makes Deal," *Los Angeles Times*, May 9, 1983.

13. Jim Conklin, interview by Mike Ritter, Las Vegas, Nevada, July 2000.

14. "American, Dane Held After Chase," *Bangkok Post*, May 31, 1979; "Two Face Possible Execution," *Bangkok Post*, June 1, 1979. In many ways, radios were more of a concern to the Thai government than marijuana because they were associated with communist sedition.

15. "Another Huge Haul of Marijuana," *Bangkok Post*, October 23, 1980; "Police Seize Three Tons of Marijuana," *Bangkok Post*, October 22, 1980; "Big Marijuana Trial Opens," *Bangkok Post*, February 17, 1981; "Drug Suspect Denies Offer of B600,000 for Release," *Bangkok Post*, February 21, 1981; "Five in Marijuana Ring Get 30–45 Years," *Bangkok Post* October 21, 1981; "American: I'm No Drug Financier," *Bangkok Post*, June 18, 1981; "Court Turns Down Appeal by Drug Trio," *Bangkok Post*; "Captain Files Appeal in Drugs Case," *Bangkok Post,* November 4, 1981.

16. Abdul, interview by Mike Ritter, Indonesia and Andaman Islands, March and May 1999; Jim Conklin, interview by Mike Ritter, Las Vegas, Nevada, July 2000. For more on Sicilia-Falcon, see Elaine Shannon, *Desperados: Latin Drug Lords, U.S. Lawmen, and the War America Can't Win* (New York: Penguin, 1988), 67.

17. "End of the Coronado Company," *Newsweek*, July 4, 1984; Ed Bridgely, interview by Mike Ritter, Palm Springs, California, July 2000. 718 F.2d 332, UNITED STATES of America, Plaintiff-Appellany v. David Rowland Lee VAUGHN, Defendant-Appellee No. 82-1717, United States Court of Appeals, Ninth Circuit, Argued and Submitted April 6, 1983. Decided Oct. 14, 1983.

18. Jim Lawton, interview by Mike Ritter, Santa Barbara, California, July 1999. "He [Conklin] knew that the 'Santa Barbara Five,' the guys that we were, the beach crew guys, were all surfers and fishermen."

19. Abdul, interview by Mike Ritter, Indonesia and Andaman Islands, March and May 1999; "We indicted James Monroe; Monroe was a big fish," said Agent Conklin.

20. William Meyers, "California's Counterculture Counselor," *High Times*, September 1985; "Counterculture's Warrior Lawyer Tony J. Serra's Specialty Is Outlaws and He's Made His Reputation Defending Them," *Los Angeles Times*, May 3, 1989; "DeMassa, Vil-

lar Bury Hatchet in Secret Deal," *Los Angeles Times*, July 26, 1986; Abdul, interview by Mike Ritter, Indonesia and Andaman Islands, March and May 1999; Lawyer Barry Tarlow described Villar as "a master manipulator, a user of people. . . . He is a man who is utterly without a conscience"; "In 1982, Villar, who is now 46, pleaded guilty to three counts of conspiracy to import marijuana and was sentenced to years in federal prison. But, five months later, he became a government informant implicating DeMassa and others in the conspiracy." "Offshoot of Coronado Co. Case, DeMassa Drug Trial Gets Off to a Testy Start," *Los Angeles Times*, October 17, 1985.

21. Abdul, interview by Mike Ritter, Indonesia and Andaman Islands, March and May 1999.

11. CONFIDENTIAL INFORMANT

1. Mike Ritter, essay, 2011.

2. Mike Ritter, essay, 2011.

3. What was sold as sticks were mostly crude imitations. As *High Times* pointed out, "the closest these sticks had ever been to Thailand was a warehouse in western Columbia where someone had hired some native labor to tie some strands of Columbian twine around some wooden match-stick size sticks"; "The star of this short season, however, has been what has become a welcome staple: pressed stickless Thai," wrote *High Times* magazine in their 1982 epitaph for the Thai stick. "The point is, very little real Thai comes on sticks anymore . . . what goes as Thai these days is a scandal." "Taster's Journal: Delicacies from the Drought and Other Observations," *High Times*, May 1982.

4. Mike Ritter, essay, 2011; "*Boutwell* Defendants Sentenced," *High Times*, October 1983. For more on the *Orca* capture, see: UNITED STATES v. C Humphrey Wc D, 759 F. 2d 743, United States of America, Plaintiff-Appellee, v. John C. Humphrey, W.C. Garbez, and Robert D. Smith, Defendants-Appellants. Nos. 83-3023, 83-3025 and 83-3026, United States Court of Appeals, Ninth Circuit. Argued and Submitted Aug. 17, 1983. Decided May 2, 1985. See also Charles Fuss Jr., Fuss, *Sea of Grass: The Maritime Drug War 1970–1990* (Annapolis: Naval Institute Press, 1996), 102. For more on the disabling of the *Boutwell*, see: "Sabotage! Coast Guard Reveals Tale of Drugs, Intrigue at Sea," *AP*, July 7, 1982.

5. David Hall, telephone interview by Mike Ritter, December 2008.

6. Mike Ritter, essay, 2011.

7. "Eight Indicted in Two Drug Cases," *Eugene Register Guard*, February 5, 1983; "Suspect Pleads Not Guilty to Pot Smuggling Charge," *Eugene Register Guard*, June 23, 1987; "Anonymous Tip Leads Police to Suspected Drug Smuggler," *Eugene Register Guard*, May 21, 1987.

8. Jim Conklin, interview by Mike Ritter, Las Vegas, Nevada, July 2000.

9. Jim Conklin, interview by Mike Ritter, Las Vegas, Nevada, July 2000.

10. Jim Conklin, interview by Mike Ritter, Las Vegas, Nevada, July 2000.

11. Jim Conklin, interview by Mike Ritter, Las Vegas, Nevada, July 2000.

12. Jim Conklin, interview by Mike Ritter, Las Vegas, Nevada, July 2000.

CONCLUSION

1. DEA Report, "M/V Encounter Bay, M/V Lloyd B. Gore, Brian Daniels," 1988. See also: "Pot-laden Ship Towed to Shore," *AP*, July 7, 1988; "The Huge Pot Deal That Went up in Smoke," *Seattle Post-Intelligencer*, July 27, 28, 1988. I was also able to watch a videotape of the entire bust thanks to James Conklin.

2. James "Abdul" Monroe*, interviews by Mike Ritter, Indonesia and Andaman Islands, March 25, 1999 and May 1999.

3. Jim Lawton*, interview by Mike Ritter, Santa Barbara, California, July 1999.

4. Jon Robinson, "Smuggler Tells His Tale," *Santa Cruz Sentinel*, April 10, 1990.

5. John Parten, grand jury testimony, Boise, Idaho, January 14, 1997; John Parten, interview by Mike Ritter, Ketchum, Idaho, October 1999.

6. Mike Carter, interviews by Mike Ritter, Mendocino, California, September 25–26, 2000.

7. Peter Lewis, "Sentencings Close Drug-Smuggling Case—Ringleaders Given Prison Terms," *Seattle Times*, July 10, 1993; "Captains Outrageous," *The Nation*, September 9, 2007; David Poland, "The Hot Button," July 21, 1998, http://www.thehotbutton.com/today/hot.button/1998_thb/980721_tue.html; Tony Thompson, *Reefermen: The Rise and Fall of a Billionaire Drugs Ring* (London: Hodder & Stoughton, 2007), 404–5.

8. James Conklin, interview by author, Las Vegas, Nevada, July 2000.

9. James Conklin, interview by author, Las Vegas, Nevada, February 2005.

10. Mike Ritter, essay, 2011.

11. "Mauian Pleads Guilty in Drug Money Laundering," *The Maui News*, May 4, 2005; "Maui Man Gets Two Years in Federal Court for Drug Scheme," *The Maui News*, May 27, 2005. "First off, they should have just said, 'You are going to face some jail time over this.' They should have let him know that, they blindsided him at the end of this after everyone had suggested something else," said Jim Conklin. "We can't let our biggest case in history get by without going to jail. He's going to have to go to jail for our benefit, for my benefit. I look the tough prosecutor, I can't let the guy walk."

12. Mike Ritter, essay, 2011.

13. Jim Avila, "Prescription Painkiller Use at Record High for Americans," *ABC World News*, April 20, 2011; for more on drug scheduling, see: http://www.deadiversion.usdoj.gov/schedules/index.html; "Majority Now Supports Legalizing Marijuana," Pew Research Center for the People and the Press, April 4, 2013; Andrew Sullivan, *The Cannabis Closet: First Hand Accounts of the Marijuana Mainstream*, ed. Chris Bodenner (Blurb Inc., 2010); Vincent Carroll, "DEA Chief Stonewalls on Marijuana," *Denver Post*, June 24, 2012; for the DEA administrator's testimony, see: http://www.youtube.com/watch?v=kFgrB2Wmh5s.

BIBLIOGRAPHY

BOOKS

Adler, Patricia. *Wheeling and Dealing: An Ethnography of an Upper-Level Drug Dealing and Smuggling Community*. New York: Columbia University Press, 1985.

Aesop. *Aesop, The Complete Fables*. Trans. Olivia and Robert Temple. New York: Penguin Classics, 1998.

Baritz, Loren. *Backfire: A History of How American Culture Led Us Into Vietnam and Made Us Fight the Way We Did*. New York: William Morrow, 1985.

Bartholomew, Wayne Rabbit, with Tim Baker. *Bustin' Down the Door: The Surf Revolution of '75*. Sydney, Australia: HarperCollins, 2002.

Baum, Dan. *Smoke and Mirrors: The War on Drugs and the Politics of Failure*. New York: Little, Brown, 1996.

Berger, Dan. *Outlaws of America: The Weather Underground and the Politics of Solidarity*. Edinburgh: AK Press, 2006.

Black, David. *Acid: The Secret History of LSD*. 2nd ed. London: Vision, 2003.

Boire, Richard Glen. *Marijuana Law*. 2nd ed. Oakland, Calif.: Ronin Publishing, 1996.

Boon, Marcus. *The Road to Excess: A History of Writers on Drugs*. Cambridge, Mass.: Harvard University Press, 2002.

Booth, Martin. *Cannabis: A History*. New York: Picador–St Martin's Press, 2003.

Botts, Andy. *Nightmare in Bangkok*. Honolulu: Poi Dog Publishers, 2007.

Brennan, Joseph. *Duke: The Life Story of Duke Kahanamoku*. Honolulu: Ku Pa'a Publishing, 1994.

Brokaw, Tom. *Boom! Voices of the Sixties: Personal Reflections on the '60s and Today*. New York: Random House, 2007.

Burdett, John. *Bangkok 8*. New York: Knopf, 2003.

——. *Bangkok Tattoo*. New York: Knopf, 2005.

Chandler, David. *Voices from S-21: Terror and History in Pol Pot's Secret Prison*. Berkeley: University of California Press, 2000.

Chepesiuk, Ron. *The Bangkok Connection: Trafficking Heroin from Asia to the USA*. Dunboyne, Ireland: Maverick House, 2011.

Chumpon, Prateep. *The History of Traditional Thai Medicine*. Bangkok: University of Bangkok Press, 2002.

Clarke, Robert Connell. *Hashish!* Los Angeles: Red Eye Press, 1998.

Collier, Peter and David Horowitz. *Destructive Generation: Second Thoughts About the '60s*. New York: Free Press, 1996.

Colnett, Wethern and Vincent Colnett. *A Wayward Angel: The Full Story of the Hells Angels*. New York: R. Marek Publishers, 1978.

Conrad, Joseph. *Lord Jim*. New York: Empire Books, 2012.

Cooper, George and Gavan Daws. *Land and Power in Hawaii: The Democratic Years*. Honolulu: University of Hawaii Press, 1990.

Cordingly, David. *Life Among the Pirates: The Romance and the Reality*. London: Little, Brown, 1995.

Dabney, Joseph Earl. *Mountain Spirits: A Chronicle of Corn Whiskey from King James' Ulster Plantation to America's Appalachians and the Moonshine Life*. Fairview, N.C.: Bright Mountain Books, 1984.

Das, Bhagavan. *It's Here Now (Are You?)*. New York: Broadway Books, 1997.

Dass, Ram. *Remember, Be Here Now*. Questa, N.M.: Lama Foundation, 1971.

Davenport-Hines, Richard. *The Pursuit of Oblivion: A Global History of Narcotics*. New York: Norton, 2002.

Didion, Joan. *Slouching Towards Bethlehem: Essays*. New York: Farrar, Straus & Giroux, 1968.

——. *Where I Was From*. New York: Vintage, 2004.

Divine, Jeff and Scott Hulet. *Surfing Photographs from the Seventies Taken by Jeff Divine*. Santa Barbara, Calif.: T. Adler Books, 2006.

Doherty, Sean. *MP: The Life of Michael Peterson*. New York: HarperCollins, 2005.

Dougan, Clark, Samuel Lipsman, and eds. *The Vietnam Experience, Volume 10: A Nation Divided*. Boston: Boston Publishing Co., 1984.

Douglas, Brett. *The Golden Gate Smuggling Company: A San Francisco Marijuana Empire*. Bloomington, Ind.: iUniverse Books, 2011.

Duke, Steven B. and Albert C. Gross. *America's Longest War: Rethinking Our Tragic Crusade Against Drugs*. New York: Tarcher, 1994.

Durden, Charles. *No Bugles, No Drums*. New York: Viking, 1976.

Eddy, Paul and Sara Walden. *Hunting Marco Polo: The Pursuit of a Drug Smuggler Who Couldn't Be Caught by the Agent Who Wouldn't Quit.* New York: Little, Brown, 1991.

Eklof, Stephan. *Pirates in Paradise: A Modern History of Southeast Asia's Maritime Marauders.* Copenhagen: Nordic Institute of Asian Studies, 2006.

Eszterhas, Joe. *American Rhapsody.* New York: Knopf, 2000.

Fellows, Warren. *The Damage Done: Twelve Years of Hell in a Bangkok Prison.* Sydney: Pan Macmillan, 1997.

Fielding, Leaf. *To Live Outside the Law: Caught by Operation Julie, Britain's Biggest Drugs Bust.* London: Serpent's Tail, 2011.

Forwell, Michael and Lee Bullman. *Blowback: Adventures of a Dope Smuggler.* London: Pan Macmillan Limited, 2010.

Fuss, Charles Jr. *Sea of Grass: The Maritime Drug War 1970–1990.* Annapolis: Naval Institute Press, 1996.

Gilboa, Amit. *Off the Rails in Phnom Penh: Into the Dark Heart of Guns, Girls, and Ganja.* 7th ed. Bangkok: Asia Books, 1998.

Gitlin, Todd. *The Sixties: Years of Hope, Days of Rage.* New York: Bantam, 1987.

Goldman, Albert. *Grassroots: Marijuana in America Today.* New York: Harper & Row, 1979.

Gooberman, Lawrence. *Operation Intercept: The Multiple Consequences of Public Policy.* Oxford, UK: Pergamon Press, 1976.

Gray, Mike, ed. *Busted: Stone Cowboys, Narco-Lords, and Washington's War on Drugs.* New York: Nation Books, 2002.

Greenfield, Robert. *Timothy Leary: A Biography.* New York: Harcourt Trade Publishers, 2007.

Forwell, Gypsy Boots. *The Gypsy in Me!* Camarillo, Calif.: Golden Boots Company, 1993.

Hall, Sandra Kimberley. *Duke: A Great Hawaiian.* Honolulu: Bell Press, 2004.

Halperin, Shirley and Steve Bloom. *Pot Culture: The A–Z Guide to Stoner Language and Life.* Foreword by Tommy Chong. New York: Abrams Image, 2008.

Heer, Friedrich. *The Medieval World.* London: George Weidenfeld & Nicolson, 1961.

Herr, Michael. *Dispatches.* New York: Avon, 1978.

Hersh, Burton. *The Mellon Family: A Fortune in History.* New York: William Morrow, 1978.

Hobsbaum, Eric J. *Bandits.* 1969. Revised with new introduction by author. New York: The New Press, 2000.

Hodgson, Godfrey. *America in Our Time: From WWII to Nixon—What Happened and Why.* New York: Doubleday, 1976.

Hopkins, Jerry. *Bangkok Babylon.* North Clarendon, Vt.: Tuttle Publishing, 2005.

Hughes, Robert. *Things I Didn't Know: A Memoir.* New York: Vintage, 2007.

Jacobs, Ron. *The Way the Wind Blew: A History of the Weather Underground.* New York: Verso, 1997.

James, Dr. Don. *Surfing San Onofre to Point Dume 1936–1942.* Photographs by Don James. San Francisco: Chronicle Books, 1998.

Jarratt, Phil. *Mr Sunset: The Jeff Hakman Story*. Los Angeles: General Publishing Group, 1997.

Jenkins, Bruce. *North Shore Chronicles: Big Wave Surfing in Hawaii*. 3rd ed. Berkeley, Calif.: Frog Books, 2005.

Jonnes, Jill. *Hep-Cats, Narcs, and Pipe Dreams*. New York: Scribner, 1996.

Jumsai, Brig. Gen M.L. Manich. *History of Thailand and Cambodia, from the Days of Angkor to the Present*. Bangkok: Chalermnit, 1979.

Jumsai, M.L. Manich. *History of Laos*. 4th ed. Bangkok: Chalermnit, 2000.

Kampion, Drew. *Greg Noll: The Art of the Surfboard*. Layton, Utah: Gibbs Smith, 2007.

Kamstra, Jerry. *Weed: Adventures of a Dope Smuggler*. New York: Harper & Row, 1974.

Kaplan, David E. and Alec Dubro. *Yakuza: The Explosive Account of Japan's Criminal Underworld*. Boston: Addison-Wesley Longman, 1986.

Kattenburg, Dave. *Foxy Lady: Truth, Memory and the Death of Western Yachtsmen in Democratic Kampuchea*. Toronto: The Key Publishing House, 2011.

Kelly, Richard. *Sean Penn: His Life and Times*. Edinburgh, Scotland: Cannongate, 2005.

Kennedy, Gordon. *Children of the Sun: A Pictorial Anthology From Germany to California 1883–1949*. Ojai, Calif.: Nivaria Press, 1998.

Kephart, Horace. *Our Southern Highlanders*. New York: Outing Publishing Co., 1913.

Lachman, Gary. *Turn Off Your Mind: The Mystic Sixties and the Dark Side of the Age of Aquarius*. London: Sidgwick & Jackson—Macmillan, 2001.

Langewiesche, William. *The Outlaw Sea: A World of Freedom, Chaos, and Crime*. New York: North Point Press, 2005.

Lattimore, Owen and Eleanor, eds. *Silks, Spices, and Empire: Asia Seen Through the Eyes of Its Discoverers*. New York: Dell, 1968.

Leary, Timothy. *Flashbacks*. New York: Tarcher–Putnam, 1997.

——. *Psychedelic Prayers and Other Meditations*. 1966; reprint, Charleston, S.C.: Forgotten Books, 2012.

LeCompte, Tom. *The Last Sure Thing: The Life and Times of Bobby Riggs*. Kent, Ohio: Black Squirrel Books, 2003.

Lee, Martin A. *A Social History of Marijuana—Medicinal, Recreational, and Scientific*. New York: Scribner, 2012.

Lee, Martin A. and Bruce Shalin. *Acid Dreams, The Complete Social History of LSD: The CIA, the Sixties, and Beyond*. Rev. ed. New York: Grove Press, 1992.

Leigh, David. *High Time*. New York: HarperCollins, 1985.

Li, Hui-Lin. "The Origin and Use of Cannabis in Eastern Asia: Their Linguistic-Cultural Implications." In *Cannabis and Culture*, ed. Vera Rubin, 51–62. Paris: Mouton & Co., 1975.

Lipsman, Samuel, Edward Doyle, and eds. *The Vietnam Experience: Fighting for Time*. Boston: Boston Publishing Co., 1983.

Lopez, Gerry. *Surf Is Where You Find It*. Ventura, Calif.: Patagonia Books, 2009.

Lowe, Rob. *Stories I Only Tell My Friends*. New York: St. Martin's Griffin, 2011.

Lundy, A. L. "Scrap." In *The California Abalone Industry: A Pictorial History*. Palm Beach Gardens, Fla.: Best Publishing Company, 1997.

Lupsha, Peter and Kip Schlegel. *The Political Economy of Drug Trafficking: The Herrera Organization*. Santa Fe: Latin American Institute, University of New Mexico, 1980.

Lysiak, Oleh. *Barely Inside the Lines*. Bloomington, Ind.: Xlibris, 2007.

MacPherson, Myra. *Long Time Passing: Vietnam and the Haunted Generation*. Bloomington: Indiana University Press, 2002.

Maitland, Terrence, Peter McInerney, and eds. *The Vietnam Experience: A Contagion of War*. Boston: Boston Publishing Co., 1983.

Maguire, Peter. *Facing Death in Cambodia*. New York: Columbia University Press, 2005.

Marez, Curtis. *Drug Wars: The Political Economy of Narcotics*. Minneapolis: University of Minnesota Press, 2004.

Marks, Howard. *Mr Nice: An Autobiography*. Edinburgh, Scotland: Cannongate UK, 2003.

Marks, Judy. *Mr Nice and Mrs Marks: Adventures with Howard*. London: Ebury Press—Random House, 2006.

Martin, Marie Alexandrine. *Cambodia: A Shattered Society*. Berkeley: University of California Press, 1994.

——. "Ethnobotanical Aspects of Cannabis in Southeast Asia." In *Cannabis and Culture*, ed. Vera Rubin, 63–76. Paris: Mouton & Co., 1975.

Massing, Michael. *The Fix*. Berkeley: University of California Press, 2003.

McCoy, Alfred W. *The Politics of Heroin in South East Asia*. New York: Harper & Row, 1977.

McGirr, Lisa. *Suburban Warriors: The Origins of the New American Right (Politics and Society in Twentieth-Century America)*. Princeton: Princeton University Press, 2001.

McMillan, David. *Escape the Past*. Singapore: Monsoon Books Pte. Ltd., 2012.

McPherson, Michael. *Rivers of the Sun*. Hilo, Hawaii: South Point Press, 2000.

Meng-Try and Ea Sorya Sim. *Victims and Perpetrators: Testimony of Young Khmer Rouge Comrades*. Phnom Penh: Documentation Center of Cambodia, 2001.

Merlin, Mark David. *Man and Marijuana: Some Aspects of Their Ancient Relationship*. New York: A. S. Barnes and Co., 1973.

Meyers, Jeffrey. *Inherited Risk: Errol and Sean Flynn in Hollywood and Vietnam*. New York: Simon and Schuster, 2002.

Miles, Barry. *Hippie*. London: Cassell Illustrated, 2003.

Miller, Joel. *Bad Trip: How the War Against Drugs Is Destroying America*. Nashville: WND Books, 2004.

Mills, James. *The Underground Empire*. New York: Doubleday, 1986.

Moore, Robin, with June Collins. *Khaki Mafia*. New York: Crown, 1971.

Neville, Richard. *Play Power: Exploring the International Underground*. New York: Random House, 1970.

Novak, William. *High Culture: Marijuana in the Lives of Americans*. New York: Knopf, 1987.

O'Dea, Brian. *High: Confessions of an International Drug Smuggler.* New York: Other Press, 2009.

Palmer, Cynthia and Michael Horowitz, eds. *Shaman Woman, Mainline Lady: Womens' Writings on the Drug Experience.* New York: William Morrow, 1982.

Parnell, Christopher. *Hell's Prisoner: The Shocking True Story of an Innocent Man Jailed for Eleven Years in Indonesia's Most Notorious Prison.* Edinburgh, Scotland: Mainstream Publishing, 2011.

Pasuk Phongpaichit and Chris Baker. *Thailand: Economics and Politics.* Oxford: Oxford University Press, 2002.

Pasuk Phongpaichit, Sungsidh Piriyarangsan, and Nualnoi Treerat. *Guns, Girls, Gambling and Ganja.* Chiang Mai, Thailand: Silkworm Books, 1998.

Pietri, Joe R. *The King of Nepal.* Bloomington: Indiana Creative Arts, 2001.

Pinchbeck, Daniel. *Breaking Open the Head: A Psychedelic Journey Into the Heart of Contemporary Shamanism.* New York: Broadway Books, 2002.

Plant, Sadie. *Writing on Drugs.* New York: Farrar, Straus, & Giroux, 2001.

Portelli, Alessandro. *The Death of Luigi Trastulli and Other Stories: Form and Meaning in Oral History.* Albany: State University of New York Press, 1991.

Pratt, John Clark, comp. *Vietnam Voices: Perspectives on the War Years 1941–1975.* Athens: University of Georgia Press, 2008.

Preston, Brian. *Pot Planet: Adventures in the Global Marijuana Culture.* New York: Grove Press, 2002.

Price, John. *Tijuana: Urbanization in a Border Culture.* Notre Dame, Ind.: University of Notre Dame Press, 1973.

Redden, Jim. *Snitch Culture: How Citizens Are Turned Into the Eyes and Ears of the State.* Port Townsend, Wa.: Feral House, 2000.

Rediker, Marcus. *Between the Devil and the Deep Blue Sea: Merchant Seamen, Pirates and the Anglo-American Maritime World, 1700–1750.* Cambridge: Cambridge University Press, 1987.

Reeves, Richard. *President Nixon: Alone in the White House.* New York: Simon and Schuster, 2001.

Rensin, David. *All for a Few Perfect Waves: The Audacious Life and Legend of Rebel Surfer Miki Dora.* New York: IT Books, 2009.

Robbins, Christopher. *Air America.* New York: Avon Books, 1985.

Ryan, Jason. *Jackpot: High Times, High Seas, and the Sting That Launched the War on Drugs.* Guilford, Conn.: Lyons Press, 2012.

Sabbag, Robert. *Smokescreen: A Misadventure on the Marijuana Trail.* New York: Little, Brown and Company, 2002.

Schlosser, Eric. *Reefer Madness: Sex, Drugs, and Cheap Labor in the American Black Market.* Boston: Mariner Books, 2004.

Schou, Nicholas. *Orange Sunshine: The Brotherhood of Eternal Love and Its Quest to Spread Peace, Love, and Acid to the World.* New York: St. Martin's Press, 2010.

Shannon, Elaine. *Desperados: Latin Drug Lords, U.S. Lawmen, and the War America Can't Win.* New York: Penguin, 1989.

Silver, Gary, ed., with text by Michael R. Aldrich. *The Dope Chronicles, 1850–1950*. New York: Harper & Row, 1979.

Sloman, Larry. *Reefer Madness: The History of Marijuana in America*. New York: Bobbs-Merrill, 1979.

Smith, Adam. *The Wealth of Nations*. Hollywood, Fla.: Simon and Brown, 2012.

Sokolove, Michael. *The Ticket Out: Darryl Strawberry and the Boys of Crenshaw*. New York: Simon and Schuster, 2004.

Southern, Terry. *Red Dirt and Other Tastes*. New York: Citadel, 2001.

Sparrowhawk, Phil with Martin King and Martin Knight. *Grass*. London: Mainstream Publishing, 2003.

Stecyk, Craig and Brewer, Art. *Bunker Spreckels: Surfing's Divine Prince of Decadence*. Cologne: Taschen, 2007.

Stecyk, C. R. III and Drew Kampion. *Dora Lives: The Authorized Story of Miki Dora*. Santa Barbara, Calif.: T. Adler Books, 2005.

Stevens, Jay. *Storming Heaven: LSD and the American Dream*. New York: Grove Press, 1987.

Sullum, Jacob. *Saying Yes*. New York: Tarcher Books, 2004.

Syamananda, Rong. *A History of Thailand*. Bangkok: Thai Watana Panich, 1988.

Taliacozzo, Eric. *Secret Trades, Porous Borders: Smuggling and States Along a Southeast Asian Frontier, 1865–1915*. New Haven: Yale University Press, 2005.

Tendler, Stewart and David May. *The Brotherhood of Eternal Love: From Flower Power to Hippie Mafia, the Story of the LSD Counterculture*. London: Panther Books—Granada Publishing, 1984.

Thompson, E. P. *The Making of the English Working Class*. New York: Vintage, 1966.

Thompson, Tony. *Reefermen: The Rise and Fall of a Billionaire's Drug Ring*. London: Hodder and Stoughton, 2008.

Torgoff, Martin. *Can't Find My Way Home: American in the Great Stoned Age, 1945–2000*. New York: Simon and Schuster, 2004.

Torrens, Herb. *The Paraffin Chronicles: A Surfer's Journey 1960–1971*. Victoria, Canada: Trafford, 2003.

Turner, Jack. *Spice: The History of a Temptation*. New York: Vintage, 2005.

Torsone, A. R. *HERB TRADER: A Tale of Treachery and Espionage in the Global Marijuana Trade*. Woodstock, N.Y.: Woodstock Mountain Press, 2009.

Verill, A. Hyatt. *Smugglers and Smuggling*. London: George Allen & Unwin, 1924.

Warner, Roger. *The Invisible Hand: The Marijuana Business*. New York: William Morrow, 1986.

Warshaw, Matt. *The Encyclopedia of Surfing*. Boston: Houghton, Mifflin Harcourt, 2003.

Waters, Harold. *Smugglers of Spirits: Prohibition and the Coast Guard Patrol*. New York: Hastings House, 1971.

Webb, James. *Fields of Fire*. New York: Bantam, 1978.

Wethern, George and Vincent Colnett. *A Wayward Angel: The Full Story of the Hells Angels*. New York: R. Marek Publishers, 1978.

Wetterhahn, Ralph. *The Last Battle: The Mayaquez, the Lost Fireteam, and the End of the Vietnam War*. New York: Avalon Publishing Group, 2001.

Wilkerson, Cathy. *Flying Close to the Sun: My Life and Times as a Weatherman.* New York: Seven Stories, 2007.

Wilson, Constance Maralyn, Chrystal Stillings Smith, and George Vinal Smith, eds. *Royalty and Commoners: Essays in Thai Administrative, Economic, and Social History.* Leiden, Netherlands: Contributions to Asian Studies, 1980.

Witcover, Jules and David Halberstam. *The Year the Dream Died: Revisiting 1968 in America.* New York: Warner Books, 1997.

Wolf, Leonard. *Voices from the Love Generation.* New York: Little, Brown, 1968.

Wolfe, Tom. *The Electric Kool-Aid Acid Test.* New York: Bantam, 1969.

——. *Mauve Gloves & Madmen, Clutter & Vine.* New York: Farrar, Straus & Giroux, 1976.

——. *The Pumphouse Gang.* New York: Bantam Paperback, 1969.

——. *The Purple Decades—A Reader.* New York: Berkley, 1987.

Young, Nat. *The Complete History of Surfing: From Water to Snow.* Layton, Utah: Gibbs Smith, 2008.

——. *Nat's Nat and That's That: A Surfing Legend.* Frenchs Forest, N.S.W., Australia: Nymboida Press, 1998.

UNPUBLISHED MANUSCRIPTS

Boyum, Bill. "Punching Out." 2007.

Bull, Doug. "Wallowing in Cruciality."

Dawson, Terry. "The Road to Anaraxta." 1997.

Wright, Dion. Untitled.

TELEVISION AND FILM

Blow. Dir. Ted Demme. New York: New Line Cinema, 2001.

The Endless Summer: The Search for the Perfect Wave. Dir. Bruce Brown. Hollywood, Calif.: Bruce Brown Films, 1966.

Glass Love. Dir. Andrew Kidman. 2006.

Krough, Emil "Bud." Interview from "The Drug Wars, Part 1." *Frontline.* PBS. Aired October 9, 2000. Produced by Brooke Runnette and Martin Smith. Written by Martin Smith, Brooke Runnette and Oriana Zill. Senior Producer Sharon Tiller. Series Reporter Lowell Bergman.

Rainbow Bridge. Dir. Chuck Wein. Los Angeles: Transvue Pictures, 1972.

The Search for Kurtz. Dir. Adrian Levy. Non-Fiction Films, 1999.

"Who Profits From Drugs?" *Frontline.* PBS. Aired February 21, 1989. Produced by Charles C. Stuart and Marcia Vivancos. Written by Charles C. Stuart. Reported by Charles C. Stuart, Marcia Vivancos, and Mark Hosenball.

INTERVIEWS

Anonymous. Interview by Mike Ritter, Maui, Hawaii, December 12, 1998. Tape recording.

Anonymous. Interview by Mike Ritter, Santa Barbara, California, July 1999. Tape recording.

Anonymous. Interviews by Mike Ritter, Seattle, Washington, August 2–5, 1999. Tape recording.

Anonymous former Thai marijuana farmer 1 and farmer 2. Interview with Mike Ritter, Pone Sawan, Northeast Thailand, January 2002. Tape recording.

Anonymous. Interview by Mike Ritter, Bangkok, Thailand, July 2010. Tape recording.

Bridgely, Edward*. Interview by Mike Ritter, Palm Springs, California, July 2000. Tape recording.

Carter, Mike. Interviews by Mike Ritter, Mendocino, California, September 25–26, 2000. Tape recording.

Conklin, James. Interview by Mike Ritter, Las Vegas, Nevada, July 2000. Tape recording; interview by Peter Maguire, February, 2005.

Conklin, James. Interview by Peter Maguire, February, 2005. Tape recording.

Dawson, Terry*. Interview by Mike Ritter, Boulder, Colorado, February 1999. Tape recording.

Deeds, Karl. Interview by Peter Maguire and Mike Ritter, Molokai, Hawaii, March 31, 1998.

Ferguson, Michael. Interviews by Mike Ritter, Oahu, Hawaii, November 2001, June 2002, August 2003, July 2007. Tape recording.

Hagee, John*. Interviews by Mike Ritter, Ponderay, Idaho and Rancho Mirage, California, April and August 1998. Tape recording.

Hall, David. Telephone conversation with Mike Ritter, December 2008. Tape recording.

Hall, Don. Interview by Mike Ritter, Palm Springs, California, April 2001. Tape recording.

Hoyt, Brian "Bombay Brian." Interview by Mike Ritter, San Francisco, May 2001. Tape recording.

Jo. Interview by Mike Ritter, Bangkok and Nakhon Phanom, Thailand, January 2002. Tape recording.

Johns, Kevin. Interview by Mike Ritter, Maui, Hawaii, October 2007. Tape recording.

Jones, Bob. Interview by Mike Ritter, Carlsbad, California, May 2001. Tape recording.

Latch, Bob*. Interview by Mike Ritter, Maui, Hawaii, April 2001. Tape recording.

Lawton, Jim*. Interview by Mike Ritter, Santa Barbara, California, July 1999. Tape recording.

Lek. Interview by Mike Ritter, Chiang Mai, Thailand, April 1999 and January 2002. Tape recording.

Livingstone, Julie. Interview by Mike Ritter, Maui, Hawaii, July 12, 1999. Tape recording.

Mancuso, Ciro. Interview by Mike Ritter, Maui, Hawaii, May 2007. Tape recording.

Marshall, Robert. Interview by Mike Ritter, Amsterdam, May 2000. Tape recording.

Martin, Bob. Interview by Mike Ritter, Maui, Hawaii, March 2001. Tape recording.

Monroe, James "Abdul"*. Interviews by Mike Ritter, Indonesia and Andaman Islands, March 25, 1999 and May 1999. Tape recording.

Musson, Bill. Interview by Mike Ritter, Maui, Hawaii, May 1998. Tape recording.

Nicholson, Tim*. Interview by Mike Ritter, Bangkok, Thailand, January 2002. Tape recording.

Ortiz, David. Interviews by Mike Ritter, Santa Barbara, California, October 1999, July 2007, and various telephone conversations. Tape recording.

Parten, John. Interview by Mike Ritter, Ketchum, Idaho, October 1999. Tape recording.

Ramirez, Rudy. Interview by Mike Ritter, Maui, Hawaii, November 1998. Tape recording.

Wakeland, Mark. Interview by Mike Ritter, Hilo, Hawaii, January 2009. Tape recording.

Whelan, Ray. Interview by Mike Ritter, Ketchum, Idaho, October 1999. Tape recording.

Williams, Craig. Interview by Mike Ritter, Maui, Hawaii, October 1998. Tape recording.

INFORMAL INTERVIEWS

Abbott, David. Interview by author, Sunset Beach, Oahu, December 2004. Notes.

Angelini, Joe. Interview by Mike Ritter, San Juan Capistrano, California, May 2001. Notes.

Bull, Doug. Personal letter to Mike Ritter, September 19, 1999.

Cutler, Bob. Conversation with Mike Ritter, Maui, Hawaii, July 2001. Notes.

Cyndi. Interview by Mike Ritter, Maui, Hawaii, July 2001. Notes.

Etcheson, Craig. Interview by author, Phnom Penh, Cambodia, August 10, 2002.

Frank "the redhead." Interview by Mike Ritter, Corte Madera, California, May 2001. Notes.

Gardner, Ed. Interview by Mike Ritter, Maui, Hawaii, December 1999.

Hagee, John*. Telephone conversation with Mike Ritter, July 2000.

Hall, David. Telephone conversation with Mike Ritter, December 2008. Notes.

Hill, David. Various conversations with Mike Ritter between 1995 and 2002, Thailand. Notes.

Huy, Him. Interview by Peter Maguire, Phnom Penh, Cambodia, March 14, 1997.

Jackson, Ron*. Telephone conversation with Mike Ritter, July 2002. Notes.

Jones, Ned*. Interview by Peter Maguire, Pupakea, Oahu, June 2004.

Lahodny, Bob. Conversation with Mike Ritter, La Jolla, California, December 1999. Notes.

Lek. Interview by Mike Ritter, Isan, Thailand, July 2000.

Linman, Mike*. Conversation with Mike Ritter, January 2002. Notes.

Long, Nek*. Interview by Peter Maguire, Kompong Speu, Cambodia, May 2005.

"Mak"*. Interview by Mike Ritter, Si Kiu, Thailand, January 2002. Notes.

Miller, Paul. Interview by Mike Ritter, Maui, Hawaii, March 2007. Notes.

Nicholson, Tim*. Interview by Mike Ritter, Bangkok, Thailand, January 2002.

Padilla, Ed. Phone conversation with Mike Ritter, Maui, Hawaii, September 7, 2001. Notes.

Rewatt, Lt. Col. (Thai Police). Interview by Mike Ritter, Bangkok, Thailand, January 2002. Notes.

Sambat Suthern*. Interview by Mike Ritter, Bangkok and Nakhon Phanom, Thailand, January 2002.

Sann, Sok*. Interview by Peter Maguire, Phnom Penh, Cambodia, May 2005.

Sherritt, Tom (Portland, Oregon). Telephone conversations with Mike Ritter, December 2007, June 2005. Notes.

Spradling, Blaine (Las Vegas). Telephone conversation with Mike Ritter, ca. 2000. Notes.

Stratton, Richard (Toronto). Telephone conversation with Mike Ritter, August 2001. Notes.

Temper, Dean*. Telephone conversation with Mike Ritter, June 2000.

Waugh, Sally*. Telephone conversation with Mike Ritter, July 1999. Notes.

Willson, Bill. Interview by Mike Ritter, Corte Madera, California, May 2001. Notes.

ARTICLES

Abercrombie, Thomas. "Morocco—Land of the Farthest West." *National Geographic,* June 1971.

"Alarming Rise in Dope Traffic." *U.S. News and World Report,* September 2, 1968.

"American Abroad Faces Tough Narcotics Laws." *Van Nuys News,* June 14, 1974.

"American, Dane Held After Chase." *Bangkok Post,* May 31, 1979.

"American: I'm No Drug Financier." *Bangkok Post,* June 18, 1981.

Anderson, Jack. "GI Drug Abuse Hushed Up." *Washington Post,* August 9, 1970.

"Anonymous Tip Leads Police to Suspected Drug Smuggler." *Eugene Register Guard,* May 21, 1987.

"Another Huge Haul of Marijuana." *Bangkok Post,* October 23, 1980.

"Armed Forces: As Common as Chewing Gum." *Time,* March 1, 1971.

Ayres, Drummond. "Pot Charges Jail Islanders in Thailand 1969." *New York Times,* March 29, 1970.

"Bad Scene: 640 Young Americans Sit in Foreign Jails on Dope Charges." *Associated Press,* January 3, 1971.

"Bangkok 'a Clearing House for Drugs.'" *Bangkok Post,* December 4, 1970.

"Beyond the Reefer." *Honolulu Star Bulletin,* January 8, 1969.

"Big Marijuana Trial Opens." *Bangkok Post,* February 17, 1981.

"Big 'Pot' Haul in Bangkok Trimaran—Suva, Fiji (UPI)." *Bangkok Post,* June 19, 1976.

"Booming Busts, Pot Is Still Legally Hazardous." *Time,* March 19, 1984.

"*Boutwell* Defendants Sentenced, Coast Guard Mutineers Draw Light Punishment." *High Times* 98 (October 1983).

Boxer, C. R. "Piracy in the South China Sea." *History Today,* December 1980.

"Breath-taking Bonfire: Six Tons of Confiscated Marijuana Go up in Smoke." *Bangkok Post,* February 18, 1981.

"Brillig Crew Fined for Pot." *Bangkok Post,* January 12, 1978.

"Brillig's Crew 'Held for Drugs'" *Bangkok Post,* November 10, 1977.

Brinson, Betsy. "Crossing Cultures: An Interview with Alessandro Portelli." *Oral History Review* 28, no. 1 (Winter/Spring 2001).

"The Brotherhood of Eternal Love: The Senate Report." *High Times* 2 (Fall 1974).

Brush, Peter. "Higher and Higher: Drug Use Among U.S. Forces in Vietnam." *Honolulu Star Bulletin*, Sept 1969.

"Build-Up of Drug Patrol." *Sydney Morning Herald*, November 3, 1974.

Burgess, John. "When the GIs Go Home." *The Washington Post*, April 21, 1974.

"Captain Files Appeal in Drugs Case." *Bangkok Post*, November 4, 1981.

"Cargo Ship Robbed in Pirate Attack." *Bangkok Post*, August 26, 1976.

Chamberlain, John. "The Brotherhood of Eternal Love." *Coshocton Tribune*, January 22, 1974.

Cherniak, Laurence. "Great Balls of Nepalese Fire." *High Times*, January 1981.

"CIA Dropped Drug Case to Save Name." *Bangkok Post*, July 31, 1975.

"CIA Shield for Thai Smuggler." *Bangkok Post*, July 19, 1975.

"'Coronado Company' Figure Arrested in New Drug Case." *Los Angles Times*, April 6, 1989.

Corpora, Thomas. "Use of Marijuana by GIs in Vietnam Is Being Studied Up." *The Washington Post*, October 1, 1967.

"Counterculture's Warrior Lawyer Tony J. Serra's Specialty Is Outlaws and He's Made His Reputation Defending Them." *Lost Angeles Times*, May 3, 1989.

"Country Boy Outslicks Big-City Drug Smugglers." *Los Angeles Times*, February 21, 1979.

"Court Turns Down Appeal by Drug Trio." *Bangkok Post*, August 17, 1981.

"A Cure Worse Than the Disease." *Time*, March 19, 1984.

"Customs Catch Two 'Pot' Boats." *Bangkok Post*, October 11, 1980.

"DeMassa, Villar Bury Hatchet in Secret Deal." *Lost Angeles Times*, July 26, 1986.

Doyle, Kate. "Operation Intercept: The Perials of Unilateralism." *The National Security Archive*, online journal published by George Washington University, posted April 13, 2003.

"Drug Suspect Denies Offer of B600,000 for Release." *Bangkok Post*, February 21, 1981.

"The Economic Impact of US Withdrawal." *The Investor*, December 1975.

"Eight Indicted in Two Drug Cases." *Eugene Register Guard*, February 5, 1983.

"Elaborate Smuggling Plot Leads to Jail." *Los Angeles Times*, January 27, 1979.

"End of the Coronado Company." *Newsweek*, July 4, 1984.

Eszterhas, Joe. "The Strange Case of the Hippie Mafia." *Rolling Stone* (December 7, 1972).

"Ex-Agent's Death Leaves Questions." *The Gainesville Sun*, April 11, 2000.

"Ex-ISM Student Dead in Soi." *Bangkok Post*, April 20, 1972.

"15 Tons of Marijuana Seized on Navy Base, 7 Suspects Held at U-tapao." *Bangkok World*, April 10, 1983.

"Five in Marijuana Ring Get 30–45 Years." *Bangkok Post*, October 21, 1981.

"Foiled Escape Leads to Heroin: Two Face Possible Execution." *Bangkok Post*, June 1, 1979.

"Former Detective Jailed." *Sydney Morning Herald*, October 10, 1978.

"40 Tons of Marijuana Destroyed." *Bangkok Post*, November 23, 1982.

"Four Arrested on Narcotics Charges." *Bangkok Post*, April 1, 1971.

Freeman, Joseph. "Western Inmate Identified in S-21 Portraits." *Phnom Penh Post*, September 3, 2012.

Fuller, Linda. "Lord of the Ring." *Orange Coast*, December, 1991.

"Gains in the War Against Drug Smugglers." *U.S. News and World Report,* June 21, 1971.

Gault-Williams, Malcolm. "Tarzan Redux: Chapter Fill-ins from the Life of Gene Smith." *The Surfers Journal,* Spring 2004.

"GI Drug Use Rises Fivefold." *Bangkok Post,* October 14, 1972.

"GI Here Mailing Pot to US?" *Bangkok Post,* October 12, 1969.

"The GIs' Other Enemy: Heroin." *Newsweek,* May 24, 1971.

"GIs Sending Marijuana to Pals Back Home." *Bangkok Post,* September 7, 1967.

Goldsmith, Heather. "Duch Remains on the Hot Seat." *Cambodia Tribunal Monitor,* April 2, 2012. http://www.cambodiatribunal.org/blog/2012/04/duch-remains-hot-seat.

Graves, William. "Bangkok: City of Angels." *National Geographic,* July 1973.

"Greener Grass---Grimmer Jails." *Newsweek,* June 15, 1970.

Grosvenor, Donna and Gilbert Grosvenor. "Bali by the Back Roads." *National Geographic,* November 1969.

"Halt Drugs or Else." *UPI,* March 8, 1972.

"Hashish Oil Plant Was Copied from Book." *Bangkok Post,* October 22, 1974.

"Heroin Ring Formed in Germany in 1955." *Bangkok Post,* August 14, 1976.

Heinl, Col. Robert D. Jr. "The Collapse of the Armed Forces." *Armed Forces Journal,* June 7, 1971.

"Higher and Higher: Drug Use Among U.S. Forces in Vietnam." *Vietnam Magazine* 15, no. 4 (December 2002).

Holbreich, Curt. "2 Members of Drug Ring Seized Again." *Los Angeles Times,* April 5, 1989.

"How the 'Full Moon Drug Syndicate' Eclipsed Mr. Asia." *Sydney Morning Herald,* August 17, 1985.

"Huge Marijuana Haul on Truck, 5670 Kilos Seized in Sakon Nakhon." *Bangkok Post,* April 9, 1981.

"Huge 'Pot' Haul Aboard Yacht: American, Dane Held After Chase." *Bangkok Post,* May 31, 1979.

"Huge Pot Haul in Rayong [15 Tons]." *Bangkok Post,* July 23, 1977.

Hughes, John. "'Pot Trail' Not an Easy Street." *The Post-Crescent* (Appleton, Wisc.), November 30, 1970.

"Indictments Target Big Drug Operation." *AP,* February 24, 1983.

"Indochina's Heroin Traffic." *Time,* July 19, 1971.

"Intergalactic Union Dopogram." *East Village Other,* July 1968.

Kampion, Drew. "When the Smoke Cleared." *The Surfers Journal* 2, no. 1 (Spring 1993).

Kamstra, Jerry. "Life with Panama Red." *Newsweek,* July 1, 1974.

Koke, Louise. "Our Hotel in Bali." http://balisurfstories.wordpress.com/2010/09/27/balis-first-surfer-and-first-expat-squabble-and-first-pommie-surfer-too/.

Kubsch, Fred. "Afghanistan Hashish Business Grows." *The Post-Crescent,* December 3, 1972.

"Land, Air and Sea Dragnet for 'Pot' Runners." *Bangkok Post,* October 13, 1980.

"Leary Cult Drug Ring Reported." *Oakland Tribune,* January 14, 1974.

Leary, Timothy. "Deal for Real." *East Village Other,* September 1968.

——. "Episode and Postscript." *Playboy Magazine* (December 1969).

——. Interview by *Playboy*. *Playboy Magazine* (September 1966).

"Leave North Shore, Arrive Lahaina: Maui 'Mellow So Drug Ring Moves In.'" *Honolulu Star Bulletin,* April 20, 1972.

MacLeish, Kenneth. "The Top End of Down Under." *National Geographic,* February 1973.

"Marijuana Between Layers of Plywood." *Bangkok Post,* June 22, 1977.

"Marijuana Plantation Discovered." *Bangkok Post,* January 8, 1979.

"Marijuana Receives USAF 'Approval.'" *Bangkok Post,* November 15, 1971.

"Marijuana Shipment Seized." *Honolulu Advertiser,* January 28, 1970.

"Mary Jane in Action." *Newsweek,* Novermber 6, 1967.

"Maui Officials Eye Drug Ring." *Honolulu Star Bulletin,* April 22, 1972.

Maxwell, Evan. "Dream of Universal Love Founders on Drug Use Beliefs." *Los Angeles Times,* February 12, 1973.

McCabe, Robert. "Drug Net Hunt." *Honolulu Star Bulletin,* August 9, 1972.

McMullen, Paul. "Marijuana Smugglers Detected." *Air Force Times,* http://www.vspa .com/k9/dm-2.htm.

"Mexico's War on Marijuana." *U.S. News and World Report,* December 29, 1969.

Meyers, William. "California's Counterculture Counselor." *High Times,* September 1985.

"Millionaire Drug Dealer Makes Deal." *Los Angeles Times,* May 9, 1983.

Mollenhoff, Clark. "Attention Focusing on Passport Frauds." *Van Nuys News,* February 3, 1974.

"MP: Villagers Grow 'Pot' for GIs." *Bangkok Post,* July 23, 1971.

"'Narcs' Have Their Eye on Maui Ring." *Honolulu Star Bulletin,* April 19, 1972.

"New Death on Leary's Ranch—Tests Planned." *Oakland Tribune,* August 4, 1969.

"The New Public Enemy No. 1." *Time,* June 28, 1971.

"New Unit to Probe Narcotics." *Bangkok Post,* October 7, 1972.

"New Withdrawal Costs." *Time,* June 7, 1971.

"Nine Arrested in WA Drug Raid." *Sydney Morning Herald,* December 29, 1976.

"Offshoot of Coronado Co. Case, DeMassa Drug Trial Gets Off to a Testy Start." *Los Angeles Times,* October 17, 1985.

O'Neill, Ann W. "Drug Kingpin's Testimony Helps Lead to Convictions." *Orange County Register,* April 1990.

Owers, Kirk. "Wasted." *Waves Magazine,* January 1, 2011.

Paglia, Camille. "Cults and Cosmic Consciousness." *Arion* 10, no. 3 (Winter 2003).

Paskowitz, Dorian. "Tarzan at Waikiki." *The Surfers Journal,* Summer 1993.

Piccalo, Gina. "A Yogi's Requiem; Bhajan Arrived in L.A. at the Dawn of the Guru and Though His Legacy Is Clouded, His Followers Remain True." *Los Angeles Times,* October 23, 2004.

"Pirates Attack Refugees 4 Times in 8 Days." *Bangkok Post,* June 7, 1980.

"Pirates Murder Ship's Captain." *Bangkok Post,* March 15, 1975.

"Police Arrest American in Big Drug Raid." *Bangkok Post,* April 18, 1979.

"Police Nab 11 in 'Pot' Farm." *Bangkok Post,* October 1, 1969.

"Police Raids Net Huge Drug Hauls." *Bangkok Post*, May 1983.

"Police Seize Three Tons of Marijuana." *Bangkok Post*, October 22, 1980.

"Pot: Year of the Famine." *Newsweek*, September 22, 1969.

"Pot Luck for US Youths." *Bangkok Post*, April 7, 1972.

"Pot and Parents." *Time Magazine*, January 26, 1968.

"A Pothead's Paradise." *Bangkok Post*, July 27, 1976.

"The President: War on Drugs." *Newsweek*, June 28, 1971.

"Raid Could Provide Clue to Nationwide Drug Traffic." *Los Angeles Times*, January 3, 1978.

"Riley the Prime Mover, Court Told." *Sydney Morning Herald*, July 4, 1978.

"Riley Says He Lied About Drugs Role." *Sydney Morning Herald*, March 27, 1980.

Roach Haleiwa II, no. 3. March 23–April 6, 1969.

"Road Chase Ends with Seizure of 389kg 'Pot.'" *Bangkok Post*, April 9, 1981.

Robinson, John. "Smuggler Tells His Tale." *Santa Cruz Sentinel*, April 10, 1990.

Schiller, Lawrence. "A Remarkable Mind Drug Suddenly Spells Danger: LSD." *LIFE* Magazine, March 25, 1966.

"Second Raid Finds Drugs Worth $30m." *Sydney Morning, Herald*, June 17, 1978.

"7 Youths Arrested in 'Pot' Den." *Bangkok Post*, September 30, 1969.

"Seventh Swimmer Sought in Marijuana Smuggling, Imperial Beach." *UPI*, November 11, 1970.

"Singapore: Reluctant Nation." *National Geographic*, August 1966.

"6 Area Men Charged as Pot Conspirators." *The Miami News*, February 10, 1982.

Skolnick, Jerome H. "Pyrrhic Victories in the Drug War." *Los Angeles Times*, October 24, 1986.

"Smuggling---the Emphasis Shifts." *Sydney Morning Herald*, February 3, 1970.

"A Smuggling Kingpin: An Interview." *High Times* (November 1967).

"Strange Doings Led to 'Pot' Raid." *Los Angeles Times*, January 8, 1978.

Suksamran, Naovarat. "A Village That Prospered Through 'Pot.'" *Bangkok Post*, June 1, 1994.

"'Sunburn' Trial Witness Details Drug Operation." *Palm Beach Post*, March 18, 1982.

"Super-marijuana Is Turning Heads—Even Some Old Ones." *Honolulu Advertiser*, January 19, 1970.

"Surfer Jailed for Life." *Bangkok Post*, December 27, 1980.

"Suspect Pleads Not Guilty to Pot Smuggling Charge." *Eugene Register Guard*, June 23, 1987.

"Tait May Name Drug Syndicate Leaders." *Sydney Morning Herald*, May 25, 1979.

"Taster's Journal: Delicacies from the Drought and Other Observations." *High Times*, May 1982.

"Timothy Liar." *LA Weekly*, May 31, 2006.

"Thai: The Dope of the Eighties?" *High Times*, May 1978.

"Thai-Based GIs Run Drug Ring." *Bangkok Post*, October 21, 1972.

"Thai Marijuana Smugglers at the Hearst Ranch." *Valley Morning Star*, November 2, 1976.

"Thai Marijuana Trade Expanded During VN War." *Bangkok World*, September 29, 1986.

"The Thai-Stick Jinx, Marijuana Mutiny in the North Pacific." *High Times* 89 (January 1983).

"Thai Sticks Newest Drug Threat." *Times Herald* (Middletown, N.Y.), April 28, 1974.

"Three Get Month for Using 'Pot.'" *Bangkok Post*, September 26, 1969.

"The Troubled U.S. Army in Vietnam." *Newsweek*, January 11, 1971.

"The Troubled Waters of the South: Piracy off Thailand's Southern Provinces." *Bangkok Post*, February 3, 1980.

"20 Armed Robbers Hold Up Foreign Tanker Captain." *Bangkok Post*, September 4, 1974.

"25 GIs Seized in Viet Raid." *The Washington Post, Times Herald*, October 13, 1967.

"2 Couples Linked to Guerico Killing." *Evening Outlook*, February 6, 1995.

"Two Face Possible Execution." *Bangkok Post*, June 1, 1979.

"237 Tons of Pot Seized in 12 Months at N-E Source." *Bangkok Post*, January 2, 1978.

"2 Sentenced in Murder." *Honolulu Star Bulletin*, November 9, 1970.

"Two Tons of Illegal Dreams: American, Thais in Marijuana Seizure." *Bangkok Post*, September 1, 1976.

Upadhyay, Archana. "Dynamics of Smuggling in Southeast Asia." *Dialogue* 5, no. 1 (July–September 2003).

Vargas, Lance. "Surf and destroy: WIndanSea's [*sic*] secret society," http://www.lancevargas.com/meda.php.

Whipple, Chris. "'We're About to Be Rammed!' Came the Signal—Then, Suddenly, Three Americans Were Prisoners in Vietnam." *People Magazine* (January 9, 1978):28+.

White, Peter. "Hopes and Fears in Booming Thailand." *National Geographic*, July 1967.

Williams, Nick Jr. "Opium-Plagued Thailand Fight New Problem: Pot." *Los Angeles Times*, December 27, 1986.

"Yacht Drama Off Vietnam Coast." *Bangkok Post*, October 14, 1977.

"Yachtsmen Towed to Saigon." *Bangkok Post*, October 15, 1977.

Zeitlin, Arnold. "Leary Named Ringleader in Statewide Drug Haul." *Sunday Post-Crescent*, December 3, 1972.

DOCUMENTS

Abdullah, Munshi. The Burke Library Archives (Columbia University Libraries), Union Theological Seminary, New York, Missionary Research Library Archives: Section 4, Munshi Abdullah Papers, 1918, http://clio.cul.columbia.edu:7018/vwebv/holdingsInfo?bibId=4737108.

Bell, Bill. Letter to the *Los Angeles Times*, May 5, 2002.

Camper & Nicholsons Boatyard. E-mail and telephone communication with Peter Maguire.

Deeds, Michael Scott. Confession of Michael Scott Deeds. Documentation Center of Cambodia, Phnom Penh, Cambodia.

Delance, Christopher Edward. Confession of Christopher Edward Delance. Documentation Center of Cambodia, Phnom Penh, Cambodia.

Hashish Smuggling and Passport Fraud: "The Brotherhood of Eternal Love." Hearing Before the Subcommittee to Investigate the Administration of the Internal Security Act and Other Internal Security Laws of the Committee on the Judiciary, United States Senate, 93rd Cong., 1st sess., October 3, 1973 (Washington, D.C.: U.S. Government Printing Office, 1973).

Liberty Information Guide, *U.S.S. Kitty Hawk*, Pattaya Beach and Thailand.

Murphy, Morgan F. and Robert H. Steele, *World Heroin Problem*. Report of special study mission, House Committee on Foreign Affairs, June 22, 1971. House Report No. 92-298. Southeast Asia is covered on 18–29. The text has been placed online in the Virtual Vietnam Archive of the Vietnam Project, Texas Tech University, in two sections: front matter and pages 1–20 (http://www.vietnam.ttu.edu/virtualarchive/items.php?item=2391101004) and pages 21–46 (http://www.vietnam.ttu.edu/virtualarchive/items.php?item=2391101004).

Reuter, Peter. "Transnational Crime: Drug Smuggling." Paper presented at conference on Transnational Crime, University of Cambridge, January 7, 2000.

Shafer, The Honorable Raymond Philip, Chairman, National Commission on Marijuana and Drug Abuse. "Marijuana: A Signal of Misunderstanding." The Report of the National Commission on Marijuana and Drug Abuse. http://www.druglibrary.org/schaffer/library/studies/nc/ncmenu.htm.

Stanton, Dr. Morris D. "Drug Use in Vietnam: A Survey Among Army Personnel in the Two Northern Corps," *Archives of General Psychiatry* 26 (1972): 279–86.

S-21 Prison Torture Manual. Courtesy of Tuol Sleng Museum of Genocide, Phnom Penh, Cambodia.

"Task Force Report: Narcotics, Marijuana and Dangerous Drugs. Findings and Recommendations." Special Presidential task force. Washington, D.C.: U.S. Government Printing Office, 1969.

Under Secretary of State Irwin, memorandum to President Nixon, June 9, 1971. Washington National Records Center, Agency for International Development, AID Administrator Files: FRC 286 75 A 13, Chron Files for April through September, 1971.

U.S. Congress, Senate, Committee on the Judiciary, Subcommittee to Investigate Juvenile Delinquency. Hearings on Drug Abuse in the Armed Forces, Part 21 (Washington, DC: GPO, 1971), testimony of Dr. Joel H. Kaplan, 24 March 1970.

World Drug Traffic and Its Impact on U.S. Security: Hearing Before the Subcommittee to Investigate the Administration of the Internal Security Act and Other Internal Security Laws of the Committee on the Judiciary. U.S. Senate, 92nd Cong., 2nd sess. (part 1, Southeast Asia, August 14, 1972).

INDEX